Mike Leigh

MANCHESTER 1824

Manchester University Press

BRIAN MCFARLANE, NEIL SINYARD *series editors*

ALLEN EYLES, PHILIP FRENCH, SUE HARPER,
TIM PULLEINE, JEFFREY RICHARDS, TOM RYALL
series advisers

BRITISH
FILM
MAKERS

already published

Anthony Asquith TOM RYALL

Roy Ward Baker GEOFF MAYER

Sydney Box ANDREW SPICER

Jack Clayton NEIL SINYARD

Lance Comfort BRIAN MCFARLANE

Terence Davies WENDY EVERETT

Terence Fisher PETER HUTCHINGS

Launder and Gilliat BRUCE BABINGTON

Derek Jarman ROWLAND WYMER

Joseph Losey COLIN GARDNER

Carol Reed PETER WILLIAM EVANS

Michael Reeves BENJAMIN HALLIGAN

Karel Reisz COLIN GARDNER

J. Lee Thompson STEVE CHIBNALL

BRITISH FILM MAKERS

Mike Leigh

TONY WHITEHEAD

Manchester University Press
MANCHESTER AND NEW YORK

distributed exclusively in the USA by Palgrave

Published by Manchester University Press
Oxford Road, Manchester M13 9NR, UK
and Room 400, 175 Fifth Avenue, New York, NY 10010, USA
www.manchesteruniversitypress.co.uk

Distributed exclusively in the USA by
Palgrave, 175 Fifth Avenue, New York, NY 10010, USA

Distributed exclusively in Canada by
UBC Press, University of British Columbia, 2029 West Mall,
Vancouver, BC, Canada V6T 1Z2

British Library Cataloguing-in-Publication Data
A catalogue record for this book is available from the British Library

Library of Congress Cataloging-in-Publication Data applied for

ISBN 978 0 7190 7236 9 *hardback*
ISBN 978 0 7190 7237 6 *paperback*

First published 2007

16 15 14 13 12 11 10 09 08 07 10 9 8 7 6 5 4 3 2 1

Typeset in Scala with Meta display
by Koinonia, Manchester
Printed in Great Britain
by CPI, Bath

For Pete Walsh – simply the best

Contents

List of plates

These stills are used with the kind permission of Mike Leigh and Thin Man Films, and were photographed by Simon Mein.

Series editors' foreword

The aim of this series is to present in lively, authoritative volumes a guide to those film-makers who have made British cinema a rewarding but still under-researched branch of world cinema. The intention is to provide books which are up-to-date in terms of information and critical approach, but not bound to any one theoretical methodology. Though all books in the series will have certain elements in common – comprehensive filmographies, annotated bibliographies, appropriate illustration – the actual critical tools employed will be the responsibility of the individual authors.

Nevertheless, an important recurring element will be a concern for how the oeuvre of each film-maker does or does not fit certain critical and industrial contexts, as well as for the wider social contexts which helped to shape not just that particular film-maker but the course of British cinema at large.

Although the series is director-orientated, the editors believe that reference to a variety of stances and contexts is more likely to reconceptualise and reappraise the phenomenon of British cinema as a complex, shifting field of production. All the texts in the series will engage in detailed discussion of major works of the film-makers involved, but they all consider as well the importance of other key collaborators, of studio organisation, of audience reception, of recurring themes and structures: all those other aspects which go towards the construction of a national cinema.

The series explores and charts a field which is more than ripe for serious excavation. The acknowledged leaders of the field will be reappraised; just as important, though, will be the bringing to light of those who have not so far received any serious attention. They are all part of the very rich texture of British cinema, and it will be the work of this series to give them all their due.

Acknowledgements

My thanks first and foremost to Mike Leigh, for finding time during a busy period for a conversation that was both frank and fascinating, and for kindly offering to check the manuscript for factual errors; his input without question resulted in a better book. (Any remaining inaccuracies are, naturally, down to me.) Abbie Browne at Thin Man Films has also been extremely friendly and helpful.

I am also exceptionally grateful to Neil Sinyard, for suggesting that I take on the project, and for being unfailingly enthusiastic, encouraging and patient during the writing of it. The pleasure of his genial company and friendship is a valued bonus. Thanks also to Brian McFarlane, who has been positive and constructive throughout, and to everyone at Manchester University Press for their kind assistance.

Anyone writing about Mike Leigh owes a debt of gratitude to Michael Coveney's detailed and sympathetic critical biography *The World According to Mike Leigh*, which is referred to numerous times throughout this book and remains a unique source of information about Leigh's life and work.

I could not have completed this book without the support and co-operation of Janek Alexander and the staff of Chapter. I am especially grateful to my friends and colleagues in the cinema department – Matt Beere, and Glen Manby and his gang of ace projectionists – and to Carol Jones and the marketing team.

My thanks also to the various friends who have offered stimulating discussion about Leigh's films, even those (and they know who they are) with whom I have sometimes been in active disagreement. Special thanks to Steve Sullivan, for the loan of rare material and for always being willing to talk comedy.

Charles Barr fostered my interest in British cinema during my studies at the University of East Anglia in the early 1980s, and it is good to have the opportunity now to acknowledge my appreciation of his influence and encouragement.

Finally, my everlasting thanks to my parents for their love and support over all these years, and to my wife Sara, who sustains and inspires me always.

Introduction: 'You've gotta laugh'

Mike Leigh may well be Britain's greatest living director. Without question, he has carved a unique niche for himself: describe a person or a situation as being like someone or something 'out of a Mike Leigh film', and few would fail to understand what you meant (which would probably be a small-scale domestic drama involving trapped, yet highly idiosyncratic, suburban characters).

And yet, when his most recent film *Vera Drake* was released in 2005, thirty-four years after his debut feature, Peter Bradshaw was able to claim in a *Guardian* profile, with total justification, that its success was 'seen as Leigh's breakthrough to a new level'.[1] Why should it have taken so long? He had hardly been inactive; he made that debut feature, *Bleak Moments*, in 1971, and although he did not make another film for the cinema for seventeen years, he built up a formidable television CV in that time, including recognised classics like *Nuts in May* (1976), *Abigail's Party* (1977) and *Meantime* (1983). Since his return to the cinema, he has consistently written and directed a film every two or three years, with occasional returns to the theatre, the medium in which he began his career. He is not, therefore, an obscure talent who has been waiting to be discovered: on the contrary, his worldview has permeated our national consciousness to the extent that there was even at one time said to be a brand of cheese named after *Abigail's Party* – a 1970s cocktail-party-style blend with pieces of pineapple in it.[2]

Yet Leigh remains something of an outsider. Even now, with his big-screen career secure, more awards have come his way abroad than at home and much of the critical response to his work in the UK has been ambivalent, as we shall see. The 'breakthrough' of *Vera Drake* was certainly preceded by a turning point in his reputation – and his success at the box office – with the release of *Secrets and Lies* in 1996, but even that came a quarter of century after *Bleak Moments*. Again one wonders – what took him so long?

It is tempting to wheel out the old arguments about (film-making) prophets being without honour in their own country – especially when that country is the UK. The British media still seem torn between crowing over any visible success enjoyed by the national film industry and weeping crocodile tears over that industry's alleged death throes. And appreciation of Leigh's international acclaim has not always been matched by appreciation of the films themselves. Compare the *Daily Telegraph*'s report from the 2002 Cannes Film Festival, at which Leigh's *All or Nothing* was premiered, with the same newspaper's – in fact the same *writer's* – review of the film when it was released in Britain six months later:

> It's a banner year for British films in Cannes, with a total of six playing in and out of competition, compared with last year's none. Of the three vying for the Palme d'Or, one (Michael Winterbottom's excellent *24 Hour Party People*) has already been released in the UK, and the other two are new projects from that ever dynamic duo of socially conscious British film-making, Mike Leigh (*All or Nothing*) and Ken Loach (*Sweet Sixteen*).[3]

> Like Marmite and *Moulin Rouge*, Mike Leigh has a tendency to divide people. To fans of his work ... he's a compassionate miserablist who finds comedy in the most painful of situations; in the eyes of his detractors, those same films are impossibly grim and full of condescension and caricature. The latter contingent will want to run away screaming after just seconds of his new drama, *All or Nothing*.[4]

It should be said that critic Tim Robey goes on to provide a largely favourable assessment of the film, while having, perfectly reasonably, some personal reservations about aspects of it. And yet he also measures its qualities against some perceived flaws in Leigh's earlier work (the 'contrived' denouement of *Secrets and Lies*, the 'often too-broad leading ladies' of past films); he cannot resist asking 'Is Leigh parodying himself?' and concludes, as he began, by *almost* giving equal voice to 'Leigh's harshest critics' who 'might have trouble finding a trace of caricature in it'.[5] The overall tone of the praise is consequently rather grudging.

Maybe something of the reason is to be found implied in Robey's bracketing together, in his report from Cannes, of Leigh and Ken Loach as an 'ever dynamic duo of socially conscious British film-making'. It is not uncommon to find the two directors mentioned together in this way, sometimes simply on the grounds that both of them have worked largely within a recognisable contemporary milieu, sometimes – more convincingly, as in Robert Murphy's *British Cinema of the 90s* – as evidence of their status as great talents and great survivors, who have maintained active careers partly by their willingness to work for television as well as the cinema.[6] Yet more often than not, indeed almost without exception, once the two directors are shoehorned together in the same category of 'socially conscious film-making', the result is that Leigh is found wanting.

Let it be said from the outset that nothing herein is intended to denigrate Loach, or to define Leigh by what (or who) he is not. My point is simply to indicate the continuing primacy of realism as a critical yardstick in the consideration of British cinema, and to suggest that this approach does Leigh no favours. Rather than celebrating the presence in the British industry of two such distinct but formidable commentators, it instead assumes that Leigh is aiming at the same territory as Loach, but somehow missing the target. Geoff Brown's comments, in the BFI's *British Cinema Book*, make a fairly typical comparison: 'Loach's realism is realism with a cause, and few other directors share his passionate commitment. Mike Leigh, who has also alternated between television and film, works in an ostensibly realist mode but often treats ordinary life as the subject for cruel satire, not compassion'.[7]

I shall go on to query the contention that, where his work falls into the area of satire (which I am interpreting as a style of social observation and commentary robust enough to encompass both caustic humour and righteous anger), Leigh's approach is cruel; I do not believe that even an angrily satirical approach necessarily precludes compassion. For the moment, let us simply note the dominance of realism as a critical ideal. Time after time, the comedy and satire in Leigh's films are treated not as an integral part of his method, but as things that get in the way. Put simply, the charge is that if he were less of a humorist, he would be more of a humanist.

As a further illustration of how realism is privileged above all else as the guiding principle, the quality to be striven for, it is interesting to consider David Lusted's comment, in (of all things) an essay on the Boulting Brothers, that 'the realist tradition remains a force in contemporary British cinema, notably in the otherwise very different campaign films of Ken Loach and actor-improvised products of Mike Leigh'.[8] A perfectly valid observation in itself, but when did any study of British films state the equally valid converse: that much of Leigh's work stands apart from Loach's as being in the same satirical vein as the 'otherwise very different' comedies of the Boulting Brothers? When, for that matter, was the observation last made that Loach's films are very well intentioned, but don't, on the whole, have many laughs in them?

If I seem to emphasise the comic in Leigh's work, it is to redress this balance; not to place humour – jokes, comedy, laughter, satire, caricature and farcical situations – as the only relevant factor, but to reassert it as a vitally important driving force which gives that work much of its distinct tone. Even in comparatively sombre films like *Bleak Moments* and *All or Nothing*, laughter and a sense of humour are seen as valid, indeed vital, responses to life. 'You've gotta laugh' is a phrase that recurs many times in Leigh's work – though it is significant that it is usually said by characters who are not joking at the time; who have either not much to laugh about (such as Brenda Blethyn's Cynthia in *Secrets and Lies*), or no discernible sense of humour at all (like Timothy Spall's Aubrey in *Life Is Sweet* (1990)). Throughout Leigh's work, laughter is a survival mechanism, and *shared* laughter is the key to a clear understanding of oneself and happy, healthy relationships with other people.

To be fully appreciated, then, Leigh needs to be seen not as a failed realist, but as a hugely successful humorist, in the broadest sense of that word. This is borne out both by what others have said about him, and by what he has said about himself. It is no surprise that Andy Medhurst, one of the most cogently perceptive commentators on British comedy, should be among Leigh's staunchest supporters; in one article he dismisses Alan Bleasdale, Terence Davies and Dennis Potter and contends that 'when it comes to making moving (in both senses of the word) pictures that evoke the horrors and humours of being English over the past twenty years ... only Alan Bennett and Victoria Wood come close to matching Leigh's success, and they too have had to look to audiences, rather than critics, for their primary recognition'.[9] His choices for comparison are significant, as is his description on another occasion of Leigh as 'the man who *I'd insist* was Britain's greatest living filmmaker';[10] the italics are mine, the feeling of a need to insist on Leigh's status is shared. (Note the cop-out use of 'may well be... ' in my opening sentence above.)

Leigh himself has on occasions chosen to locate the origins of his working methods (of which more later) not just in the principles of improvisational theatre, but also in a more pragmatic and specifically comic tradition:

> A humorist is what I am, yes, and you know what that means. I love the tragi-comic and I am a lampooner in a way. And yes, I'm a student of humour, and how it works, of timing and structure, feeds, gags, punchlines, pay-offs and double-jokes. But that humour is never in script form – it grows *organically* out of discussion and improvisation and my structuring ... Keaton, too, did what I'm doing *many* years ago; show up, say 'okay, let's get a collapsing car and see what we can do with it', and if it doesn't work, do it again. It's exactly the same thing.[11]

On a similar note, the actor Martin Jarvis, Leigh's fellow student at RADA, has described him admiringly as 'a brilliant comic actor' whose final-year portrayal of Costard in *Love's Labour's Lost* 'owed more to Stan Laurel than Stanislavsky'.[12] And in the introduction to the published screenplay of *Topsy-Turvy*, Leigh's affectionate celebration of the theatre and those who work in it, he chose to cite it specifically as 'a film about all of us who suffer and strain *to make people laugh*' (my italics).[13]

The whole question of realism has been prominent in much recent assessment of British cinema, in particular modifying the notion of a bipolar film culture that could be fairly summed up as 'Ken Loach versus Ken Russell': an identifiably realist tradition (documentary, 'kitchen sink' and so on) pitted fairly and squarely against a more fantastical approach (which may cover anything from Powell and Pressburger to Hammer horror or the *Carry On* films). Charles Barr was among the first to suggest an alternative position, namely that what he defines as 'sobriety' on the one hand and 'excess' on the other not only exist side by side but 'interact and interpenetrate, all the time and in a variety of ways'.[14]

Of course, as Barr goes on to say, this risks seeming like a statement of the obvious, since a very great deal of cinema – and much other art – depends on a fusion of the real and the unreal. We have certainly been conditioned to expect that narrative cinema should be, on the one hand, 'real' or recognisable enough to engage us and, on the other, 'unreal' or exceptional enough to excite and entertain us. But, as Barr states, British cinema seems to thrive on a tension between the two, often creating a negotiation between them and exploring the resulting dynamics. Alan Lovell also makes the point in a more recent essay:

> I think contemporary scholarship has fallen into a trap by posing excess and restraint against each other. British cinema is often most exciting when restraint and excess interact with each other. *Brief Encounter* provides a classic example of what can be achieved when the interaction takes place, and of the problems created when one dominates the other.[15]

Brief Encounter (David Lean, 1945), often cited as a quintessentially British film, is indeed best appreciated as a work in which the tension between melodrama and realism clearly reflects its heroine's state of mind, torn as she is between loyalty to hearth and home and her desire for escape. As Richard Dyer succinctly puts it, 'No film is more of a melodrama than *Brief Encounter*. Yet the film itself asks not to be treated as melodrama but as realism'.[16] A reading which acknowledges this duality sensibly takes into account the improbability of Noël Coward, a gay man writing in the 1940s, creating a story of forbidden love which is quite so bereft of passion as has routinely been claimed. It also allows for more common ground with the near-simultaneous *The Wicked Lady*

(Leslie Arliss, 1945), often supposed to represent the opposite pole of unbridled, vaguely irresponsible escapist fantasy.

This notion of interaction makes sense of a great deal of British cinema history and many of its most iconic texts. *The Third Man* (Carol Reed, 1949), voted best British film of all time in the 'BFI 100', an industry poll of the 100 most highly regarded British films, commissioned in 1999 by the British Film Institute,[17] blends political background seamlessly with bold expressionism – as did Carol Reed's earlier *Odd Man Out* (1947). Humphrey Jennings, the British cinema's greatest ever documentary-maker, was also one of its greatest visual poets; in Brian Winston's words, 'a surrealist who became an arch-realist'.[18] More recently, the work of directors like Sally Potter and Andrew Kötting – not to mention Danny Boyle's *Trainspotting* (1995) – has continued this bracing mixture of real and unreal. Dilys Powell's definitive description of Ken Russell as 'an appalling talent' surely hinges on the co-existence of craftsmanship (the talent) and waywardness (the ability to appal); and, despite Russell's own denunciation of the *Carry On* series as 'crap',[19] *his* marriage of bio-pic and flamboyant imagination is surely spiritual cousin to *their* combination of pastiche and burlesque. Finally, to cite a personal favourite as an example, if realism and fantasy go hand in hand, then what could be more natural than that the Ministry of Information's very specific request for a film to improve Anglo-American relations as the Second World War drew to an end should be answered by the highly organised hallucination that is *A Matter of Life and Death* (Michael Powell and Emeric Pressburger, 1946)? Here, as in *Brief Encounter*, though more explicitly, the negotiation of the real and the fantastic enacts a specific conflict in the psyche of its hero.

I do not think it is merely my own affection for Powell and Pressburger's work that makes it irresistible to suggest comparisons with Leigh's. They seem equally to create films that one engages with either fully or not at all; all or nothing, in fact. The complaint that Leigh's comic devices distract from what is assumed to be a guiding principle of realism surely echoes Richard Winnington, famously grumbling that *A Matter of Life and Death* saw Powell and Pressburger moving 'even further away from the essential realism and true business of the British movie than their two recent films *I Know Where I'm Going* and *A Canterbury Tale*'.[20] And just as Richard Combs has pointed out that *The Life and Death of Colonel Blimp* (Powell and Pressburger, 1945) 'cannot really be accounted for without its contradictions being taken into account',[21] so there are ambivalences in Leigh's work that simply cannot be ironed out or wished away. They need to be taken into account, to be dealt with and worked through, for they are essential to the way his films operate.

A fundamental ambivalence between the real and the unreal can also be found in comedy itself. This may, in the cinema, be expressed in formal terms, by narratives which are sufficiently plausible to remain engaging and absorbing while audiences nevertheless note with pleasure the arrival of familiar personalities from the repertory companies of, say, Ealing Studios or the Boulting Brothers. The appeal of genre parody is likewise rooted in the discrepancy between the identifiable form and the unlikely or ridiculous content (as in the *Carry On* or *Monty Python* films). The tension between real and unreal can also operate on a deeper thematic level: in farce comedy, where the recognisability of the characters and their plight is necessary to anchor the situation as events get ever more wildly out of control; or in slapstick, which depends on laughter at extravagant comic violence coupled with an awareness that it is all make-believe and the 'victim' is not really hurt at all.

The classic double act of straight man and clown is also predicated on the conflict between the realism of the world as we know it (conformity or pragmatism) and the fantasy of the world as we would like it to be (anarchy or wish-fulfilment). Arguably, the more complex the relationship between the members of the double act, the richer the comedy, because the greater the range of interplay between the two impulses. Hence, I think, the reason why Laurel and Hardy remain the most enduringly popular comic double act of all time, both with audiences and successive generations of comedians. Ken Dodd implies this when he notes that

> Laurel and Hardy formed the perfect symmetry of comic incongruity ... The straight man, for instance, may represent the world as bureaucracy would want it to be, and the outwardly comedic character supplies the world as it is. Sometimes the comic world flies off into the idealistic fantasy of how we would like the world to be, but the straight man – with suitable cynicism – shows us that it is impossible.[22]

The duality that Dodd implies is essential. Both impulses, the pragmatic and the anarchic, need to be present, the precise dynamic between the two defining an individual's response to the joke or comic situation. When we see John Cleese, in character as Basil Fawlty, thrash his car with the branch of a tree because it will not start, we must recognise, firstly, that on a rational level this is a ridiculous action, but also, secondly, that it is something most of us have felt like doing at one time or another. Without the first reaction, the beating of the car would seem perfectly reasonable; without the second, it becomes merely fatuous ('too silly to laugh at', as some members of my own family would say).[23]

Some comedy films, such as Ealing's *Passport to Pimlico* (1948) and *The Ladykillers* (1955), can themselves be read as enacting a process of wish fulfilment and its resolution one way or another. Indeed, much comedy effects a compromise between conformity and anarchy by allowing a limited period of licence during which anarchic impulses may be worked out, akin to the traditions of carnival or festive rituals. The enacting of a compromise between the real and the unreal – the world as it is and the world as we would like it to be – can be found at the core of our impulse towards laughter; just as it can also be read in Nietzschean terms as a negotiation between order and chaos, or in Freudian terms as a way of reconciling social constraints and individual impulses. Is it really any wonder that comedy is often regarded as saying something fundamental about human nature and experience?

These dynamics, between realism/pragmatism and fantasy/anarchy, are complex in the area in which Leigh has frequently operated, that of satirical comedy, but as we shall see the simultaneous amusement at *and* identification with human folly is central. In Leigh's films, the 'real' can be said to be the worlds the characters inhabit, which are highly recognisable and constructed with great care and commitment to authenticity. The 'unreal' is the heightened comedy, the stylisation and comic excess, with which Leigh and his actors portray many of the characters and the situations in which they find themselves.

The tendency to deploy caricature is probably the aspect of Leigh's style that has most consistently come in for criticism, and I think it is fair to say that he is less comfortable with the term than I am. My own inclination is to resist pejorative connotations and to defend caricature robustly as a valid comic method – after all, no serious commentator ever asked why Gerald Scarfe or Ralph Steadman or Steve Bell can't draw properly. Leigh is more wary of the word – not surprisingly, given that it has been used so often as a critical stick to beat him with – and he insists that only one of his films, *High Hopes* (1988), can truly be said to use caricature to make its satirical points.[24] Out of deference to this, I shall, as often as possible, use such synonyms as seem appropriate in context to describe the character portrayals elsewhere in his work: exaggeration, mannerism, stylisation, broad comedy – though probably not that mealy mouthed term, larger-than-life characterisation.

What his films undoubtedly do is to use these styles, however one wants to describe them, to present characters in all their glorious, defiant individuality, full of quirks and idiosyncrasies. But it should also be noted that they embrace a range of behavioural styles; the characters who are portrayed most idiosyncratically, who hover on the edge of stylisation (or caricature) are those who are least in touch with the real world and their place in it. They defy the limitations of what we have been conditioned to think of as 'naturalistic' or 'realistic' behaviour precisely because the personas these characters are presenting are *not* quite real. Obsessed with the world as they would like it to be, they lack a purchase on the world as it is, and are intent on keeping up appearances, maintaining a façade or an image that they wish to present to others – or which is simply intended to keep themselves and their lives on an even keel. And when that façade collides with the 'real' and begins to disintegrate, their control over a given situation will frequently lapse, resulting in farcical comic chaos.

This is the key to the particular form taken in Leigh's films by the dialectic between the real and the unreal characteristic of many British films and fundamental to much comedy. He works painstakingly with his actors to create fully rounded characters whose lives and personalities are too complex to be shoe-horned into the tidy conventions of 'realist' drama derived from theatrical concepts of the 'well-made play'. Some of these characters are portrayed according to accepted codes of 'naturalism'; these are the ones who are secure in themselves and their relationships with others, who can see the world as it is and know how to survive in it as best they can. Others appear more exaggerated; the ones who are less secure, less comfortable in who they are and where they fit into the world around them. In the former group we find the characters with a sense of humour, a sense of play, an ability to laugh with each other and to maintain an ironic self-awareness. In the latter group are the characters who insist that 'you've gotta laugh', but hardly ever actually do so.

Notes

1 Peter Bradshaw, '*The Guardian* Profile: Mike Leigh', *The Guardian*, 7 January 2005
2 See Patrick Barkham and Diana Blamires, 'Snack Hits of the 70s Are Height of Retro Chic', *The Guardian*, 16 December 2004
3 Tim Robey, *Daily Telegraph*, 18 May 2002
4 Tim Robey, *Daily Telegraph*, 18 October 2002
5 *Ibid.*
6 Robert Murphy, 'A Path Through the Moral Maze', in Robert Murphy (ed.), *British Cinema of the 90s* (London, BFI Publishing, 2000), p. 6
7 Geoff Brown, 'Paradise Lost and Found: The Course of British Realism', in Robert Murphy (ed.), *The British Cinema Book* (London, BFI Publishing, 1997), p. 195
8 David Lusted, 'British Cinema Aesthetics and Hybridity', in Alan Burton, Tim O'Sullivan and Paul Wells (eds), *The Family Way: The Boulting Brothers and British Film Culture* (Trowbridge, Flicks Books, 2000), p. 191
9 Andy Medhurst, 'Mike Leigh: Beyond Embarrassment', *Sight and Sound*, 3: 11 (November 1993), p. 7
10 Andy Medhurst, *Sight and Sound*, 10: 3 (March 2000), p. 36
11 Quoted in John Hind, *The Comic Inquisition: Conversations with Great Comedians* (London, Virgin Books, 1991), p. 78

12 Martin Jarvis, *Acting Strangely: A Funny Kind of Life* (London, Methuen, 2000), p. 32
13 Mike Leigh, *Topsy-Turvy* (London, Faber & Faber, 1999), p. vii
14 Charles Barr, 'Introduction: Amnesia and Schizophrenia', in Charles Barr (ed.), *All Our Yesterdays: 90 Years of British Cinema* (London, BFI Publishing, 1986), p. 24
15 Alan Lovell, 'The British Cinema: The Known Cinema?', in Murphy (ed.), *The British Cinema Book*, p. 239
16 Richard Dyer, *Brief Encounter* (London, BFI Publishing, 1993), p. 49
17 The full list of 100 films can be found at www.bfi.org.uk/features/bfi100
18 Brian Winston, '*Fires Were Started ...*' (London, BFI Publishing, 1999), p. 10
19 *Carry On Darkly*, a Blackwatch production for Channel 4, first broadcast 30 September 1998
20 Richard Winnington, *News Chronicle*, 8 November 1946
21 Richard Combs, 'Less Sophistication at the Second Showing', *The Listener*, 17 October 1985, p. 8
22 Quoted in John Hind, *The Comic Inquisition*, p. 176
23 This incident takes place in the *Fawlty Towers* episode 'Gourmet Night', first broadcast on BBC TV on 17 October 1975. It will come as no surprise that this is not an example chosen entirely at random, but it seems to me to have a certain paradigmatic value: *Fawlty Towers* was voted the favourite TV programme – *not* just comedy programme – of all time in another of the BFI's industry polls, and Cleese has reckoned that the attack on the car is 'the single moment people like best in all [the] shows'. He goes on to acknowledge that 'everyone says "I've felt like doing that", but it's so obviously a ludicrous thing to do, to punish a vehicle' (quoted in John Hind, *The Comic Inquisition*, p. 157)
24 Interview with the author, 5 April 2000

'Really wants to direct': formative years

1

It comes as something of a surprise to discover that Leigh, a famously proud Salfordian, was actually born in Welwyn, Hertfordshire – because, as the old joke goes, his mother was there at the time. Phyllis Leigh was in fact staying with her parents in 1943 while his father, Abe, was serving abroad with the Royal Army Medical Corps. A matter of days after the birth, however, Phyllis returned with her new baby to Salford, where Abe had worked before the war, at Salford Royal Hospital. When Abe returned to Salford after the war, the family lived above his surgery in the working-class area of Higher Broughton.

The family was part of Manchester's Jewish community:[1] Abe's parents had both emigrated from Russia, while Phyllis's mother and father had come to London from, respectively, Germany and Lithuania. As a child, Leigh was a keen cinemagoer, experiencing a traditional diet of British and Hollywood features, newsreels, cartoons, serials and slapstick shorts. His more formal education took place at North Grecian Street County Primary and then Salford Grammar School. It was shortly after he started at the latter that the family moved to Cavendish Road, 'a more suburban middle-class area'.[2] Leigh describes himself as 'pretty badly unmotivated at secondary school',[3] and, no doubt like many a natural rebel, now regrets convincing himself that he did not need to know about subjects, like geography, which now interest him passionately. Drama seems to have been his salvation, however. Salford Grammar had a good track record in school plays: Albert Finney had only just left the school, and Leigh appeared in *The Government Inspector* and *Androcles and the Lion*, as well as producing a play called *God's Jailer*, which he apparently came across in the school library. At the same time he was writing, directing and performing in revues for Habonim, the Zionist socialist youth movement, which provided him with most of his social life. He was also developing his skills as a cartoonist; an interesting talent in the light of his later reputation as a caricaturist.

Staying on, without much enthusiasm, for A levels in Art, History and English, he was unsure what to do next, but the advertisements in *Plays and Players* turned his thoughts to drama school. The new drama department at Manchester University might have been an option, but Leigh's eye was on London. It is tempting to speculate that this was because his *real* ambition was to work in films rather than in the theatre (a career in theatre being a more viable proposition in the regions than one in film-making) but Leigh does not think that his plans were quite so well worked out at this stage. The desire to leave Manchester was his prime motivation; he was keen to leave home, as he felt stifled and repressed by family life. Making films was certainly an ambition, but he was not particularly aware at this time of what the role of a film director actually was: 'Sure, I wanted to make movies, but in my fantasies. I didn't know what it meant actually. I knew about films a bit, not much, because you watched them, but I'd never seen a foreign film – i.e. a film not in English'.[4] In the event, he won a scholarship to RADA, which he has described as both a 'fluke'[5] and 'the most wonderful and also the most mystifying thing that had ever happened to me',[6] and arrived in London in 1960.

Rather like Norman in *Bleak Moments,* who says that 'it's easy enough to know what it is you don't want to do ... it's not so easy to know what it is you really do want to do', Leigh seems to have found the experiences of his early career most useful in helping him define ways in which he preferred *not* to work in the future. However, he seems also to have taken something away from most of them that helped to shape his working methods. In those days, he considers that what was taught at RADA was 'not much beyond the territory of elocution lessons',[7] though he qualifies that by pointing out that the grounding in stage technique was nonetheless useful – and he is also at pains to say that RADA has since then changed greatly and become a much more forward-looking place. In the early 1960s, however, he found that the new wave of dramatists like Beckett, Osborne and Wesker were little valued there; Pinter was dismissed as 'rubbish' by a senior teacher when Leigh directed a student production of *The Caretaker* in his second year. One of the few memorable and useful classes, however, was one in which Peter Barkworth put two students together to improvise a scene, having first briefed them separately with contradictory information. Suddenly Leigh began to appreciate how an authenticity of performance could be achieved through a natural, organic exploration of character through improvisation. He was also intrigued by the exercises derived by director James Roose-Evans from Lee Strasberg's Actors Studio in New York.

During the year he subsequently spent on a foundation course at Camberwell Art School, Leigh experienced a further revelation with the realisation, in life class, that real life, all around him, was the true raw material of art:

> I realised that what I was experiencing as an art student – and what I definitely hadn't experienced as an actor – was that working from source and looking at something that actually existed and excited you was the key to making a piece of art. What that gave me as a film-maker, playmaker, storyteller, and as an artist generally, was a sense of freedom. Everything is up for grabs if you see it three-dimensionally, and from all possible perspectives, and are motivated by some kind of feeling about it.[8]

Other inspirations included one of the first films he saw after getting to London, John Cassavetes's semi-improvised *Shadows* (1959), and the innovative improvisatory techniques used by Peter Brook in developing his 1964 production of Peter Weiss's *Marat/Sade*.

His appetite for cinema was fed further by his joining the London School of Film Technique (now the London Film School), where he made the most of the chance to meet visitors like Jean Renoir, Fritz Lang, John Huston, Alfred Hitchcock and François Truffaut.

In 1965, Leigh formed a theatre company with David Halliwell, a fellow RADA student who had found the place similarly constricting. The purpose of the company was to get Halliwell's first play, *Little Malcolm and His Struggle Against the Eunuchs*, staged; Leigh had agreed to direct it, an experience that left him convinced he should only direct his own work in future. He got his chance to do so when he was invited to work at the Midlands Arts Centre (MAC) in Birmingham by the director John English. 'There was going to be a company of actors doing plays ... I was going to be the assistant director of this company of actors', he recalls. 'I arrived there in the September of 1965 and there was no company. They still hadn't got it together basically, they were still getting the place finished and getting more money. There was this arts club for teenagers and young people, people fifteen to twenty-five, so instead, my brief was to do experimental drama in this studio theatre'.[9] These somewhat chaotic working conditions aside, Leigh found the atmosphere at MAC 'extremely bourgeois'[10] and overall rather negative, but he was able to put some of his ideas into practice, directing one of his favourite plays, Beckett's *Endgame*, as well as creating work of his own, starting with *The Box Play* (1965), which Leigh devised with a group of young adults. In this project he was able for the first time to develop his ideas about improvisation, the crucial difference from the method he would later evolve being that he gave the actors their roles rather than, as would later become his practice, inviting them to discuss real people they had known as a basis for characterisation. *The Box Play* was followed by two more pieces developed in collaboration with young actors at MAC, which bore the rather splendid titles *My Parents Have Gone to Carlisle* and *The Last Crusade of the Five Little Nuns* (both 1966).

Leigh subsequently spent a year at the Royal Shakespeare Company (RSC): 'I'd written to Peter Hall at the same time I wrote to John English, and at some point they said, well, there's a job going if you want it, assistant director at Stratford'.[11] Leigh had previously auditioned for the RSC, and received a dismissive account of his efforts from the casting director, whose judgement was: 'Very wooden. Does not really think what he is saying when acting. Really wants to direct. Told him that's what he should do'.[12] And, rather aptly in view of that last comment, it was during his time with the RSC that Leigh, among other projects, at last worked on an improvised play with professional actors, as opposed to the keen and talented amateurs at MAC. It was at this point that he experienced one further liberating revelation that would inform his working methods in the future: 'I saw that we must start off with a collection of totally unrelated characters (each one the specific creation of its actor), and then go through a process in which I must cause them to meet each other, and build a network of real relationships; the play would be drawn from the results'.[13] Apart from the resulting play, *NENAA* (1967), however, he regarded his time with the RSC, true to form, as invaluable for teaching him how *not* to do things; eventually he fell out with the management and his contract was terminated.

Back in London, his work included an improvised play, *Individual Fruit Pies* (1968), for E15 Acting School, where he first met Alison Steadman, whom he would marry in 1973. After a brief return to Manchester, where he devised and directed *Epilogue* (1969) for the joint drama department of Sedgley Park College and De La Salle College, and *Big Basil* and *Glum Victoria and the Lad with Specs* (both 1969) for the Manchester Youth Theatre, he returned to London once more, still anxious to break into films. The break came after one final, disastrous attempt at directing someone else's work, a troubled production of Brecht's *Galileo*, in Bermuda, to which Leigh had been co-opted by actor Earl Cameron. 'I decided this was *it*', he has said. 'I was never, ever, going to direct anything again except my own work'.[14] He teamed up with Les Blair, a friend from Salford Grammar whom he had re-encountered at MAC, and together they formed a production company with the aim of filming a play of Leigh's which had opened in 1970, just before the *Galileo* fiasco, at the Open Space Theatre in London. An agent had put Leigh in touch with Charles Marowitz, who ran the venue, and Marowitz gave him a late-night slot in which to develop a play. The result was *Bleak Moments*, and, says Leigh, 'we sensed straight away that we could really take these characters and expand it into a film'.[15]

By the time of *Bleak Moments* in both its stage and film versions, Leigh had arrived at a very sure understanding of the way he wanted to work, and he has continued to follow this practice ever since, often in the teeth of as much scepticism and misunderstanding as appreciation and acclaim. Quite properly, out of respect for the integrity of himself and of his actors, he has always refused to discuss his working methods in detail, and this book does not concern itself with them; I believe in any case that it is much more valuable to look in detail at the end results – to concentrate on the product, not the process. However, it does seem to me that some brief encapsulation of the principles by which Leigh's films are conceived and developed is vital to a genuine understanding of them, and I trust that I am not misrepresenting those principles in the following account.

A Mike Leigh film begins when he recruits a group of actors, who agree to work with him not knowing what character they will be playing or what the film will be about. Leigh, who at this point will himself have many ideas as to possible themes he could explore, then works with each key actor individually to invent a character. As this process goes on, the actors can improvise in character with absolute security and confidence. Where appropriate, they will be sent out to ask for directions, or do the shopping, or some other mundane but everyday task 'in character'. If this all sounds heavy going, a little like 'method' acting at its most solemn and intense, Leigh is always keen to point out that he and his casts also have a good deal of fun and laugh a lot; Janine Duvitski, for one, has concurred that while working with him, 'I don't think I ever stopped laughing the whole time'.[16]

From this extensive research and discussion, the world of the film is evolved and a screenplay is prepared – though not necessarily written down. Once it is fixed, however, this script is strictly adhered to. Leigh's films are *not* improvised, and he is understandably irritated by the continuing misconception that they are: all the improvisation occurs in the preparation and rehearsal. (There are, of course, occasional on-set amendments and suggestions, but no more than in the shooting of most other films.) What he does do is enhance the authenticity of the performances by giving the actors no more information than their characters know: Alison Steadman, for example, was not aware that her character's daughter suffered from bulimia until she saw a preview of *Life Is Sweet*; and in *Vera Drake*, nobody but Imelda Staunton knew in advance that her character was an illicit abortionist, the other members of the cast only discovering this, during rehearsals, at the moment when their characters found out.

Appearing in one of Leigh's films is, in short, a great leap of faith. An actor is required to sign up knowing very little about it beyond the detail of his or her own character, even during filming. No wonder Leigh likes to work with many of the same actors on a regular basis; but the number and, perhaps above all, the quality of those actors speak for themselves. Almost unanimously, they confirm that his working methods are a bit scary at first, but ultimately afford them a freedom of expression that is genuinely liberating. The confidence they are required to have in him is fully repaid by the confidence he has in them. Jim Broadbent says that working with Leigh is 'hugely stimulating and rewarding';[17] Timothy Spall calls it 'an experience of totally organic creativity';[18] Brenda Blethyn considers it an 'ultimate acting experience';[19] Imelda Staunton found it 'shocking, terrifying, exhilarating'.[20] Stephen Rea 'would regard it as a required experience for actors';[21] Philip Davis sums it up as 'not only extremely hard and worthwhile, there is nothing else like it';[22] and the late Katrin Cartlidge once said: 'It's not an acting job; it's a life experience, a profoundly fascinating and philosophical journey that's like climbing Mount Everest'.[23] It is not so much the case that Leigh gets great performances out of his actors, as that he and they work *together* to create great performances. At the time of *Vera Drake*'s UK release, Sam Mendes noted that Leigh 'has consistently pushed three generations of actors to give the performances of their lives',[24] and he has certainly contributed as much as any other single film-maker to the rich tradition of fine British character acting. If one were looking for the contemporary equals of past masters such as Alastair Sim, Alec Guinness, Margaret Rutherford or Joan Greenwood, one would surely have to include the likes of Timothy Spall, Jim Broadbent, Brenda Blethyn and Alison Steadman.

Before turning to a detailed examination of the features Leigh has made for the cinema, and an overview of his television work, I would like to make two observations. Firstly, although I have worked closely with the screenplays of the films where these have been published, I have tended to iron out their use of idiomatic English, replacing, for example, ''E's 'avin' a 'eart attack' with 'He's having a heart attack'. In doing so my intention is not to lose the flavour of the dialogue; I just feel that the former style looks fine within a complete screenplay but is more jarring when taken out of context.

Secondly, although close readings of the films and their characters form the core of this study, I hope I am not falling into the trap of treating Leigh's protagonists as though they are 'real' people with an independent existence away from the control of their creator and his actors.[25] It is rather that, because of the meticulous and thorough processes that go into developing Leigh's characters, *any* aspect of their lives, whether it appears on screen or not, is inescapably *already* under his control. I hope that in analysing them in such detail I am simply according them the same respect that he does.

Notes

1 In a 2006 interview, Leigh described Mancunian Jewishness as 'a very special condition, with its own abrasive humour, a combination of funny aggression and Northern cockiness – blunt and direct' (quoted in Aleks Sierz, 'All My Work Has a Certain Jewishness in It', *Daily Telegraph*, 17 April 2006)
2 Quoted in John Hind, *The Comic Inquisition: Conversations with Great Comedians* (London, Virgin Books, 1991), p. 84
3 Quoted in Michael Coveney, *The World According to Mike Leigh* (London, Harper Collins, paperback edition, 1997), p. 44
4 Interview with the author, 5 April 2005
5 Quoted in John Hind, *The Comic Inquisition*, p. 78
6 Quoted in Michael Coveney, *The World According to Mike Leigh*, p. 57
7 Interview with the author, 5 April 2005
8 Quoted in Graham Fuller, 'Mike Leigh's Original Features', in *Naked and Other Screenplays* (London, Faber & Faber, 1995), p. xiv
9 Interview with the author, 5 April 2005
10 *Ibid.*
11 *Ibid.*
12 Quoted in Michael Coveney, *The World According to Mike Leigh*, p. 74
13 *Ibid.*, p. 75
14 *Ibid.*, p. 80
15 Interview with the author, 5 April 2005
16 Quoted in Michael Coveney, *The World According to Mike Leigh*, p. 117
17 Quoted in Peter Bradshaw, '*The Guardian* Profile: Mike Leigh', *The Guardian*, 7 January 2005
18 Quoted in Mick Brown, 'Life Is Bittersweet', *Telegraph Magazine*, 12 October 2002
19 Quoted in Kenneth Turan, 'The Case for Mike Leigh', *Los Angeles Times*, 22 September 1996; reprinted in Howie Movshovitz (ed.), *Mike Leigh Interviews* (Jackson, University Press of Mississippi, 2000), p. 89
20 Quoted in Peter Bradshaw, '*The Guardian* Profile: Mike Leigh'
21 Quoted in Alan Riding, 'An Original Who Plumbs the Ordinary', *New York Times*, 26 September 1996; reprinted in Howie Movshovitz (ed.), *Mike Leigh Interviews*, p. 100
22 Quoted in Michael Coveney, 'In a Class of His Own', *Observer Magazine*, 4 July 1993; reprinted in Howie Movshovitz (ed.), *Mike Leigh Interviews*, p. 41
23 Quoted in Kenneth Turan, 'The Case for Mike Leigh'; reprinted in Howie Movshovitz (ed.), *Mike Leigh Interviews*, p. 89
24 Quoted in Peter Bradshaw, '*The Guardian* Profile: Mike Leigh'
25 Indeed, I am very anxious not to suggest any such thing, having on occasion had the experience of arguing precisely the opposite case. Taking part in a public debate in which my role was to defend Neil LaBute's biting *In the Company of Men* (1996), for example, I was told that LaBute had been somehow 'dishonest' in resolving the role of the main female protagonist. This kind of debate about what characters 'would' or 'wouldn't do' seems to me to miss the point, since all we have to go on is the evidence provided by the writer and/or director who created them in the first place.

'A kind of language': *Bleak Moments*

2

Having formed their company, Autumn Productions, Leigh and Blair set about raising the necessary finance for their first feature, sending letters to anyone whom they thought might be willing and able to support them. In the event, the BFI Production Board coughed up the minimum permissible amount of £100, but the vast majority of the funding came from Memorial Films, run, with Michael Medwin, by their fellow ex-Salford Grammar School pupil, Albert Finney. Memorial Films put up an initial £14,000, and then, when the production went over-budget, a further £3,000. Leigh was, finally, a film-maker.

Bleak Moments lacks the robust comedy that punctuates most of Leigh's later films; it also does not have the strong narrative structure of his subsequent work. Leigh himself once called it 'the slowest film ever made with jokes in ... like watching paint dry',[1] but it firmly established him as a superb, meticulous chronicler of suburban anxiety and repression. In any case, he is right on both counts. It *is* a slow film, but it *does* have jokes in it.

The slowness is part of its method. The narrative focuses on a group of characters who cannot communicate, for whom talk is 'an evasion of what's going on', in the words of the central figure Sylvia (Anne Raitt), and Leigh makes us sit through their various encounters and conversations – frequently non-conversations – in their excruciating entirety. The point – that all the characters, to varying degrees, have problems in expressing their feelings and saying what they really mean – could have been conveyed in a few representative gestures, actions or exchanges, but *Bleak Moments* never resorts to that kind of dramatic shorthand. Scene after scene is played out virtually in full. The technique might appear theatrical rather than cinematic, which would hardly have been surprising given Leigh's career up to this point – but in fact the effect is so uncompromised by the received dramatic conventions of either medium that critic Irving Wardle, reviewing the opening night of the original theatre production, mistakenly thought that the actors were making it up as they went along, the hesitancy betraying an over-reliance on improvisation.[2] It was an understandable enough misconception at the time, but it has dogged the perception of Leigh's work ever since.

The film's jokes exist despite the lack of overtly comic devices to alleviate the overall mood of melancholy. The kind of sequence mentioned above, in which halting conversations and hesitant small talk take place in semi-formal social situations, of course provokes the laughter of exceedingly painful recognition but, more than that, the ability to make jokes, to get jokes, to retain a sense of humour and a sense of play are vital in defining the characters.

Thoreau's maxim that 'the mass of men live lives of quiet desperation'[3] hangs heavily over *Bleak Moments*. Sylvia copes with a tedious job as a typist, a dependent younger sister, and above all with loneliness. The possibility of companionship exists through her faltering, nervous courtship of a teacher named Peter (Eric Allan), although such is his own reticence and lack of social skills that he constantly threatens to become part of the problem rather than the solution; just one more thing for Sylvia to cope with.

With her somewhat unflattering, old-fashioned clothes and hairstyle, Sylvia is reminiscent of a Victorian governess like Jane Eyre. (Reinforcing the Brontë connection, *Wuthering Heights* is prominent among the books she owns; the Penguin edition, as it happens, which will loom large in Leigh's later film *Career Girls* (1997).) The opening sequences eloquently sketch in the detail of her work and home life. The credits run over a brief initial silence, then over piano music (Chopin's E flat Nocturne), which is probably being played by Sylvia, although we will only realise this, and appreciate its significance, much later. The film opens on a shot of a suburban street: shooting took place in West Norwood and Tulse Hill, and the brief but evocative glimpses of the locations add a suitably autumnal feel. We see Sylvia walk by in the middle distance and then, in the next shot, meet Peter, with whom she walks a little way before they go off in separate directions: 'See you tomorrow'. There is then a cut to Sylvia in the office where she works as secretary to a chartered accountant. Her fellow typist, Pat (Joolia Cappleman), is bright, breezy, superficially chatty; Sylvia is obviously bored. Their boss (Christopher Martin) enters and asks Pat for 'two million copies' of a document. Seeing that she is genuinely nonplussed, he relents and admits that he wants a single copy. And here, less than five minutes into *Bleak Moments*, we have had Leigh's first example of a joke that fails, that simply does not function *as* a joke: Pat doesn't get it; Sylvia looks bored and vaguely contemptuous; the boss himself does not even seem to think it very funny. He follows this up with another witticism, saying that the copies should be 'one top and two bottoms, like a beauty queen at a freak show', to exactly the same responses all round.

We next see Sylvia at home with Hilda (Sarah Stephenson), her twenty-nine-year-old sister, who has a learning disability. In a superbly telling and economic piece of shot composition, they are eating together but not together, Hilda seated at the table in the living room, while Sylvia looks through the serving hatch from the kitchen.

Next day, Sylvia meets Peter again. He clearly wants to ask her out, but can only bring himself to ask whether Hilda would like to be taken for a walk on Sunday. This presumably being agreed upon, we cut to Sylvia preparing Hilda for his visit, telling her: 'You should like Peter – he's a teacher'. However, when Peter arrives (Eric Allan making hilariously heavy weather of opening and closing the garden gate) it is immediately evident that Hilda does not like him at all. He has brought her some Pontefract cakes as a present (one can imagine Leigh's glee in thinking up that particular detail), but she shows no interest. He puts them on the arm of the sofa ('Maybe she'd like them later') and she angrily swipes them onto the floor. Peter and Sylvia make awkward conversation. They never do go for their walk, but have tea and biscuits instead. Offers of tea and coffee function throughout the film as a stalling or diversionary tactic, designed to get the characters through uncomfortable silences or embarrassing moments. Indeed, at various times, tea, coffee, nuts, biscuits, cigarettes, sherry and Maltesers, not to mention those Pontefract cakes, are all offered to one character by another as attempts to make a social situation run more smoothly. After Peter has gone, there is a short scene with Sylvia and Hilda sitting side by side on the couch. Sylvia appears to grab Hilda's hair; Hilda punches Sylvia violently on the shoulder, then cries. Sylvia yells out in pain, looks despairing, and then semi-comforts Hilda by almost forcing her sister's head down onto her own lap.

The next day Sylvia is back at work, listening to Pat babbling enthusiastically about a spiritualist meeting she has attended, but not contributing anything to the conversation. That evening, she is drinking sherry alone in her bedroom when a young northerner called Norman (Mike Bradwell), who is just moving into her garage, calls round with a couple of friends (Malcolm Smith and Donald Sumpter) and explains that they are using the garage to start up production of an alternative magazine.

The next daytime scene is of Hilda at a day centre for adults with learning disabilities, performing mundane tasks for a rather unsympathetic senior trainee, together with another girl who constantly talks and asks trivial questions despite the lack of response from the others:

there is a clear parallel with Sylvia's tedious office job. Walking home, Hilda can hear Norman playing his guitar and singing 'Freight Train'. Norman's music is a form of self-expression denied to most of the other characters; even though his guitar playing is not particularly good, he obviously enjoys it, and is often seen or heard singing. As Hilda listens, she looks curious and uncertain, but her response to the music seems positive, and every bit as instinctive as her dislike for Peter.

That evening, Sylvia baths Hilda and they can hear Norman playing and singing again ('Cocaine Blues'). Having dried Hilda, Sylvia combs her hair in front of the mirror, leaving it flowing rather than pinned up in her usual style. Reaching a decision, she goes out to ask Norman in for coffee, and he shyly accepts. As an early example of the variations in character representation in Leigh's films, Sylvia is, here as throughout, portrayed in a low-key, unobtrusive fashion, while Norman's natural diffidence and self-consciousness are expressed through a series of pronounced mannerisms. Scruffily dressed and with an unkempt beard and hair, he is hesitant, uncomfortable, laughing nervously, avoiding eye contact and punctuating every sentence with 'like'. Yet for all his idiosyncrasies he is a more endearing companion than the uptight Peter. He has enough of a sense of humour to make Sylvia smile by revealing that he is really from Scunthorpe, not, as he previously claimed, Doncaster ('When people say where do you come from, and you say Scunthorpe, they laugh') – although he seems embarrassed rather than amused when he asks Sylvia what she does and she makes the obviously ridiculous claim to be 'the President of Venezuela'.

When Norman observes that knowing what one does *not* want to do in life is easier than discovering what one does want to do, Sylvia confesses a 'fantasy about writing'. Norman has earlier told her that 'anyone can write what they want' for the next edition of his magazine, but the subject now peters out; he does not invite her to contribute, and she seems unable to volunteer. Their faltering conversation is finally killed stone dead when she offers him the use of her spare room should he ever wish to stay the night – an offer which he clearly does not know how to take.

On a subsequent evening, Pat is due to look after Hilda while Sylvia and Peter go out together. Hilda has expressed a wish to see Norman play, so he is invited in, and Hilda is enjoying his music when Pat arrives. She immediately embarrasses Norman by asking Sylvia 'Is this your young man?' in a stage whisper, then interrupts Norman's guitar playing, to which Sylvia and Hilda are listening appreciatively, by chipping in 'Very good, isn't he?', fumbling for her chocolates, and insisting on showing Sylvia a birthday card intended for someone named Eileen. 'Don't stop because of me', she says when Norman has finally ground to a halt and the mood has been destroyed, 'I was enjoying it. Why don't you play something we can all join in? Something happy?' She also chastises Sylvia for letting Hilda touch the guitar: 'She could easily break it'. At this point in the film Pat, like Norman, seems amusingly mannered; unlike him, she is also immensely irritating. As with other characters in Leigh's work, however, we will come to realise that the mannerisms are significant; if Pat's chatty, bustling, fussing persona seems out of tune with codes of dramatic realism, it is because it *is* unreal, a façade covering up a deep unhappiness.

Peter now arrives and is introduced to everyone, though Hilda refuses to say hello to him, causing another awkward moment, which is broken by Sylvia's decision to make 'a brew-up'. As the group sits together taking tea, there is a rapid, eloquent series of silent close-ups of their faces as they repeatedly glance at one another, look away again, avoid each other's gaze. With twenty-four shots in slightly less than a minute – almost the equivalent in Leigh's canon of the shower scene in Hitchcock's *Psycho* (1960) – the sequence demonstrates how Leigh can use brisk editing every bit as effectively as the long, unbroken takes for which he has later become more celebrated. As Michael Coveney puts it, 'the camera merely scans each tense and furtive face in the sitting room, and you ache for someone to scream. But this is a world of stifled cries and whispers'.[4]

Hilda and Pat leave, and Sylvia goes to get ready, leaving Norman and Peter together. Their conversation emphasises the contrast between them: Norman is his usual gauche and uncomfortable self, while Peter's idea of small talk is 'Do you read much?' and 'Where did you go to school?' – which he follows up by grilling Norman on how well he did there and why he did not do A levels. Both the benefits and the limitations of education are demonstrated in this scene: Norman is slightly ashamed of his comparative lack of learning, while Peter takes the lead in their conversation with a readily assumed, if rather headmasterly, authority; yet we have seen how Norman is involved in creative pursuits, with his music and with the magazine he is producing, whereas Peter's intellectualism seems somewhat sterile. And when Norman reveals that he has stayed down south because 'I ran into this bird, like', it is the turn of Peter, the epitome of a middle-aged virgin, to be embarrassed.

Peter takes Sylvia for a meal in a Chinese restaurant, which is deserted apart from a lone, truculent diner (Reginald Stewart), who sits in a corner uttering pleasantries like 'Oi, give us some peaches and cream, will you?' Despite the lack of customers, the waiter (Ronald Eng) is impatient: Peter and Sylvia do not move to their table, take their coats off, or choose their meals quickly enough for his liking, and he irritably corrects them when they order by naming the food rather than quoting the numbers on the menu. Sylvia is mildly amused by all this, whereas Peter is taciturn but clearly annoyed ('It's just that I get very angry with waiters who don't do their job', he complains when they are safely back at Sylvia's house). Throughout the meal, his attention is more focused on his food than on Sylvia, and his conversation is true to type. We learn that all his friends are in other parts of the country, including one in Leicester whom he dismisses as 'materialistic'. 'Very strange way to describe a friend', observes Sylvia, before revealing that she has no school friends locally because she did not go to school in England. On familiar conversational ground now, Peter asks where she did go to school. 'Scotland', she replies, and goes off into a comic fantasy: 'Did you know that the haggis in Scotland tend to run about in the Highlands as opposed to the plains, and they developed two little short legs on one side'. He smiles thinly, but after a short silence retires to safe territory: 'Did Hilda go to school in Scotland as well?' Throughout the meal, and as they leave, Sylvia exchanges glances with the other diner, whose reactions are hard to read. He does not seem noticeably amused by either Peter or the waiter, and there is certainly no suggestion that he would provide any better company for her. Perhaps the implication is that in her desperation she seeks reciprocity with any potentially sympathetic soul – in which case it is significant that, just before they leave, she repositions herself so that she has her back to him.

Scenes in the restaurant are inter-cut with others taking place at Pat's house. For once, this provides some respite from the 'real-time' encounters of the rest of the film (and a real-time depiction of the entire meal would of course be unfeasible in any case). Pat lives with her mother (Liz Smith), who is confined to her bed. While Pat busies herself in the kitchen, her mother chats to Hilda. She recalls a widower whom she once invited round for tea, much to the annoyance of Pat, who, she tells Hilda, 'don't half get on my wick'. Pat enters the bedroom and becomes embarrassed by her mother's false teeth, which she insists on moving from the bedside table to a box on the dressing table. This being out of her reach, the old lady protests vigorously. The situation soon degenerates further; after another argument about the positioning of the false teeth, Pat asks, 'You're ready for your slave to bring your tea, are you?' and complains that she is 'fed up' of the situation. Hilda is upset by their arguing and starts to cry; Pat bustles her out, leaving her mother leaning out of bed, shouting and banging the bedroom door in frustration. Pat offers to take Hilda home, shouting 'You old witch!' at her mother as a parting shot.

Back home, Hilda goes to bed and Pat sits with her, knitting and talking. The scene emphasises the wish-fulfilment involved in the way she looks after Hilda. She seems to us over-protective and patronising, even playing the childish game of 'this little piggy', but, as Ray Carney observes, 'Leigh makes clear that the real game being played is an inner game – one Pat is playing with herself'.[5] Pat is fantasising about having children of her own; she even makes the rather bizarre statement that 'I might be getting married next year', which hardly seems likely from any evidence we are given. Carney notes how her treatment of Hilda is very different from Sylvia's: 'While Pat's performance of Mommy, like all impersonations, is mechanical and monotonic, Sylvia's is fluid, inventive, and genuinely responsive. While Pat's role-playing depends on feeling superior to and in control of Hilda, Sylvia treats her as an equal'.[6]

Sylvia and Peter return, and Sylvia comes upstairs to see Hilda. She invites Pat to stay for coffee, but Pat declines; Sylvia looks rather disappointed and worried, as if the potential intimacy of being alone with Peter at this stage in their date makes her anxious. Pat goes downstairs and she and Peter indulge in what Carney calls a 'semi-comic Mexican standoff':[7] he does not realise that he is blocking her access to her knitting-bag, which she wants to retrieve before leaving; she cannot bring herself to ask him to move, and 'for a long moment they stand face to face paralysed by confusion. What makes the moment so bizarrely hilarious is the gratuitousness of their mutual embarrassment. If either character simply said what he or she was thinking, the entire misunderstanding would evaporate'.[8]

After Pat's departure there is an even more painfully protracted sequence involving Sylvia and Peter – perhaps the best and most agonising example of Leigh's refusal to compress the film's key sequences. They sit separately, rather than together on the couch, neither knowing what to say to the other. Sylvia makes coffee. Peter at first refuses a sherry, but Sylvia, beginning to tease him, has one, 'so you'll have to join me'. Such challenges to his sense of control over a situation rattle him. 'Enjoy yourself', she says as she hands him the glass – an instruction taken ironically by us, and surely also by her. (There is a contrast here with the scene in which she bought the sherry, in which a cheerful wine seller told her to 'enjoy yourself' – though her expression suggested that she didn't expect to.)

Peter sets off on another of his limited topics of conversation, asking if she listens to the radio much, and then whether she prefers to watch television or radio. This enables her to tease him again, saying that she finds it easier to watch the radio. Unamused, he says, 'I'll rephrase my question', and goes on to do so at some length, throwing in references to Marshall McLuhan for good measure. Tellingly, he likens the ability to communicate with learning a foreign language, and explains how difficult he finds it talking to Hilda since his usual conversational gambits do not seem appropriate. Sylvia replies that in her opinion conversational gambits are only ever 'an evasion of what's going on', further discomfiting him. She offers more sherry and he again declines, but she smiles 'Too late!' and promptly fills his glass to the brim so that he has difficulty drinking from it. As she sits back down, on the couch this time, Peter launches from complimenting the design of the couch to expounding on his theory that 'design is a kind of language', listing a long succession of artefacts from furnishings to clothes to modes of transport. Throughout this part of the conversation, Leigh holds Sylvia alone in medium shot on the left of the screen with an empty space to the right, while Peter is consistently framed in close-up or medium close-up. The effect is to emphasise her loneliness and need for companionship, compared to Peter's willingness to exist in a self-contained world of his own.

By now Sylvia is becoming giggly, perhaps due to the cumulative pressure of the evening, or the sherry, or both. She offers him some nuts and then admits that she has none, before revealing that 'I was just saying something to you in my head – it was quite amusing'. He asks what, and she tells him it was an invitation to take his trousers off. At first she passes this off as a joke, then changes her mind and states that it was not. He moves towards her and the pause is almost unbearable as she puts her head on his chest, he caresses her shoulder and neck and then, finally, they kiss each other on the lips. Neither knows what to say after a moment of such intimacy, and Sylvia, after *almost* looking as though she is about to invite him upstairs, eventually resorts to asking if he would like another cup of coffee 'or something'. While she is in the kitchen, Peter looks frustrated, anguished, and eventually says, 'Would you mind if I changed my mind about the coffee? I should be getting along'. After he has left, Sylvia goes to the garage to see if Norman wants to come inside 'for a binge', but he is just leaving to go to a West End folk club; there is a terrible sadness in the realisation that his night out is only beginning just as Sylvia's has spluttered to a premature, unfulfilled end.

Next morning, we see a pointedly empty shot of the spot where Sylvia and Peter habitually meet on the way to work. Neither, we assume, has wanted to be passing at their usual time for fear of seeing the other. Some time later, Sylvia and Peter meet by chance outside the local library and have yet another conversation which never gets off the starting blocks, during which Sylvia says, 'It's just like Romeo and Juliet all over again, isn't it, Hilda?' There is a pause. 'Well, I'd better go', she says.

Sylvia and Hilda return home, where Norman unexpectedly announces that he is moving out of the garage. Hilda is visibly upset, and Sylvia is clearly taken aback. After Norman has left, in a wonderfully incongruous moment, she tries to cheer up Hilda – or herself – by singing a quick burst of 'Three Old Ladies Locked in the Lavatory' – except that she sings 'Two', perhaps with the implication that this is a premonition of their future together as two trapped elderly spinsters. It is only now, at the end of the film, that we discover that Sylvia can play the piano, and that it was probably her playing at the very beginning; she plays the same piece of Chopin now. Hilda also looks surprised – it would appear that Sylvia either has kept her musical ability a secret, or at least has not played for some time. Perhaps something of the life force represented by Norman's music has communicated itself to her? But in Leigh's films we will learn not to expect great – and artificial – epiphanies and revelations in the lives of the protagonists. Sylvia's comment to Hilda at the end of the scene sums it up perfectly: 'We must buy you a new cardigan – some time'. Change, perhaps. But not much. And not yet.

Before the film ends, though, there is one final encounter, one last instance of bottled-up emotions. Pat visits them again, and is seen saying to Hilda, 'Come on, come and tell me all about it'. Yet Pat's stifling attempts to mother Hilda are now explicitly revealed as a cover for her own desperation. 'I really came round to get out of the house', she admits, and when Sylvia asks after her mother, Pat reveals that she is getting no better. Precisely encapsulating the ethos of the whole film, she says, 'I don't think we should talk about it', before collapsing in a flood of uncontrollable, long-suppressed tears.

A little later, Sylvia says that Pat can take Hilda to the cinema, but declines to go with them. They leave, and now Sylvia is left alone. Our last sight of her is sitting near the piano, looking at it. She goes over to it, and starts picking out a tune, with one finger.

Michael Coveney rightly observes that this ending leaves us with 'the sense of the grinding continuity of unfulfilled lives ... unrelieved by the sort of cathartic climax that characterises most of Leigh's subsequent work'.[9] The bittersweet tone, however, is exactly what we will come to expect of the conclusion to so many of Leigh's films, as is the leaving of unanswered questions. The last words exchanged between Sylvia and Peter were 'see you again' – but will they? Will Pat eventually be better off without her dependent mother – or merely lonely, life already having passed her by? Is Sylvia as trapped by Hilda as Pat is by her mother? Her return – if that is what it is – to the piano maybe hints at a new determination towards self-expression, but little in her life has really changed.

She is in most ways more 'alive' than any of the other characters, but only because she is more aware of the ludicrousness and the pathos of all their lives, including her own. Does that make her better off, because more resilient, or worse off, because more aware of being trapped?

She is certainly isolated, and not entirely a sympathetic character; but then Leigh does not here, and will not in the future, deal in characters who are simplistically likeable, or too good to be true. It is, for example, an uncomfortable moment when Sylvia introduces Hilda to Norman by saying, 'She's a bit dopey, aren't you?' Her teasing of Peter during the evening they spend together seems a little cruel – after all, she is not exactly doing much herself to lighten the tension – and it is certainly not calculated to win him over. By the end of the evening, by which point in their date she seems to have all but given up on him, she seems simply to want to increase his discomfort. Her comment about Romeo and Juliet the last time they meet is another example of a private joke, since Hilda is unlikely to understand the reference, and Peter can hardly be expected to find it funny. When Sylvia tells Norman she is president of Venezuela, she is presumably hoping that he will respond in kind – along the lines of 'Oh yeah? Travel must get you down a bit' – but he cannot. Throughout the film, Sylvia's jokes work only insofar as they amuse *her*; they create alienation rather than intimacy, and thus only serve to isolate her more.

Of course, she is not the only one; as we have seen, her boss's comments and jokes, intended to create an atmosphere of genial familiarity in the workplace, have exactly the opposite effect. But we never get to know him well enough to know how aware he is of his failings. We do get to know Sylvia well enough to appreciate that her sense of humour is a defence mechanism; she might hope that people like Norman will get the joke, but if they do not, at least she has amused herself and maybe kept a potentially awkward situation at arm's length. As Carney says, 'she understands what her creator does: that even embarrassment and discomfort can be sources of entertainment if you look at them in the right way'.[10]

In this way Sylvia stands alone among the characters in *Bleak Moments*, and Carney is right to point out a crucial connection between her attitude and Leigh's own style of social observation:

> For a character like Sylvia (or for the viewer) to be able to see the wacky humour in a situation (rather than being offended, wounded, or morally outraged by it, as Peter invariably is) is to inhabit the same imaginative position that Leigh does as an artist – half-inside and half-outside the experience, slightly above it and yet still in touch with it, emotionally exposed and vulnerable to it but not overwhelmed by it.[11]

I would not go quite so far as Carney does on this point: it seems to me that Leigh intends us to feel as ambivalently about Sylvia as about most of the other characters and, fantasies about haggis and the presidency of Venezuela notwithstanding, I am not sure how comfortable I am with the use of 'Sylvia' and 'wacky humour' in the same sentence. But it is certainly well observed that the position of being 'half-inside and half-outside' is endemic to the role of social satirist; and that the fundamental humourlessness of the other characters, especially Peter and Pat, is what places them in such marked contrast to Sylvia.

As we have seen, Pat is uptight, unfulfilled and emotionally repressed. Like Norman, she has conspicuous verbal mannerisms, such as self-consciously mouthing words for no apparent reason, instead of speaking them out loud, and asking 'Sure?' as a reflex action every time Sylvia declines her offer of a Malteser. Her body language can be equally revealing, as in the way she approaches Sylvia's house, walking slightly faster than she really needs to. Her constantly thwarted need to assume control – and the unhealthy way this need manifests itself in the desire to mother the vulnerable Hilda – is highlighted in a conversation near the end of the film, but before her final, tearful collapse. Pat wants to take Hilda to a spiritualist meeting; Sylvia does not want her to go. Pat offers her a book, sure that if Sylvia read it, 'you'd be able to understand'. Sylvia continues to refuse, and Pat becomes almost hysterical: 'You've got to let me take her! Please, *please*, Sylvia!' She insists that 'once I've made up my mind about something, I'm going to do it' and threatens to take Hilda from the day centre. Sylvia calmly points out that she cannot do this, and Pat continues to protest. Leigh allows Sylvia the last word: 'Look, I'm sorry, Pat, but she's just not going, okay?' Yet we are not permitted to see Pat as a *totally* dislikeable character; this scene, in which she is seen at her most petulant and manipulative, comes *before* her final hysterical outburst reveals the full extent of her emotional vulnerability and despair, in the light of which we are less inclined to leave the film judging her harshly. Not for nothing has Leigh been compared to Jean Renoir in that everyone has his (or her) reasons.

Even Peter is a sufficiently rounded character for us to feel at times a little sorry for him, since we appreciate that his schoolmasterly behaviour is protection against his crippling shyness and emotional repression. We sense, however, that he would never admit as much to anyone else; significantly, it is only when Sylvia leaves him alone after they have kissed that he looks truly distressed and vulnerable, never when any other character is present. He and Pat are two of a kind in that their insecurity makes them control freaks and, as Carney notes, both of them 'are humourless. They are incapable of getting outside themselves even for a second. They are unable to entertain any perspective on experience other than those they are already up to their eyebrows in'.[12] This ability to see things from another's point of view, to have a perspective on who one is and how one fits into a larger picture, is what distinguishes Sylvia from the others, and is closely linked to her sense of humour, flawed as it sometimes is.

Peter's lack of humour is definitively laid bare in a scene that takes place shortly after his disastrous evening out with Sylvia. We see Peter in the school staff room, where a younger colleague (Susan Glanville) approaches him by asking, 'Do you like *Peanuts*?' He looks startled, perhaps remembering Sylvia's teasing of him with the offer of nuts that she hadn't got. But it turns out to be a question about the Charles Schultz comic strip; she wants to discuss with him a project she is working on for the 'thirds', about humour: 'They should understand why they laugh ... Jokes, of course – collate them, categorise them, so that they begin to understand that really there are only about four or five classifiable sorts of joke ... good jokes and bad jokes – why are jokes good, why are jokes bad sometimes?' What does Peter think of the project? 'Well, thirds', he replies, 'I don't think they've got much sense of humour at that age'. Not, one feels, that he would recognise a sense of humour anyway, in 'thirds' or anybody else. His fellow teacher may be in danger of grinding all the enjoyment out of the subject of jokes, and one has to question her judgement in asking the opinion of anyone so determinedly serious. (When she asks him who his favourite cartoonist is, he looks utterly baffled.) But at least she is not trying to avoid the notion of humour altogether, as Peter does, and her division of jokes into good and bad, while somewhat earnest, is still a distinction worth making – not least in the context of Leigh's films, which are often wrongly accused of using humour to belittle his characters.

These characters, in *Bleak Moments* and after, are rounded and, as we have seen, complex enough to evade clear-cut judgements. In this respect, they are closer to real life, in which we are regularly forced to re-evaluate and reassess the people we meet in the light of new perspectives and insights, than realist conventions might allow. It is worth noting the cheeky – and very easily missed – variation on the standard movie disclaimer that appears in the credits of *Bleak Moments*: 'Any similarity between characters in this film and persons living or dead is entirely intentional'. (Leigh now describes this as a 'totally irresponsible' joke, and admits that 'we did it in a very innocent and amateur way'.[13])

Here we see one of the fundamental differences between Leigh's work and that of a social realist like Ken Loach. Loach's films are about issues, and seek socio-political *answers*; Leigh's are about people, and ask *questions* about ordinary lives. And he intends us to go away from them still asking questions; as he has said, 'I defy anyone to walk away from one of my films with a clear, simple, conclusive message, because there isn't one. On the other hand there's always stuff to walk away and ponder'.[14] For this reason, while Loach's characters usually represent something ideologically, Leigh's characters do not represent anything except themselves as individuals. And they *are*, triumphantly, individuals, with all the associated idiosyncrasies and quirks this implies.

Leigh is, for example, superb at observing verbal mannerisms, such as Pat's habit of asking 'Sure?' after the refusal of a Malteser. He brilliantly captures the rhythms of everyday speech with all its hesitations, repetitions and occasional inarticulacy. This style of dialogue is not to everyone's taste, but for many serves as a refreshing antidote to the overwritten, hyper-articulate speech patterns of so much excruciatingly bad film and TV dialogue.[15] Nor is any detail wasted. Pat's repeated 'Sure?' is subtly significant in two later moments. Firstly, when Pat's mother tells Hilda that she does not like Maltesers, it hints at a whole world of dreadful domestic incompatibility; and secondly, when Sylvia asks Peter, 'Are you sure?' when he declines a glass of sherry, it is by contrast meant teasingly as a challenge, rather than involuntarily as a mannerism.

This appreciation of individuality informs both the form and content of Leigh's work. *Bleak Moments* already sees him refusing to fight shy of full-blooded comic characterisation, even edging towards what in most 'realist' drama would look like stylisation or caricature, evidenced here by Pat and Norman. Furthermore, while most of his protagonists are, as noted above, hard to pin down with definitive value judgements, those who come off worst in his films are frequently the ones who try to iron out individuality in others, whether it is Pat bullying her mother and Hilda, or the Chinese waiter who becomes testy when Sylvia and Peter do not conform to his system for ordering food.

In his eschewing of pat narrative resolutions, and his celebration of key characters in all their unclassifiable complexity and occasional quirkiness, Leigh is clearly striving – as he has continued to do ever since – for truth as opposed to realism. Or, rather, as opposed to what dramatic conventions have conditioned us to accept as 'realistic' (think, as an obvious example, of the way in which monochrome, via its association with documentary, still has irresistible connotations of 'the real'). For all that, it may be that the deliberately low-key tone, unglamorous characters and lack of dramatic incident in *Bleak Moments* led to Leigh being given the convenient label 'realist', thus raising expectations that he has been saddled with ever since.

Nevertheless, the film received some excellent reviews. *The Observer* called it 'a remarkable debut', *The Guardian* found it 'striking and entirely original', and the *Evening Standard* made the important point that 'it pierces you with the truth of everyday repression in a corner of life you might never have looked into by yourself'. In America, Roger Ebert's *Chicago Sun-Times* review judged it 'a masterpiece, plain and simple'.[16] In the *Monthly Film Bulletin*, Victoria Wegg-Prosser's perceptive review noted how the film works both as a tragi-comedy and as 'a telling indictment of a society which provides education and a tolerable degree of affluence, but fails to teach people how to understand themselves, and thus to communicate with others. The flat, two-dimensional photography, the exaggerated slowness and repetition of the action, the over-acting of Peter and Pat – all these aspects heighten the total inability of the characters to come to terms with and break out of their physical and mental state'.[17]

Without a doubt, *Bleak Moments* was successful in delicately evoking that 'world of stifled cries and whispers'; a world in which emotions are sublimated into food and drink, into music, into lists of artefacts, but never actually expressed. Its slow pace – and the patchy sound quality – notwithstanding, it was a great calling card, revealing much promise for Leigh's future career. He would not make another feature film for the cinema for seventeen years.

Notes

1 Quoted in Michael Coveney, *The World According to Mike Leigh* (London, Harper Collins, paperback edition, 1997), p. 85
2 *Ibid.*, p. 84
3 Henry David Thoreau, 'Economy', in *Walden* (1854, New American Library edition, 1960), p. 10
4 Michael Coveney, *The World According to Mike Leigh*, p. 86
5 Ray Carney and Leonard Quart, *The Films of Mike Leigh: Embracing the World* (Cambridge, Cambridge University Press, 2000), p. 36
6 *Ibid.*, p. 37
7 *Ibid.*, p. 38
8 *Ibid.*, p. 39
9 Michael Coveney, *The World According to Mike Leigh*, pp. 85–6
10 Ray Carney and Leonard Quart, *The Films of Mike Leigh*, p. 44
11 *Ibid.*, p. 49
12 *Ibid.*, p. 45
13 Interview with the author, 5 April 2005
14 Quoted in Nigel Andrews, 'Monumental Achievement', *Financial Times*, 12/13 October 2002
15 It is probably unfair to single out a specific film, but I feel some justification of this comment is called for, so I will simply cite the most recent example I have seen. *The Great Ecstasy of Robert Carmichael*, premiered at the 2005 Edinburgh International Film Festival, seemed to me to typify the kind of British film that

looks very impressive, but whose ambitions towards gritty realism are scuppered by clunking, unconvincing dialogue

16 I am quoting the *Observer, Guardian* and *Evening Standard* reviews from the programme note issued by the Institute of Contemporary Arts in London when it screened *Bleak Moments* in 1984 as part of a retrospective of productions by Memorial Films; and Roger Ebert's review from Coveney, *The World According to Mike Leigh*, p. 87

17 Victoria Wegg-Prosser, *Monthly Film Bulletin*, 39: 461 (June 1972), p. 108

'A long time in the womb': the TV films

3

'Oh, it's Beaujolais. Fantastic! Won't be a sec, I'll just pop it in the fridge'. Has any beverage in any work of art ever excited quite so much comment or controversy as that bottle of red wine in Leigh's 1977 play – and its TV adaptation – *Abigail's Party*?

Abigail's Party was just one of the nine feature-length productions which Leigh 'devised and directed' (his preferred credit at the time) between 1973 and 1985. The success of these meant that, as Garry Watson observes, 'most British viewers were aware of Leigh long before the arrival of *High Hopes* in 1988',[1] even though few of them would have had the chance to see *Bleak Moments* during its limited London run. Leigh has recalled of those heady days of British television drama that 'you could get eight or nine million viewers in one evening. ... I don't know how long it will take for eight or nine million people to see *Secrets and Lies* for all its success. It'll take quite a while'.[2]

When Leigh describes his TV years as 'a long time in the womb',[3] the comment is double-edged: he acknowledges that he was protected by (mainly) the BBC as well as waiting to be fully 'born' as a film-maker. For all that, the cinema was still where his sights were set, with the opportunity to have his work seen more than just once or twice (and even at the time of writing, in 2006, only three of his TV features are available on video or DVD in Britain), in more places across the world, and, of course, on the big screen. Yet his TV films see him doing considerably more than marking time; all of them make entertaining, often compulsive viewing, several are classics of the medium, and the signs of his developing preoccupations and techniques that are evident with hindsight make them even more fascinating. By grouping them together in a single chapter I do not mean to imply that they are inherently inferior to the films he has made for the cinema, but merely to concentrate the focus of this book on the latter, and perhaps to suggest that the TV features are, like Leigh's work for the theatre, subjects worthy of a separate study.

The period in question – broadly, the 1970s through to the mid-1980s – is widely perceived as an unproductive one for the British cinema. The (partly tongue-in-cheek) contention that 'while America has come up with *Apocalypse Now* and *Star Wars* we've been busy making *Confessions of a Plumber's Mate* and *Holiday on the Buses*'[4] is more than a little unfair to Ken Russell, Nicolas Roeg, Mike Hodges, Alan Parker, Derek Jarman and the *Monty Python* team, among others, but it was certainly a period during which a lot of aspiring British film-makers struggled to get a break. 'The truth is', Leigh has said, 'had it not been for the BBC, and I'm not just talking about me here but a number of film-makers, I can't bear to think what would have happened'.[5] Martyn Auty's analysis substantiates this view:

> In the late 1960s and throughout the 1970s, virtually all Britain's best known producers and directors were to be found in television companies, predominantly within the BBC, but also at Granada, Thames and London Weekend. The roll call of these years is impressive: Ken Loach, Tony Garnett, Jack Gold, Michael Apted, Mike Hodges, Alan Clarke, Kenith Trodd, Stephen Frears, Mike Leigh, Karel Reisz, Alan Parker, Mark Shivas, Graham Benson, Franc Roddam, Roland Joffe, Jim Goddard, Richard Eyre, Margaret Matheson, and so on.[6]

It was the backing of one of the above mentioned, the pioneering producer Tony Garnett, that proved crucial in establishing Leigh's TV career. As David Robinson once put it, 'a *Catch-22* logic' militated against Leigh's working methods when it came to getting into movies: 'British films are financed on the strength of advance scripts (ill-advised through investors' judgement of them often appears); and since Leigh cannot offer an advance script … '.[7] Garnett, who had admired *Bleak Moments* on both stage and film, was well aware of this problem and saw TV as Leigh's way of gaining the reputation he would need if he was going to make the move into the cinema in the way he wanted to: 'His conditions were expensive, not for the scale of the thing – there were never going to be Cossacks coming over the hill – but for the time required. I knew nothing would happen for him until he got established. So I decided that I would give him one of my last available slots'.[8]

The resulting film, *Hard Labour* (1973), is essentially a character study of a middle-aged Salford housewife, Mrs Thornley (Liz Smith). Though she says perhaps less than any other major character in the film, Mrs Thornley dominates it spiritually, and Leigh's camera occasionally privileges her – holding her in a one-shot and gradually moving into a close-up, for example, as she placidly reads the newspaper while her family bickers around her; or keeping her at the front of the frame, asleep in bed, as her husband (Clifford Kershaw) arrives home from the pub, puffing, panting and stomping his way around the bedroom before roughly waking her up for sex (a ritual, we will learn, of Saturday nights – the one day in the week when he does not go out to work as a night watchman).

Mrs Thornley is worn down by the daily grind of her family – her argumentative daughter (Polly Hemingway) and upwardly mobile daughter-in-law (Alison Steadman), as well as her dyed-in-the-wool, chauvinistic bully of a husband – by her job cleaning for a middle-class lady called Mrs Stone (Vanessa Harris), and by the church, principally represented in the film by a bossy nun who calls round collecting for a jumble sale ('I hope you've got something good for me, have you? Because we need at least fifty pounds, you know, if we're going to have the conjuror again'). The title *Hard Labour* flags up the long hours Mrs Thornley works, as well as what will become a recurring theme in Leigh's work, that of having children ('You have to suffer to bring children into the world'). It also, surely, implies the way in which a woman of her class and generation can effectively be imprisoned by social expectations of loyalty to husband, family, employers and church. It is Mrs Thornley's religion that supplies the immediate context for the breathtaking sting in the film's tail, when she goes to confession and tells a priest, who can barely tear himself away from the *Manchester Evening News Sporting Pink*, that 'I just don't love people enough' and even feels guilty about not enjoying the perfunctory, enforced sex she has with her husband: 'When he's near me, I don't like to touch him – when he wants me to do something for him'. This sad, hopeless ending – the priest merely sending her away to say 'Five Hail Marys, one Our Father, and a Glory Be' – elevates *Hard Labour* from poignant comedy-drama to near-tragedy.

Leigh and Garnett next worked together on the first few of a planned series of five-minute shorts for the BBC. Like many other people, Leigh was a great fan of the witty and rather surreal children's programme *The Magic Roundabout*, which was broadcast in five-minute episodes before the main evening news (hence being seen by many adults arriving home from work) and he 'suddenly thought you could do this with characters – a series of full-length self-contained dramas lasting five minutes'.[9] He envisaged thirty or so of these, which could be screened either in a regular slot, such as before the later evening news bulletin, or more randomly throughout the schedules. Sadly, only five were made before the BBC got cold feet and abandoned the project, and those five – *The Birth of the 2001 F.A. Cup Final Goalie, Old Chums, Probation, A Light Snack* and *Afternoon*, all made in 1975 – were never broadcast until a 1982 TV season of Leigh's work. They are a mixed bunch, but *Afternoon* (three women drinking together) and *Old Chums* (two men having a conversation but not quite communicating) in particular are wittily observed and well-shot conversation pieces, which make one wish that he had been let loose on more of these tantalising vignettes.

Also in 1975, Leigh had made *The Permissive Society*, the first of his two half-hour studio plays for BBC Birmingham's *Second City Firsts* strand. This is another acute study of a nervous courtship, between a shy young man and his rather prim girlfriend, whose stilted conversation is in marked contrast to the earthy badinage between the boy and his brassy sister. A year later he made the second, *Knock for Knock*, which has sadly been wiped ('Stupid', Leigh calls it. 'The amount of space anyone needs to keep a tape ... '[10]). Its unavailability is all the more regrettable for depriving us of what sounds like a hilarious performance from Sam Kelly, in his first collaboration with Leigh, as a hyperactive insurance salesman.

However, 1976 also saw Leigh transplant the leading characters from his 1973 theatre play *Wholesome Glory* into the British countryside, creating one of his most popular television films in the process. *Nuts in May* is the only one of his films to use exterior locations so extensively, dealing as it does with Keith and Candice-Marie Pratt (Roger Sloman and Alison Steadman), a middle-class couple from Croydon, as they set out on a camping holiday in Dorset.

Although Leigh's previous films had involved characters who are more or less exasperating or dislikeable – Peter and Pat in *Bleak Moments*, the family members who harass Mrs Thornley, especially her husband, in *Hard Labour* – Keith Pratt is perhaps his first authentically monstrous creation. He and Candice-Marie are a pair of self-satisfied prigs, though, being Mike Leigh characters, they are also rounded enough to be thoroughly credible – which is precisely what makes them so appalling. Their vegetarianism and preference for health foods and free-range eggs are not in themselves risible; what makes them ridiculous, even obnoxious, is their self-righteousness about it all. Their initial objection when their fellow camper Ray (Anthony O'Donnell) asks if they mind him smoking is that it's bad for *him* ('It's just that Keith and I believe that smoking damages your health'), not uncomfortable for *them* (which Keith seeks to objectify by referring to it in the most generalised terms, pontificating that 'air polluted by one person has to be breathed by everybody else'). Although they complain about the noise from his radio, they are quite happy to sing and play their guitar and banjo at equal volume; this being an activity they enjoy, they cannot for a moment conceive of anyone else disapproving of it or finding it irritating. And even if one accepts their twee musical performances as a relatively harmless eccentricity, it is the way they then insist that Ray joins in with them that is so inexcusable – and so toe-curlingly embarrassing.

Keith works for social services, 'organising pensioners' holidays, meals on wheels, that sort of thing', according to Candice-Marie – and one can imagine him in his element, sorting out the lives of those too frail or vulnerable to answer back. He bosses Candice-Marie about, taking charge, lecturing her and striding ahead of her on their trips out, forcing her to keep up with him. 'I wish I had the guidebook', she complains as he marches round Corfe Castle. 'How am I supposed to know what all these numbers are?' 'Well, I'm telling you, aren't I?' he replies. And telling people is what Keith does best; most notably, as the film approaches its climax he repeatedly orders another camper, the recalcitrant Finger (Stephen Bill), to 'be told!' when he sets about lighting an open fire on the campsite.

In short, Keith is a control freak. 'There's no point in having a schedule if you don't stick to it', he tells Candice-Marie, with all the self-assurance of one who has drawn up the schedule himself precisely so that he has something to stick to. When people don't do what he tells them, he retreats into himself, becoming uncharacteristically quiet. (Candice-Marie is prone to winding him up even further at such moments by undiplomatically pointing out that people are ignoring him.) And when the control freak finally loses control of himself, it is spectacular. The moment comes during the argument with the rowdy biker Finger and his girlfriend Honky (Sheila Kelley). Keith is right, of course, that lighting a fire on the campsite is a foolishly dangerous thing to do, but he becomes progressively more pompous, antagonising Finger by quoting rules, declaring it his business to 'protect the life of the countryside and our heritage', and wittering on about his power to make a citizen's arrest. When Finger persists in going ahead, Keith is eventually driven to chase him, eyes blazing, brandishing a large piece of wood and repeatedly yelling, 'I'll knock your head off!' However, the loss of self-control is too much for Keith, and he collapses in tears, sobbing, 'I was only trying to advise you for your own good!' before running off alone into the woods.

At the very end of the film, Keith, now camping in a farmer's field and thus deprived of even the most basic of facilities, makes his way gingerly through a barbed wire fence and across a field of pigs, spade in one hand and toilet roll in the other. It is a far cry from the jolly song he and Candice-Marie were singing over the opening credits, about how they would 'be with Mother Nature, and laugh and sing and play'. Mother Nature, alas, has obstinately failed to submit to Keith's control or to follow his schedule.

Leigh next returned to the north of England, to Oldham, for *The Kiss of Death* (1977), which is again basically a character study; although, unlike Keith Pratt, the protagonist here, Trevor (David Threlfall), is young enough and open enough to show the possibility of change and development. At the start of the film, his shy, guffawing manner and sloping gait are indicative of a young man not quite psychologically out of adolescence. His tendency to chortle when uncertain or vaguely embarrassed also contrasts rather markedly with his job as an undertaker's apprentice. Michael Coveney identifies him as the first example of a recurring figure in Leigh's work: 'the articulate egomaniac, the critical motormouth, the dissident yelper at what happens to other "inadequate" people'.[11] Personally I think we *have* seen at least a version of this type before: Sylvia, in *Bleak Moments*, while no motormouth, uses a nervy, brittle humour to keep potentially discomfiting situations or emotions at arm's length, without ever quite managing to create a rapport with anyone in the process. Once again, the difference is that although Trevor does this too, he is young enough not to be yet locked into a rigid behaviour pattern – or a hopeless future.

The potential for Trevor's emotional development comes with his relationship – if one can call it that – with a local girl called Linda (Kay Adshead). His penchant for a kind of humour which fails to connect is reflected in several of her comments to him at key moments. 'Are you being funny again?' she demands angrily when, after he has stood her up and she has stormed round to the pub and hit him, he then calls round to her house; and her parting shot in the film, following a disastrous night out at a disco during which she has briefly flirted with his mate Ronnie (John Wheatley), is 'What are you laughing at, eh?' Following on from the discussion about humour between two essentially humourless people in *Bleak Moments*, references to jokes, to laughing or being funny, will continue to figure in Leigh's work, and the references will frequently be made by people who are not amused at all, or between characters who are incapable of sharing laughter in a given situation.

The major scene in *The Kiss of Death* occurs towards the end, and has been justly compared to that long scene between Sylvia and Peter for its agonisingly accurate depiction of emotional reticence. Trevor, as noted above, has visited Linda's house, and she vents her anger on him. They are interrupted when the next-door neighbour calls to say that her mother has fainted on the stairs. Suddenly, Trevor's professional training makes him able to deal with the situation capably and efficiently and we – and Linda – see a different side to him. It is crucial to Leigh's method of characterisation, however, that this is not a miraculous transformation; Trevor remains recognisably his slightly goofy, immature self, saying 'Hello Dolly!' to the recovering mother on learning that this is her name, and playfully pushing the wet face-cloth into Linda's face before replacing it on the old lady's forehead.

Having seen him in a slightly different light, Linda's attitude softens. They return to her house, next door, and she makes him a mug of coffee. 'You can kiss me if you like', she tells him. 'Do you want to?' He looks unsure, but nods shyly. Slowly, eventually, he puts down his mug and moves across to sit by her. She repeats 'Come on', and he gradually moves in closer. Suddenly, she bursts out laughing at his inexperience, recovering herself but asking outright, 'Don't you know how to kiss anybody?' Now Trevor starts to giggle, appears to recover, moves in for a kiss, chortles again, then grabs her face and kisses her fiercely on the lips. She invites him upstairs, and he gets the giggles again, nervously and uncontrollably. 'You'd better go then, hadn't you?' she says.

Trevor is clearly not yet ready to relax into physical intimacy, let alone to take on the emotional commitment of a relationship. Yet, just as he had earlier been unexpectedly moved by having to visit the scene of a cot death, the incident with Linda does seem to have an effect on him, maybe signalling the possibility for change. At this stage, though, a possibility is all it is: although he does agree to go to a disco with her, having earlier told her that he hates them, he does not enjoy it and the evening is not a success. The following day, Trevor attends a wedding – the undertaker's car occasionally being used for this purpose – and chats to a little bridesmaid outside the church. He relates to her more easily than to most of the adults he encounters in the film, pointing up his own comparative lack of maturity; when he asks her, 'You not got a boyfriend? ... Why not?' we cannot help thinking that someone could be asking him the same question about a girlfriend – except that she is a little girl, and he appears to be in his late teens or even (as David Threlfall was at the time of filming) his early twenties. Just as she prefers to play with her friends, so the last shot in the film is of Trevor and Ronnie driving off together in the wedding car, heading for Blackpool. (Leigh's planned ending, which he did not have time to shoot, might have reinforced this sense of their being essentially boys at play rather than young adults ready to settle down, by showing them picking up two free-spirited female hitchhikers, whose personalities would clearly have been more appealing to them than the somewhat predatory small-town girls back home.)

And so to *Abigail's Party* and – among a range of other comestibles and fashion accessories – that much discussed bottle of Beaujolais. A straightforward TV version of Leigh's original play (also first seen in

1977), it is a multi-camera studio production rather than a film – even if it does not *quite* take place on a single, three-walled set (one tiny scene takes place in the bathroom, and there is a brief reverse-angle shot to give a glimpse of the 'fourth wall'). Regarding it as 'really quite a mess' with 'patchy, inconsistent lighting, and even the odd microphone in shot',[12] Leigh vowed he would never again direct a piece in a studio – and never has. Given all that, not to mention the fact that both the stage and television versions were hastily mounted when other productions fell through, it is, as Michael Coveney puts it, 'a cruel irony'[13] that *Abigail's Party* remains the most widely recognised and best-remembered piece Leigh has ever written and directed. Its status in the popular consciousness rests at least in part on the massive viewing figure of sixteen million achieved by its third broadcast, when, as Coveney notes, 'there was an ITV strike, an unattractively highbrow programme on BBC2 (Channel 4 had not yet been invented), and a raging storm throughout the British Isles'.[14] Its reputation, for better or for worse, has also hinged in no small part on a review written for the *Sunday Times* by Dennis Potter at the time of its original transmission. Potter famously judged it to be 'based on nothing more edifying than rancid disdain, for it was a prolonged jeer, twitching with genuine hatred, about the dreadful suburban tastes of the dreadful lower-middle-classes'.[15] As Coveney ruefully observes, it was after this that 'words like "condescension" and "patronising" started to appear regularly' in reviews of Leigh's work.[16]

The play is all about a cocktail party taking place at the home of Beverly (Alison Steadman) and Laurence (Tim Stern); the three guests are Angela and Tony (Janine Duvitski and John Salthouse), a couple who have recently moved into the street, and another neighbour, Susan (Harriet Reynolds), a divorcee whose fifteen-year-old daughter Abigail is having a party of her own across the road. Laurence and Beverly have been married for three years, and as their cocktail party progresses, it becomes obvious that their relationship is falling apart. This lends *Abigail's Party* something of the bitter flavour of Edward Albee's *Who's Afraid of Virginia Woolf?* – except that in place of that play's emotional histrionics we are here presented with icy sarcasm, casual insults and thinly disguised contempt. As the play develops, their bickering turns nastier. There is a disturbing moment when Laurence goes to make a sandwich: 'I hope it chokes you!' Beverly tells him and when he charges back into the living room brandishing the sandwich knife, she jokes that 'I'm going to get stabbed', to which he replies, 'Don't tempt me'. Shortly afterwards, they get into an actual physical tussle when vying for supremacy over the record player. Later, as the play builds to its climax, they argue over a painting, which Laurence hates but Beverly wants to bring downstairs to show to the others; defending it as erotic rather than pornographic, she suddenly accuses him of being 'dead from the waist down anyway, let's face it' and, as the slanging match continues, tells him to 'Drop dead!' – which he does shortly afterwards, from a heart attack.

These are not, then, likeable characters. Yet the idea that Leigh invites us to do no more than 'jeer' at them for their 'dreadful suburban tastes' is patently ridiculous. Ray Carney is nearer the mark when he notes the scrupulously assembled, egregiously garish 1970s fashions which comprise the play's sets and costumes, and says of Beverly and Laurence: 'Their stereotypical externals are only dramatic externalizations of their stereotypical internals. Their off-the-peg clothing only matters as evidence of their off-the-peg souls'.[17] They aspire to things without asking why they are doing so. Laurence works hard – too hard – to provide a home in which he spends hardly any time, for a wife he hardly ever sees. Beverly shows off kitchen appliances that she never uses ('I'm not much of a cook'). And, yes, she puts Beaujolais in the fridge. Quite why this single detail among so many should have become a matter of such debate, or such a stick to beat Leigh with, is anyone's guess – one can only assume that it must have touched a nerve with many people. Michael Coveney reports a debate 'on the whole vexed topic of wine bottles in fridges'[18] in the letters page of *The Times*, and it even rates a mention in Kenneth Williams's diaries. (Having left the play at the interval, he singles out the Beaujolais moment as typical of how the 'frightful' audience of 'Hampstead sophisticates ... fell about, loving their superiority'[19]). Julie Burchill resurrected the controversy when, among the many pot-shots she took at Leigh in her excoriating review of *Naked* in 1993, she contended that 'Beaujolais is considered by all decent wine writers to be at its best chilled ... Beverly was actually in the vanguard of taste'.[20] Quoting this in 1996, Coveney waded back in against Burchill, pointing out that what she says was hardly true in 1977.[21]

All of which rather goes to prove that it does not really matter. Tastes change, but more importantly, so does the accepted wisdom of people like 'decent wine writers'. I have no idea whether Leigh either knows or cares about the 'best' way to enjoy Beaujolais, either in 1977 or at any other time, and I am not about to ask him. The whole point, surely, is that accepted wisdom and received values prevent one thinking for oneself. The satire in *Abigail's Party*, it seems to me, is not aimed at 'dreadful suburban tastes' but at the ways in which such tastes are defined and perpetuated. There is nothing inherently wrong with social aspirations, unless one loses sight of *what* one is aspiring to, and why.

What risks getting lost amid all the arguments is the fact that, behind the comic mannerisms, these are fully three-dimensional characters with credible feelings and motives. Laurence puts his work before his home life ('It's not a nine to five job, you know that') and expects Beverly to deal with the domestic arrangements ('Beverly isn't very organised: she doesn't believe in making shopping lists', he sneeringly tells their guests). Unable to drive, having failed her test three times, and with no job – she used to work in some capacity as a beautician – Beverly is all but trapped at home, and if this domestic environment is to be her world, then she is going to *make* it hers and control it. 'This is my house, and if you don't like it, piss off!' she tells Susan near the end of the play when emotions and events are all but out of control; and it has been indisputably *her* house from the very start. She presides tyrannically over the social occasion, flirting with the boorish, near-monosyllabic Tony, forcing cigarettes and nibbles on everyone, bullying Susan into having gin and tonic instead of the sherry she asked for, and then giving her 'a little top-up' so many times that she is eventually sick. No longer having any independent existence away from the house, Beverly is a monster, but we can see why she has become this monster; she is not just a comic turn, but a real character study.

Laurence professes to be something of an art lover – but early in the play we see him having a telephone conversation with a client during which he speaks in a series of clichés ('at your service'; 'he who pays the piper calls the tune'; 'up with the lark'), and the examples of art and culture that he professes to like seem rather like clichés themselves: Shakespeare ('not something you can actually read'), Van Gogh, Lowry, Beethoven and 'light classical' music. These all sound like works that Laurence thinks he is *supposed* to like rather than matters of individual taste. Beverly's preferences may be equally second-hand, equally shaped by received values, but she does, for example, genuinely seem to enjoy her Demis Roussos record, and justifies it not because it's great music, but because she and the majority of the others in the room happen to like it. She may well add that if *she* likes her Beaujolais chilled, that's how she's going to enjoy it, thank you very much. 'The trouble with you, Laurence', she tells him, 'is if somebody doesn't happen to like what you like, then you say that they've got no taste!' Her own tastes may be questionable to some; they could certainly be seen as evidence of superficial, rather than thought-out, aspirations – but beneath Leigh's lamentation of the spiritual poverty of her lifestyle can be detected a small celebration of her feistiness in defending it, and this is not something which is ever accorded to the supercilious Laurence.

Michael Coveney says that 'the whole point about Beverly is that she is childless, and there is a sense in which that grotesque exterior carapace is a mask of inner desolation',[22] and we might indeed conclude that she craves someone to mother from her tendency to talk down to people ('Do you want me to make you a little sandwich?'; 'Would you like to slip your little jacket off?'). But when she tells the others that the physical aspects of having children revolt her ('Having to do all that breast feeding and changing nappies, that would make me heave'), it is not clear whether she is speaking from the heart or covering up the truth. It may be that not having children is one more factor which contributes to her inner loneliness, but I think it is an over-simplification to suggest that childlessness is 'the whole point' about her or that Leigh is in some way blaming her for it, using childlessness as being somehow symbolic of wider inadequacies. When all the accusations and counter-accusations are done with, is it really too much to suggest that Beverly, frightful though she may be, at least comes over better than either of the two men in the play? As we reach the extremely black conclusion – one character lying dead, another distraught and grieving, a third stricken with cramp, her unsympathetic husband trying to relieve her, and the last panicking over what mayhem has broken out back at her home – we surely feel more sympathy for Beverly than for either the boorish, bullying Tony, who will not even *allow* Angela to learn how to drive, or the quarrelsome workaholic Laurence, who has just fulfilled Beverly's earlier prediction that 'you're going to kill yourself'. We certainly have come to understand her more. Alison Steadman's portrayal of the character remains a career-defining performance and, as with Keith in *Nuts in May*, it is *because* she and Leigh make Beverly so believable that she is so terrifying. A two-dimensional caricature would be much easier to ignore and to forget.

Leigh's next film, *Who's Who* (1979), set in and around a firm of London stockbrokers, is generally regarded as one of his least successful, perhaps because in this case he really does have very little sympathy for the characters or the world they inhabit. That said, it produces a great comic creation in Alan Dixon (Richard Kane), a splendidly Pooterish middle-aged clerk, fixated with unctuous reverence on the activities of British royalty and the aristocracy, including one or two of the firm's clients. His smug delight when he receives a signed photograph of Margaret Thatcher, complete with a letter from her secretary, would almost be touching, were it not so pitiful. This he files away with all his other autographed photos of politicians and TV personalities, and his even more pathetic collection of 'royal refusals'. (The letter to Mrs Thatcher was presumably one of congratulation: *Who's Who* was made in the year she became Prime Minister, and the film gains an added resonance from the retrospective knowledge that the years of her premiership saw a rise in the influence and affluence of exactly the kind of rich City kids it portrays.)

Alan's place in the British class system is wonderfully encapsulated in one neat visual touch, which acts as the punchline to an extended sequence in which he and his wife April (Joolia Cappleman) are seen at home playing host to a Mr Shakespeare (Sam Kelly), who is there to photograph the pedigree cats that April breeds, and to Miss Hunt (Geraldine James), who has come to buy one of them. This is intercut with a dinner party taking place at the flat shared by two of the well-off younger members of the firm, Nigel (Simon Chandler) and Giles (Adam Norton). After Alan has said goodbye to Shakespeare and watched him drive away, he turns and looks off camera. Leigh cuts to a shot looking through the window of the flat at the party going on inside – whereupon the curtains are closed. The cut creates an illusory link between the two locations, and symbolically sums up Alan's chances of ever being allowed into that upper-class world, which he can only observe, as Leigh says, 'from his voyeuristic, lower-middle-class perspective' on the outside.[23]

The scenes featuring Alan are very enjoyable – and his interaction with Sam Kelly's increasingly astonished and exasperated photographer is a particular pleasure – but Leigh's heart does not seem to be in the depiction of the privileged young people at the dinner party in quite the same way. He has said that this party was 'more improvised than almost anything else that I've done, and it shows',[24] but I suspect the reasons may go slightly deeper than that. The near interchangeability of the two hosts' names, Nigel and Giles, almost says it all; despite the best efforts of all concerned, they and their friends do not seem to exist as rounded characters of the kind that Leigh's working methods usually create. Finally one is left wanting to see rather less of them, and more of Alan's desk-bound younger colleague Kevin – and not just because Kevin is played by Philip Davis, who will go on to give such excellent performances in other films by Leigh. Kevin is the film's most endearing character, one of Leigh's knowing jokers, using humour as a survival mechanism. When someone asks him, 'How's your flat hunting going?' his response is, 'All right – I killed two this morning'. Right at the end of the film, he teases Alan with talk of a visit to 'Manor Park House'. Not wanting to appear ignorant of a stately home's history, Alan attempts to join in, and Kevin leads him on with misleading information about its fictitious inhabitant, Frederick Fotherington-Farquart. 'He was a very rich man, Kevin', opines Alan sagely. 'Well, no, not really', counters Kevin. 'He lost all his money didn't he? ... In the slump'. 'The Thirties were a very bad time for everyone, Kevin', intones Alan. 'Yeah, well, of course, he died in 1896', replies Kevin, devastatingly.

If *Who's Who* ended up a somewhat meandering work that never quite coalesces, Leigh's control over both character and narrative reasserted itself triumphantly in his next film, *Grown-Ups* (1980). While he was editing *Who's Who*, Leigh was also involved in casting meetings for a planned project for the Royal Shakespeare Company. This ultimately foundered because the actors were also appearing in other plays for the company at the same time, denying Leigh the unrestricted access he needed for his usual preparation and rehearsal processes, and he sees *Grown-Ups* as a kind of running for cover: 'After the RSC abortion, I was plugging back into a world I knew about, things that directly concerned me: hell in the suburbs'.[25]

Grown-Ups is particularly well constructed, building logically to an excruciatingly funny set piece that leaves viewers horrified even as they are howling with laughter. A young couple, Dick and Mandy (Philip Davis and Lesley Manville) move into a council house in Canterbury, next door to the privately owned home of Ralph Butcher (Sam Kelly), who used to be one of their schoolteachers, and his wife Christine (Lindsay Duncan). In a manner that will become familiar in Leigh's films, the contrasts between the two couples are seen most markedly in juxtaposed scenes of them in their respective bedrooms. Early in the film, before we have met the Butchers, Dick and Mandy are cuddling up in bed in their new house. 'Seems funny, don't it, sleeping in a strange room', he says. 'It's nice, though', she replies, 'having a home of your own – start a family now, can't we?' 'What if there's ghosts?' he asks, evading the issue. Later, nearly half way into the film, she raises the subject again, saying that she will stop taking her contraceptive pills. Dick, who is just back from a boozy session at the pub, disagrees, but even so they still snuggle up together. We immediately cut to their neighbours: Ralph is marking homework in bed, his briefcase placed ominously between them – no snuggling on the cards here. 'Is the end in sight?' asks Christine wearily, unable to get to sleep because the light is still on and Ralph insists on reading his pupils' essays out loud. 'No', he tells her bluntly.

Later, after another visit to the pub, Dick and Mandy argue more aggressively as they get into bed. 'I've told you, Dick, I'm coming off the pill', she insists. 'Yeah, and I've told you you're not, till I say so', he says. They issue threats and counter-threats: he will force the pill down her throat; she will refuse to make love; he will go elsewhere for sex. Yet by the end of the film, there is harmony and, eventually, a kind of redemption. The last time we see them in bed together, they are embracing tenderly. She has forgotten to take the pill; he says it doesn't matter.

'Do you want to have a baby an' all, then?' she asks in surprise. 'Yeah, why not', he says. 'Only normal, ain't it?' This has been immediately preceded by another contrasting scene with the Butchers in bed, Ralph reading and Christine sitting bolt upright. Realising she is angry and unhappy, he snaps at her, 'What do you want?' 'I'll tell you what I want', she replies. 'I want sex, and I want love, and I want a family. That's what I want!' He returns uncomprehendingly to his book.

Into this mix are thrown two other characters: Mandy's rather taciturn and not very supportive schoolfriend Sharon (Janine Duvitski) and, most unforgettably, her unmarried older sister Gloria (Brenda Blethyn). Gloria is constantly inviting herself round to visit Dick and Mandy – to bring them things, to have tea, to go for a drink with them, and maybe, she speculates, one day to babysit for them, perhaps even staying overnight ... She is clearly desperate to escape from living with their mother and, crucially, to feel *needed*. It is Gloria who propels the narrative towards its comic climax: one Saturday afternoon she has called round while Mandy and Sharon are out shopping, and has irritated Dick by talking all the way through the sports programme *Grandstand*. Moreover, she has brought an overnight bag with the intention of staying over. After much arguing, Mandy throws Gloria's coat and bags out of the house, and slams the front door on her when she goes out after them. Gloria runs round and re-enters through the back door, and this time is physically pushed outside. Crying hysterically now, she runs to the Butchers' house; the front door is open as Christine is washing the car, and before anyone can stop her, Gloria has rushed up the stairs and locked herself in the bathroom. It takes some time, and much reassurance that Dick is not waiting for her outside the door, to coax her out, and when she is finally escorted downstairs, the sight of Dick lurking outside makes her panic and set off for the bathroom again. Moments later, Gloria, Dick, Mandy, Ralph and Christine are piled in an undignified scramble on the staircase, with Gloria trying to get back upstairs and everyone else trying to stop her, while Sharon watches warily from the front door.

A sublimely funny sequence, demonstrating ensemble comic playing at its best, this works so well partly because of its seamless blend of broad comedy and pathos, and partly because the narrative has led up to it so logically and so plausibly. Every detail, every moment of slapstick and raucous recrimination is absolutely right for the characters and the situation. Both *Nuts in May* and *Abigail's Party* build towards powerful climactic scenes; here, for the first time, but not the last, Leigh and his actors brilliantly orchestrate a sequence of escalating comic chaos that is simultaneously so hilarious and so uncomfortable that we are not sure whether to laugh or to cry.

Leigh's co-ordination of character and narrative in *Grown-Ups* is tremendously confident and accomplished. While he is continuing to develop his narrative skills, the progression of the plot is, crucially, always motivated by the protagonists. Characterisation is never subservient to the exigencies of narrative. His work continues to show very little sympathy for characters who are so trapped in their own identities that their minds are closed off to new ideas or experiences; characters who do not have the ability to think for themselves, or who stop others from thinking for themselves. Amid the array of rich, full-blooded comic characterisations in *Grown-Ups,* Sam Kelly comes near to stealing the show with his portrayal of the pedantic, self-righteous Ralph, whom he endows with a splendidly irritating mannerism – a kind of subdued harrumphing noise, as though he is perpetually trying to clear his throat without ever doing anything so vulgar as coughing.

Home Sweet Home (1982) is equally well constructed, though its tone is more dolorous, less relieved by scenes of outright farce – which is not to say that it does not contain some painfully funny moments. It is, as Ray Carney says, 'Leigh's loneliest film',[26] a portrait of lives being lived in physical proximity to each other but spiritual isolation. Stan (Eric Richard), Gordon (Timothy Spall) and Harold (Tim Barker) are three postmen who work together and live in the same neighbourhood. Stan is separated from his wife, who left him eight years ago; he has a fourteen-year-old daughter, Tina (Lorraine Brunning), who lives in a care home. Gordon is married to Hazel (Kay Stonham), with whom he is in a permanent state of open hostility, not least about the fact that, having lost four stones herself, she now wants him to diet too, despite his repeated insistence that 'I ain't fat!' Harold is also married, though we learn about half way through the film that his wife June (Su Elliott) has for some time been having an affair with Stan. Harold does not seem to notice, but then he tends to exist in a world of his own, reciting jokes and intoning the lyrics of popular songs, mechanically rather than as a means of creating a rapport, and often without making eye contact (or any other sort) with whoever he is speaking to.

Not that the other characters are ready communicators either. Stan and Tina have difficulty talking to each other, and indeed at the beginning of the film he skips a pre-arranged Sunday visit to her, instead picking up a woman (Sheila Kelley) in a laundrette. He takes her first to a pub, where she babbles nervously and he barely contributes to the conversation, obviously seeing this as nothing more than a necessary prelude to sex. Later, back at his house, we see her getting dressed and preparing to leave. 'Love a cup of tea', she says, but he does not move. She explores the subject of tea, and her love of it, a little more, and he looks at his watch. He cannot give her a lift home, as he has to go 'somewhere'. 'Better be getting off', she says eventually. At the front door, he finally asks her what her name is; 'Janice', she replies, before limping away, seemingly in pain from polio and not very sure of which way to get home. It seems unlikely that they will ever see each other again.

When Stan does finally visit Tina, a social worker named Melody (Frances Barber) pushes him into having her stay at his house for most of the following weekend. In a marvellously melancholy scene in his back garden, he tries to chat to Tina, asking her if she recalls an incident some years ago, when he thought she had got lost but she turned out to be hiding. She at first does not respond, seeming not to remember, then reveals that she does by correcting him on a detail of the story; he now seems to lose interest, and changes the subject. They never seem to be having the conversation at the same time as one another, and so it goes nowhere.

We first learn about Stan's affair with June when he calls round to see her; she initially does not want to have sex with him, but allows herself to be persuaded upstairs. 'Did you like that?' he asks afterwards. 'It was all right', she says. She complains that she has not seen him for six months. 'I wouldn't be here if I didn't want to see you, would I?' he replies. After he has left, June takes to her bed for the rest of the day, allegedly with a terrible headache. Harold, in his plodding way, tries to look after her, but irritates her by putting the tea in her cup before the milk, and offering her a biscuit ('Don't be stupid, Harold!'). They might almost be strangers; 'Live with someone all your life ... they don't know anything about you', mutters June. Harold, staring fixedly ahead, responds to her complaints of a headache with a mini-stream of consciousness: 'Why don't they have aspirin in the jungle? Cause the parrots eat 'em all. Where do parrots learn to talk? They go to the polly-technic'. He says he will go downstairs, adding, 'Give me a shout if you want anything'. 'I don't want anything from you!' she tells him. 'You all right?' he asks. 'Yes! Go away!' snaps June, telling him, 'You don't know what I've been through today!' 'What have you been through today?' he asks, not unreasonably. 'Nothing', she says, and he departs none the wiser.

In fact the revelation of the affair does not come until much later, after Stan has taken Tina to Gordon and Hazel's house for Sunday lunch during her weekend visit. Stan and Gordon have been to the pub, and when Gordon returns – loud, unsteady and demanding, 'Come on, woman, get the bleeding dinner on the table!' – it is clear that he and Hazel are on a collision course. They are still arguing when everyone later goes back to Stan's for a cup of tea. Hazel, who we have seen in an earlier scene flirting with Stan when he stops off at her house on his rounds, goes into the kitchen and Stan follows her. While Gordon sits demanding to know what they are doing, they kiss and embrace. This is seen by Tina, and also by June, who has inopportunely arrived, wanting to speak to Stan. She never gets the chance, however, as Gordon and Hazel are now in full flow, him wanting to go home, her wanting to go for a drink with Stan. As they storm out of the house, Harold is passing by, and spots June. 'What you been doing?' he asks innocently. 'Ask *him* what she would have been bleeding doing if we hadn't been round here!' says Hazel of Stan, whom she calls a 'dirty sod'. June rushes off, followed by the bemused Harold; Stan bundles Tina into his car to take her back to the care home; and Gordon and Hazel are last seen outside Stan's house, flinging abuse, threats and recriminations, and finally physically struggling with each other.

Later, back at their home, June tells Harold that she is having an affair with Stan. His unwillingness to believe that such a thing could happen makes him even slower on the uptake than usual, and he keeps asking inane questions like 'Why?', 'What do you mean?' and 'You're joking, ain't you?' as she attempts to spell it out for him. Leigh recalls that during the improvised rehearsal of this scene, Tim Barker genuinely could not believe that the revelation was true: 'He was devastated, and he tapped into those real feelings, which is why it's such a good scene'.[27] It is certainly another of those instances where one laughs almost in spite of oneself: Barker's mournful face and nonplussed manner are terribly sad, yet one also feels like shaking him out of his hilarious obtuseness.

The film ends with another fine display of non-communication. Melody, who always seemed more absorbed in herself than with her clients, has left social services, and her replacement Dave (Lloyd Peters) – who also seems to be her jilted lover – calls round to see Stan about Tina's future. As Dave maunders on, wandering from professional jargon to personal grudges to pocketbook political analysis, Stan sits saying hardly anything, while outside Tina waits and listens alone. It is a wry and touching coda to a film which demonstrates Leigh's growing ability to deal with big themes and emotions – being married, having children, loneliness, despair, adultery – through a depiction of ordinary lives which is honest enough to be both funny *and* sad. Timothy Spall, working here with Leigh for the first time (and making glorious comic business out of propping his bicycle up on its pedal against the kerb; of course, it falls over, out of shot, seconds later), has summed up as well as anyone why Leigh's style is so unique, and why it matters: 'The minutiae of people's repetitious lives becomes of the utmost importance. And his people are never seen anywhere else, except when they are destroyed in the tabloid newspapers or in patronising documentaries. If you were to tell me you think Mike's patronising, I'd accuse him of the dead opposite: of elevating, and of making amusing and tragic, what most people in life go through'.[28]

Leigh certainly achieved this again in his next film, the genesis of which apparently came during the shooting of *Home Sweet Home*:

> I was in the bath, listening to the radio very early in the morning, and this story came on about two unemployed kids in Warrington or St Helens or somewhere who had committed suicide. And I thought – I always go through something like this – what we're doing is irrelevant. *That's* what we should be doing. Something about unemployment. We were two or three years into Thatcher, it was already an issue, and it lingered in the back of my mind.[29]

Meantime was eventually made in 1983, by Central Television for Channel 4, making it the only one of Leigh's TV features not to be produced by the BBC. It provides something close to a definitive portrayal of a large section of Britain four years into Margaret Thatcher's premiership, capturing the period's high unemployment and disaffection, especially among the young urban population. At the heart of the film is the relationship between two brothers, Mark (Phil Daniels) and Colin (Tim Roth), both in their early twenties and living with their bickering parents, Mavis (Pam Ferris) and Frank (Jeff Robert) in an East End tower block. Mark is another of Leigh's motormouths, spiky, streetwise and able to runs rings around most people with a caustic wit. Colin is shy and slower-witted, and Mark seems to treat him with the same offhand derision he has for everyone else, habitually addressing him as 'Dobbin' or 'Muppet'.

Like both his sons, Frank is unemployed, although he clearly sees himself as a victim and them as somehow responsible for their own situation. Frank grumbles his way through the film, bemoaning the cessation of National Service (not that he actually did it himself) and the decline in morals ('Look at that. Sixteen years old. Schoolgirl, showing her all in a paper'). His lack of rapport with Mark and inability to match him mentally are highlighted by the contrast between Mark's joking, which is designed to challenge, to provoke and wrong-foot people, and Frank's complete lack of any sense of humour. In one scene he sits unsmiling at the television while a studio audience shrieks with laughter at whatever he is watching; and he responds to one of Mark's verbal sallies with a grumpy, 'Who's he think he is, Ernie Wise?' – cack-handedly referring to the straight man of the famous double act rather than the comic. Mavis is sour, bad-tempered and thoroughly ground down by life; though even she is allowed her moment of sympathy when we see her at the bingo hall, desperately trying to keep up with the caller despite a succession of pens that do not work, and wondering whether fate is conspiring to prevent her from winning a major prize.

Mark seems to spend his days wandering around, or in betting shops and pubs, sometimes in the company of Coxy (Gary Oldman), an aimless skinhead with a propensity for racism and violence. Mark has the measure of Coxy and treats him with calculated contempt (later in Leigh's career, when Mark's provocative verbal dexterity is combined with Coxy's potential for destructive behaviour in *Naked*'s Johnny, the result is a *really* dangerous character), but he is worried when Colin starts keeping company with him too. Although Coxy seems to befriend him and takes him to visit Hayley (Tilly Vosburgh), a young friend of the group, in her flat, he cruelly taunts Hayley while they are there, almost reducing her to tears, and later shuts Colin up in a cupboard as a joke.

Meanwhile Mavis's sister, Barbara (Marion Bailey), who lives in middle-class Chigwell with her husband John (Alfred Molina), offers to pay Colin to decorate their house. Mark, who feels that the offer is demeaning and patronising, gets to Barbara's house first on the day that Colin is due to start work and urges Colin to return home with him. As Colin sits, neither moving nor saying anything much, the power-play between Barbara and Mark becomes tense and riveting. Unlike other aspirant middle-class housewives in Leigh's work both before (*Abigail's Party*) and since (*High Hopes*), Barbara is articulate and alert, and the only other character in the film who is a match for Mark. When he 'accuses' her of talking posh, she points out that she had elocution lessons at college: 'In them days, people didn't want to employ you unless you spoke nicely. Especially at a bank, in the city. You can't pick up the phone to a customer and say, "Wotcher, cock, what can I do for you then, eh?"' 'Can't you?' replies Mark. 'No', she goes on. 'You have to say, "Good morning, this is the National Westminster Bank, may I help you please?"' 'What about the afternoons?' challenges Mark, and she tops him: 'Oh, well, you had to use your imagination then, didn't you?'

When a Mike Leigh character can engage in this kind of imaginative role-play and combative repartee, it is a sign of self-awareness. Unlike Beverly, for instance, Barbara knows quite well why she has created an affluent lifestyle for herself and what she wants from it – and on one level Mark even seems to respect this, at least in comparison to his own parents. Her tragedy is that it has involved getting trapped in a loveless marriage to the solemn, pompous businessman John. On this occasion, Mark wins the battle of wills. Colin, who believes that Mark wants the decorating job for himself, walks out, and Mark leaves soon afterwards. When John returns home from work that evening, Barbara has been drinking heavily: 'You must be feeling very merry', he says, seemingly oblivious to the fact that in this case 'merry' is absolutely the least appropriate euphemism for 'drunk' (and recalling Angela's similarly maladroit comment that 'We're all getting a little bit merry, aren't we?' in *Abigail's Party*). Fed up with his high-handed attitude, she eventually tells him to 'Fuck off!' – and a smile of small triumph spreads across her face.

Mark and Colin arrive back home separately, Colin enveloped in his voluminous parka, which he refuses to remove. When Mavis and Frank realise that Colin has walked out on Barbara's offer of a job, and that Mark was responsible, they harangue both of them in the bedroom that the brothers share. Colin, hitherto cowed and withdrawn, now snaps, ordering them to 'Shut up!' and telling them that 'It's my room – get out!' And, very taken aback, they do. Left alone together, the brothers reveal a stronger bond than at any previous point in the film. Mark asks Colin where he has been all day, reassuring him unaffectedly, 'Come on, tell us. I love you'. He also says that he is desperate to leave home. In the morning, he discovers that Colin has had his head shaved. He suspects that this is again down to Coxy's influence, but Colin denies it and says that he already regrets his new skinhead look. 'No one tells you what to do?' asks Mark approvingly. 'That's right', agrees Colin. Mark looks at him a bit more admiringly now, and gives him a new nickname: 'Kojak'. 'Don't call me that', says Colin, but he is smiling. As their parents continue to argue in another room, we see the brothers sharing a joke and exchanging smiles for the first time.

It is a bleak ending, because nothing about their circumstances has actually changed, but a touching one, because we sense that their ability to survive and carry on is strengthened by the bond between them and the independence of spirit that they may now be able to share. Mark may have found something as close to a kindred spirit as he is ever likely to, and his protective instincts for his more vulnerable brother are not in doubt; rightly or wrongly, he has closed ranks to cut out the influence on Colin of Barbara and her well-meaning patronage on the one hand, and the dangerous, unpredictable Coxy on the other. Our last sight of Coxy in the film is a marvellously resonant shot of him inside a large tin drum, rolling around and banging the inside of it with a stick in a frenzy of pent-up aggressive energy. Gary Oldman's performance may well be the most memorable in a film fairly loaded with excellent work from its then little-known cast (one of Leigh's favourite actors, Peter Wight, also turns up as the hilariously laid-back, quasi-hippy estate manager sent to check out the repairs needed in the family's rented flat).

Four Days in July (1985), which followed *Meantime*, again approached a specific socio-political situation from a familial perspective. The issue of having children had already surfaced in Leigh's films, for example in *Hard Labour*, *Abigail's Party* and *Grown-Ups*; *Four Days in July*, which is set in Belfast, leads up to the near-simultaneous births of two babies. One of them is born to Lorraine (Paula Hamilton), the wife of an Ulster Defence Regiment soldier, the other to Collette (Bríd Brennan), a Catholic woman. Moreover, the theme of children – when to have them, how to bring them up, how many to have, whether to have them at all – runs through the film from first to last. The opening shot succinctly encapsulates both theme and setting: three children run or cycle, away from the camera, down a back alley between rows of houses. They reach a point where the alley crosses a road, and pause matter-of-factly to allow armed Land Rovers to cross from left to right. Towards the end of the film, the two husbands, the soldier Billy (Charles Lawson) and the injured Catholic man Eugene (Des McAleer), find themselves in a hospital waiting room with another expectant father, a Mr Roper (John Hewitt), who moans incessantly, not least about the prospect of having children. 'Years of not sleeping at night ... by the time you get any peace, you're too old to enjoy it', he forecasts bitterly. 'The cost of raising them – feeding and clothing them. And whenever they do grow up, you never know. Get themselves into trouble. Disgrace you. What is there for them in this country anyway? Nothing!' Asked by Billy why he does not therefore emigrate, Roper contends that 'Everywhere in the world's as bad as this place ... You're better off never being born at all'. Alas, it seems his words may have come tragically back to haunt him when he is called by the Sister (Ann Hasson) to have 'a wee word' – it does not sound as though it will be good news. In the final scene, Lorraine and Collette have had their babies, and they and the Sister discuss the prospect of bringing them up, concluding that one never knows what the future will hold. 'People give their children everything, and give them all the love they can, but you don't know if a child's going to turn on you', says Collette. The misanthropic pessimism of Roper gives way to recognisable hopes and fears for the future, expressed simply through the desire to do what one can, love one's children and hope for the best.

It is typical of Leigh to have approached the film in this way: 'I simply wanted to respond to whatever I found in my investigation of Northern Ireland and all I wound up saying, really, was something very fundamental and basic about people'.[30] It is also typical that, while observing fundamental experiences common to both the Protestant and Catholic couples through the two births, he did not aspire to an antiseptic even-handedness which, while it might have *looked* like a mark of documentary-style realism, would have ended up missing the all-important quality of truth about the people and the situation – truth, however necessarily subjective, being more vital to a film-maker like Leigh than the illusory realism of apparently impersonal documentary. Shane Connaughton, who plays the plumber Brendan, has recalled: 'The Protestant side, and some of the Protestant actors, felt that they didn't get a fair crack of the whip'.[31] Michael Coveney aptly notes that this effectively translates into 'a fair crack of the crack',[32] since, unsurprisingly, Leigh's sympathies are most potently reflected in the warm, collective humour of the Republican Catholic group. This is especially evident in the long scene between Collette, Eugene, Brendan and Dixie (Stephen Rea), a stand-in window cleaner who reports that his predecessor is 'having a rest – cardiac arrest' and teases Brendan with questions like, 'What's the name of the ship in the film *Mutiny on the Bounty*?' Their conversation is much more endearing than the macho banter conducted by Billy and his fellow soldiers in front of Lorraine. Likewise, when the soldiers sing 'The Sash' during the Battle of the Boyne commemorations on 11 July (one of the film's four consecutive days), they do so in drunken, rowdy, rabble-rousing style, first around the bonfire and then back at Billy's home; later Collette and Eugene sing the same song softly and gently – if ironically – as they lie lovingly in bed together. Nevertheless, the soldiers are far from one-dimensional characters, and are convincingly allowed to express their frustration at the situation they are in, in their opinion 'overtrained and underused, babysitting a pack of loonies'.

Leigh has not made a feature film for television since *Four Days in July*, but his contribution to the medium remains both memorable and significant. *Primetime*, a magazine dedicated to covering the cultural impact of television, featured an article on Leigh in its second issue in 1981, reporting that *Grown-Ups* 'drew an audience of 4½ million in the *Playhouse* slot that usually attracts around ½ million' and that *Nuts in May* 'was seen by 8½ million people'.[33] Add to that the sixteen million who watched *Abigail's Party* during that ITV strike and you have viewing figures to compare with royal weddings, major sporting events or *The Morecambe and Wise Christmas Show*. (Who did Leigh think he was, Ernie Wise?) Public awareness and appreciation of Leigh's work were high by the mid-1980s, then, but his ambition was still to make another feature film for the cinema. *Meantime* had only missed out by months on benefiting from a change in Channel 4 policy, whereby work produced for their 'Film on Four' strand would be made on 35mm with a view to a cinema release prior to TV transmission. Leigh had been unlucky on that occasion; now he was poised to take advantage of the situation.

Notes

1 Garry Watson, *The Cinema of Mike Leigh: A Sense of the Real* (London, Wallflower Press, 2004), p. 5
2 Quoted in Mirra Bank, 'Mike Leigh', from *Films in Review* (January/February 1997); reprinted in Howie Movshovitz (ed.), *Mike Leigh Interviews* (Jackson, University Press of Mississippi, 2000), p. 118
3 *Ibid.*
4 Michael Simkins, *What's My Motivation?* (London, Ebury Press, 2003), p. 270. Simkins incidentally tops and tails his book with an account of his audition for the role of Frederick Bovill in *Topsy-Turvy*.
5 Quoted in Philip Bergson, 'Questing', *What's On*, 11 January 1989, p. 66
6 Martyn Auty, 'But Is It Cinema?', in Martyn Auty and Nick Roddick (eds), *British Cinema Now* (London, BFI Publishing, 1985), p. 58
7 David Robinson, *The Times*, 12 January 1989
8 Quoted in Michael Coveney, *The World According to Mike Leigh* (London, Harper Collins, paperback edition, 1997), p. 89
9 Quoted in Richard Dacre, 'Devised and Directed: The Television Work of Mike Leigh', *Primetime*, 1: 2 (Autumn 1981), p. 25
10 *Ibid.*, p. 25
11 Michael Coveney, *The World According to Mike Leigh*, p. 22
12 *Ibid.*, p. 114
13 *Ibid.*, p. 112
14 *Ibid.*, p. 114
15 Dennis Potter, *Sunday Times*, 6 November 1977
16 Michael Coveney, *The World According to Mike Leigh*, p. 119
17 Ray Carney and Leonard Quart, *The Films of Mike Leigh: Embracing the World* (Cambridge, Cambridge University Press, 2000), p. 97
18 Michael Coveney, *The World According to Mike Leigh*, p. 119
19 Russell Davies (ed.), *The Kenneth Williams Diaries* (London, Harper Collins, 1993), p. 541
20 Julie Burchill, *Sunday Times*, 7 November 1993
21 Michael Coveney, *The World According to Mike Leigh*, p.120
22 *Ibid.*
23 Quoted in Graham Fuller, 'Mike Leigh's Original Features', in *Naked and Other Screenplays* (London, Faber & Faber, 1995), p. xxiii
24 Quoted in Michael Coveney, *The World According to Mike Leigh*, p. 133
25 *Ibid.*, p. 150
26 Ray Carney and Leonard Quart, *The Films of Mike Leigh*, p. 150
27 Quoted in Michael Coveney, *The World According to Mike Leigh*, p. 162
28 *Ibid.*, p. 160
29 *Ibid.*, pp. 171–2
30 Quoted in Graham Fuller, 'Mike Leigh's Original Features', p. xx
31 Quoted in Michael Coveney, *The World According to Mike Leigh*, p. 177
32 *Ibid.*
33 Richard Dacre, 'Devised and Directed', p. 23

'A different world': *High Hopes* 4

By the time of Leigh's long-awaited return to the big screen, in 1988, Margaret Thatcher had been the British Prime Minister for nearly ten years. She had won a third consecutive election victory in the 1987 general election, with a majority of 102 seats – a mere forty-two less than in her previous term of office, despite the deeply divisive year-long miners' strike of 1984–85, and a bitter internal dispute over Westland Helicopters in 1986 that led to some high-profile cabinet resignations. *High Hopes* represented Leigh's uncertainty about what anyone opposed to Thatcherism could practically do in the face of such an apparently unstoppable political force: 'I just felt that I wanted to express the frustration and confusion that a lot of ordinary socialists like myself were feeling'.[1] Also, his father Abe had died in 1985; Leigh was teaching in Australia at the time and understandably felt a terrible frustration at having to miss Abe's funeral. His feeling that he ought to create a stronger bond with his mother also informs one of the key character relationships in *High Hopes*.

The film opens with a long shot, the screen masked on either side to frame a single male figure walking towards us. The image is then widened to normal screen-size, revealing the man to be just one of a large number of pedestrians in a London street. The effect is to isolate a single character but then immediately place him in a crowd of other, similar figures; this powerfully suggests, not for the last time in Leigh's work, that what we are about to see is only one story among many possible ones, all equally valid.

The character in question is Wayne (Jason Watkins), a hapless young newcomer to London who, we will shortly discover, left his family home in Byfleet following an argument with his mother over pies ('I was supposed to get steak and kidney pies, and I got pork pies instead'). Fortunately for Wayne, he comes across Cyril Bender (Philip Davis) and his partner Shirley (Ruth Sheen), a good-natured, willing-to-help couple who live in a small flat near Kings Cross station. They immediately sympathise with Wayne's all too obvious naivety: he has vague ideas about getting a job on a building site and seems to be looking for his sister ('Vivien Bennett – do you know her?'), though his only contact for her is a piece of paper given him by his mother and bearing the address Ballswood House, minus any street name.

Cyril and Shirley's amiability derives from the fact that they are largely contented in their life together. They are, however, seriously divided on the matter of whether or not they should have a baby. Shirley would like a child; at the moment plant care is the main outlet for her nurturing, caring instincts: she grows cacti (with a succession of jokey nicknames, ranging from 'Thatcher' and 'Denis' to 'Dick', 'Turd' and 'Brains'), keeps a small garden on the roof of their apartment block and, when they visit Highgate Cemetery, is as interested in the plants and flowers as in the political theory that Cyril declaims in front of Karl Marx's tomb.

Cyril rationalises his resistance to fatherhood as a desire for society to be just and fair before he brings a child into it, and says that 'It's an overpopulated world as it is' – placing him in contrast to Shirley's more pragmatic attitude that 'the world ain't never going to be perfect'. Yet he chastises their friend Suzi (Judith Scott) for thinking in political slogans, theories and abstractions and for not actually doing anything. He does of course have a point: he accurately exposes inconsistencies in Suzi's theorising ('one minute she's talking about revolutionary socialism, the next she's starting a business') and when he asks her what good talking about issues is, she comes up with the self-perpetuating justification that 'it gets it clear, in your brain ... so when you're out in the street, talking to people, you know what you're talking about'. Cyril is at least self-aware and blunt about his own lack of action: asked by Suzi, 'Well, what do you do?', he replies, 'Sit on my arse'.

It is therefore not hard to guess that Leigh's sympathies lie, however reservedly, with Cyril rather than Suzi; he has said that '*High Hopes* was of course born of my own such feelings of inertia'.[2] (His next film, *Life Is Sweet*, will also include a character for whom received ideals again do not encompass a desire actually to achieve anything or to make changes.) Yet Shirley can cut through Cyril's posturing with a simple expression of affection. A little later, he says to her: 'I'm a dead loss – don't do nothing, sit here, moaning ... Don't know why you don't clear off'. 'I would ... if I didn't love you', she replies. She starts to cry, they hug, and she reminds him that one must make the best of the world as it is. This reinforces one of the film's major themes: that in an imperfect world there is salvation of a kind to be found in personal relationships.

This theme is especially evident in the treatment of Cyril's elderly widowed mother (Edna Doré), whom he worries about and occasionally visits, though clearly not often or for long. Mrs Bender still lives in the family home, one of the few council tenants left in what is now a very middle-class area ('They buy these houses for sod all', says Cyril. 'They sell 'em for a fortune'). She no longer knows any of her neighbours, is unable to get about easily and has little discernible life beyond her domestic routine. She seems rather older than her seventy years, tired, confused and vaguely irritable.

The film frequently emphasises Mrs Bender's vulnerability by isolating her in environments where her discomfort and disorientation are painfully obvious – notably in two excruciatingly funny extended scenes which place Mrs Bender as the passive centre of comic chaos. Both involve her daughter, Cyril's neurotic, social-climbing sister Valerie Burke (Heather Tobias) and her boorish husband Martin (Philip Jackson); and in the first she is also at the mercy of her ghastly, snobbish next-door neighbours, Laetitia and Rupert Booth-Braine (Lesley Manville and David Bamber).

Valerie's first appearance in the film immediately establishes her selfishness. She has called round to see her mother to deliver her Christmas present – a blood pressure gauge! – two months late. Although Mrs Bender has no transport and Valerie and Martin have a car each, she blames the delay on her mother's not wanting to visit them for Christmas. When Mrs Bender complains about Valerie's large dog because it will 'take me a week to get all them hairs off the furniture', Valerie deals with the matter to her own satisfaction by replying 'Give you something to do, won't it?'

Valerie's lack of concern for her mother, and the equally unfeeling attitude of the Boothe-Braines, are shown up in sharp relief in the first of those two extended sequences, in which Mrs Bender locks herself out of her house. When Laetitia Boothe-Braine arrives home, she at first ignores and then patronises the distressed Mrs Bender ('You have got yourself into a pickle, haven't you?'), and only invites her into their home when there is absolutely no alternative – although her shopping basket on wheels is not allowed over the threshold. Anxious to get rid of Mrs Bender, Laetitia phones Valerie, who can likewise hardly be bothered coming to fetch her. She lies to get Martin to go for her mother ('she's had a serious accident'), then turns up anyway, but forgets the keys that are supposed to be the reason for her visit because she is more preoccupied with over-dressing herself in a futile attempt to impress the Boothe-Braines. Blaming her mother for her own mistake ('She's changed the lock'), she seizes the chance to have a look around their house, barging into Rupert's basement study with a cry of 'Ooh, look what they've done to your coal hole, Mum!' Only when Cyril and Shirley appear on the scene is Mrs Bender properly looked after; we sense that her future well-being depends on them and their genuine concern for her.

The second major set piece occurs a little over a week later, at Mrs Bender's seventieth birthday party, which takes place at Valerie and Martin's house. Martin, who we have already seen to be thoroughly boorish and crude, drives Mrs Bender there, tearing through the streets, jolting her about in the back seat of his car and cracking jokes at her expense that she barely understands ('There's a couple of old geezers in my boozer, cream their jeans over you – get their pacemakers going at seventy-eight, you would'). He then abandons her to visit his mistress (Cheryl Prime), whom he berates and bullies ('I've only got about ten minutes, I've got somebody in the car'), eventually kissing her violently as he pushes her onto the sofa and leaving her moments later, the screenplay tells us, 'breathless and upset'.[3]

As Cyril and Shirley arrive for the party, Valerie is at her most egregious: bossy, insensitive, self-righteous and, in her obvious nervousness, emitting more than ever her characteristic humourless laugh. She is also wearing a hat that appears to be an imitation of the one Laetitia was wearing on the day that Mrs Bender locked herself out. 'Is that for me?' she asks of the parcel that Cyril and Shirley have brought, then, on learning that it is a shawl for Mrs Bender's birthday, immediately blurts out, 'Oh, she won't like that'. The directions in the screenplay confirm that she is 'bordering on the hysterical' and gets herself 'into a terrible state'[4] about the arrangement of an ornamental chess set, having very obviously lied about knowing how to play. When Mrs Bender arrives, Valerie practically frog-marches her around, trying to force her to have champagne ('We have got all the drink that money can buy! Why has she got to have a cup of tea?'), then eventually proposes a toast 'to Mum's birthday cause it could be her last'. In the stunned silence that follows, she bursts into a particularly long and mirthless laugh, which turns into deep sobbing. She then proceeds to get drunk, while Martin lectures Cyril on business methods and unsuccessfully tries to chat up Shirley. Valerie recovers sufficiently to produce a cake, with which she practically tries to force-feed Mrs Bender. This provokes another argument between her and Cyril, during which Valerie accuses Cyril and Shirley of being drug addicts and of having a breakdown. Cyril counters: 'You're disgusting ... you fill the house with expensive tat, you ain't sober, it ain't her birthday party, it's got nothing to do with her, it's for you'. The camera lingers, in a strikingly unexpected but strangely tender shot, on a close-up of Mrs Bender's bewildered face as the shouting match goes on around her.

The comparison between the Burkes and the Booth-Braines goes deeper than the mere fact that they treat Mrs Bender abominably. Both couples are thoughtless and selfish on a much broader level, which reinforces Leigh's dislike of the socio-political trends they represent: the complacently privileged and the on-the-make *nouveaux riches*. Martin and Rupert are equally callous in their business dealings: we see Rupert gloating to Laetitia at one point that 'Jeremy Rutland-Barrington will have to go'; while Martin outlines to Cyril his ideal that 'you let other wallies do the dirty work, and you sit in happy valley collecting the dosh'. Laetitia, while reluctantly providing shelter for Mrs Bender, lectures her that 'you'd be far better off buying yourself a nice little modern granny-flat ... if you were to put your house on the market, I think you'll find you've been sitting on a gold mine'; and in the mutual recriminations flying at the birthday party, we learn that Cyril objected when Valerie and Martin wanted Mrs Bender to buy her council house ('The only reason you wanted to buy that house is so you could sell it off later when she's gone'). We recognise that the difference between the Booth-Braines and the Burkes is principally one of class, of the contrast between the upper-class couple's effortless superiority and the middle-class pair's underlying insecurity.

Of course, the other thing that the Burkes and the Booth-Braines have in common is that all four of them are overtly stylised characters played to the hilt by the actors concerned. It is worth reiterating here the degree to which our preconceptions of what is 'realistic' are to a great extent shaped by *dramatic* 'realism'. We are all, unless unusually insulated from the world around us, used to seeing and meeting people in real life who would defy credibility if placed in a film; what dramatic convention defines as 'caricature' may well therefore be perfectly true to a given character. As Alison Steadman has said: 'Have you never sat on a bus, on a tube, walked down the street, and seen somebody or spoken to somebody and thought to yourself, I don't *believe* that person? Life is full of the most extraordinary characters'.[5] Lesley Manville has likewise insisted: 'If you think Laetitia is over the top, you should meet some of the women *we* found researching in the country, at the opera, in Harrod's'.[6] It is unfortunate that the prevailing critical insistence on the primacy of 'realism', and narrow definition of what that 'realism' actually is, have led to the word 'caricature' acquiring such a pejorative connotation. It is, surely, a valid comic method, and in the context of narrative drama it therefore seems more useful to ask how it is being used, and to what ends, than to deplore its existence.

The truth is that Leigh's bravura use of caricature, his films' refusal to tone down rich, sometimes broadly comic characterisations to conform to expectations of 'realist' drama, is a deadly serious comic strategy, far from the careless use of behavioural tics that his detractors have often alleged. The effect could perhaps be better described as *heightened* realism: an exaggeration to get at a deeper truth. Leigh has said himself that 'one needs a different kind of language to depict different characters. I've used that combination of naturalism and caricature quite consistently'.[7] But he does not simply wish to make fun of character types who provoke his amusement or his disapproval by caricaturing them; it is far more complex than that. His use of caricature – or exaggeration or heightened realism – within the highly recognisable milieu of his narratives creates tension between 'the world as it is' and 'the world as we would like it to be' in a way that is absolutely central to his style and themes.

In his 1900 essay on laughter, Henri Bergson discusses the comic primarily in terms of automatism, the point at which someone ceases to behave like a human being and is reduced to acting like a machine; what he calls a 'mechanical inelasticity, just where one would expect to find the wide-awake adaptability and the living pliableness of a human being'.[8] As I suggested in the introduction, the most caricatured characters in Leigh's films are those who most tend to fall into this trap, those with the least purchase on who they are and how they fit into the world; who are least secure in their sense of self. Hence while the Booth-Braines have the complacent confidence of those accustomed to wealth and power ('What made this country great was a place for everyone and everyone in his place', Rupert tells Cyril), they are just as anxious to keep up appearances, to maintain a social role, as the aspirant Burkes. Their values and lifestyles are no less superficial: Rupert buys £150 tickets to an opera about which he can remember nothing later the same evening. His sole intention is to impress; he smugly tells Mrs Bender that 'We're going to the opera', then narrows his eyes coldly when she fails to respond.

Valerie is probably the broadest character of all, and the most ridiculed; not even Rupert or Laetitia is subjected to quite such physical humiliation as the tumble she takes when Martin shoves her out of the way during Mrs Bender's party. She is, crucially, also the character with the least sense of self, adrift somewhere between her roots and the middle-class lifestyle that she aspires to. Even a supporter of Leigh like Andy Medhurst has felt that this harsh portrayal leaves 'a nasty taste in the mouth',[9] with its overtones of the kind of snobbery Dennis Potter detected in *Abigail's Party*. But Valerie, surely, is not being mocked merely because she has aspirations, but rather because she does not know what she aspires *to*. She is bound up by received notions of what an affluent and desirable lifestyle consists of, the superficiality of her ideals encapsulated and exposed in her slavish copying of Laetitia's hat. She does not actually think for herself about what values or quality of life she may be striving for and, worse, her ambition makes her blind to other people's needs, especially her mother's.

Cyril and Shirley are on two occasions contrasted with both the Burkes and the Booth-Braines in sequences involving domesticity, love and sex. In the first such sequence, nearly a quarter of an hour into the film, Cyril and Shirley arrive home after visiting Mrs Bender. They discuss her past – she worked in a canteen during the war, but never returned to employment after having her first child – and her present voting habits ('working-class Tories, stabbing themselves in the back'). This leads into a discussion about having a child and whether Shirley would return to work afterwards – which is what leads in turn to Cyril's comment that the world is already overpopulated. Then the helpless Wayne turns up on their doorstep again, and they agree that he can spend the night in their spare room. They tease him gently, at first telling him that he will have to sleep with Cyril, then amused that he doesn't realise what is going on when Cyril rolls a joint. Later, they snuggle up in bed and, as Wayne plays his radio in the next room, play-act being angry parents, giggling, 'I'll give you a smack!' and 'What do you think this is, a bleeding disco?' They laugh affectionately, enjoying their shared jokes – until the issue of having a child is raised as Shirley sighs and says, 'I hope I don't have a kid that's a bit thick'. Their mutual sense of humour is vital to their relationship, but once again we see that the issue of having a child is an underlying problem.

The next morning we meet the Booth-Braines for the first time. They have scarcely entered the film before we see them preparing for sex with what is clearly a ritual game, involving a teddy bear that they nickname 'Mr Sausage'. In their infantile play, they displace all sexual desire onto this bear, giggling 'Mr Sausage deserves a smack!' and 'Mr Sausage is coming to get you!' as they undress on the stairs.

After a couple of very brief scenes – Valerie presenting Mrs Bender with her belated Christmas present, and Cyril dealing with a stroppy receptionist in his job as motorcycle courier – we see Valerie barging into Martin's office to demand cash because she claims to have left her credit cards at home; he refuses to give her any. Later, he arrives home and, in retaliation for his earlier withholding of funds, she serves him bread and water for his evening meal, much to his irritation. Having made her point, Valerie then reveals that she has cooked a meal after all. However, Martin now perversely refuses it, preferring to go to the pub, and it ends up being given to the dog.

There is no evidence of any affection at all in the Burkes's marriage – Martin has his mistress, whom he plainly treats as badly as he does everyone else, while Valerie lavishes attention on the dog. Their discussion in this dinner-table scene is thoroughly characteristic. 'You trying to be funny?', asks Martin when she presents him with the bread and water; when Valerie replies, laughing nervously, that she isn't, he asks, 'What're you laughing at then?' 'I'm not laughing', she protests, promptly doing so involuntarily and mirthlessly. This is followed by an exchange about Martin's ability to take a joke ('Take a joke? I could take a joke, I don't get this joke'). It is a wonderfully ironic discussion of laughter and jokes by people who are clearly neither enjoying their situation nor genuinely finding any amusement in it; another illustration of the importance in Leigh's work of a sense of humour, and a contrast to the real, bonding laughter that Cyril and Shirley enjoy.

Unlike Valerie with her nervous laugh and Martin with his smug wisecracks that amuse nobody but him, Cyril and Shirley *share* jokes. They laugh together, touch and kiss each other with genuine affection. The fact that we see them cuddling in bed, sharing physical and emotional warmth, is crucial to our understanding of their relationship, as it was in *Grown-Ups* and will be for couples in Leigh's future films from *Life Is Sweet* to *Vera Drake*. Ray Carney's extended analysis of their joking and sense of play comprehensively demonstrates how Cyril and Shirley's laughter is a sign of their humanity, their sense of self and their ability to engage with the world around them. Their behaviour is healthily, spontaneously responsive – the antithesis of the inelasticity which Bergson defines as inappropriate and therefore ridiculous. In that sense, their characterisation as a couple can be seen as a development of Sylvia's faltering attempts to connect with other people through jokes in *Bleak Moments*, which were not always successful, but at least showed her to be capable of imagination and spontaneity.

This is how *High Hopes* works: the caricatured characters are the ones who are inelastic, locked into behaviour patterns designed to keep up the images they have of themselves and which they wish to project to the world. As Carney says, 'our rigidity is traceable to feelings of uncertainty. We wrap ourselves up in our own views out of a desire for security'.[10] Here, then, is a further variation on the theme of the world as it is (which Cyril and Shirley are able to engage with) and the world as we would like it to be (an illusion which the keeping-up-appearances 'performances' of the Burkes and the Booth-Braines are designed to perpetuate).

The second set of contrasts comes in a tighter, briefer sequence, showing the three couples engaged in bedtime conversations. As implied above, the ways in which people behave in the most private, intimate space in their homes is significant – certainly in Leigh's films, which repeatedly centre on domestic life, whether it is that of a suburban family or of William Schwenck Gilbert and Sir Arthur Sullivan.

The Booth-Braines, who might as well be speaking different languages as they get ready for bed, 'discuss' the opera they have just seen, which Rupert hardly even remembers. He is more concerned with what he has eaten: 'two steaks, same day, totally different'. Laetitia, meanwhile, preens herself: 'I thank God every day I've been blessed with such beautiful skin: you really are a very lucky boy. You take me for granted'. It is, in effect, not a conversation, but two barely interacting monologues.

Next we cut to the Burkes in bed together. While the Booth-Braines earlier displaced their sexual desire onto the teddy bear, Martin and Valerie's pillow talk is just a continuation of the bickering and hostility which informs every other aspect of their relationship: 'You start' – 'No, you start' – 'You get on top' – 'No, I don't want to get on top', and so on. Valerie's attempt to initiate sex by telling him 'You're Michael Douglas ... I'm a virgin' seems as bogus and inadequate as all her other role-playing. In any case, Martin has never heard of Michael Douglas, and the idea of Valerie as a virgin just makes him roar with laughter before turning away to sleep.

Finally we see Cyril and Shirley, just back from the pub, cheerful, loving and a little tipsy. In contrast to the Booth-Braines's childish sexual rituals, or Valerie's mechanical attempts at role-play, they once again engage in spontaneous play-acting, purely for their own amusement, this time revolving around the trivial fact that Cyril is too drunk to take his boots off. They also indulge in suggestive jokes: 'If I can't ease it off, I'll give it a good tug', says Shirley. There is a shift of mood as she becomes reflective and Cyril asks her to use a contraceptive; the tension continues as they bicker about each other's families, but then as they agree on the simple pleasure of being together in their flat, we see that, as the screenplay tells us, 'they both smile. Warmth has returned'.[11]

It is crucially Cyril and Shirley, then, whose outlook makes them open, adaptable, responsive, capable of change; and it is in them that we see hope for Mrs Bender's future as she grows older and more dependent. Her daughter, son-in-law and neighbours will certainly offer little comfort, locked as they are into their own rigid behaviour patterns. As Carney observes, 'while Valerie and Martin, and Rupert and Laetitia are completely defined by external, public, received roles, Cyril and Shirley dive beneath them (or, in the spatial imagery of the rooftop scene, rise above them)'.[12]

The rooftop scene to which Carney refers is the last in the film. Shirley tries to take Mrs Bender home after her birthday party, but memories crowd in upon the old lady – of her sister Freda, of a family rift – 'I never took him away from her' – and of unjust childhood humiliation: 'How was I supposed to see? I caught my shoe in the tramline. What'd she have to smack my legs for? ... They both stood there, laughing at me. In front of all them people!'

It now dawns on Cyril that his mother needs more care and attention; she spends the night at their home, and the next morning he and Shirley take her up on the roof of their block of flats. They show her St Pancras station, where her late husband used to work, her house behind the nearby gasworks, and landmarks like St Paul's Cathedral. Suddenly she can see connections between things, between various places that she knows and recognises. It would be wholly out of keeping with the scene's scope and tone to suggest that she can see her own environment 'clearly and at once, as in a poet's eye', as *A Matter of Life and Death*'s Dr Reeves can through his camera obscura, but everything is relative; in terms of this one ordinary life, we sense that she has gained a perspective usually denied to someone of her class, gender and generation. 'It's the top of the world!' she exclaims, and one feels that only in a Mike Leigh film could James Cagney's famous last words from *White Heat* (Raoul Walsh, 1949) be paraphrased with such delightful poignancy by a seventy-year-old lady in failing health.

Thus the film ends on a warm, quietly optimistic note, suggesting high (well, moderately so) hopes for the future through a newly discovered continuity between the generations – which might now even include the next generation, with the implication that Cyril and Shirley have finally agreed to have a baby. It is this sense that the main area of conflict in their relationship may have been resolved that makes for a satisfying conclusion here, as opposed to the deliberate *lack* of conclusion, the feeling of lives grinding on, at the end of *Bleak Moments*. As is usual in Leigh's work, the characters make important decisions and undergo significant events, but do not experience artificial transformations or have their lives miraculously changed. Their journeys and their victories are on a small, recognisable, human scale and thus, while not what we might be used to in terms of the conventions of high drama, are wholly credible. Leigh's stories are certainly well crafted and finely structured, and they almost always lead to an emotional catharsis of some kind, but their conclusions usually suggest nothing more melodramatic than life going on, not radically different from before, but informed by the enhancement to be found in human relationships discovered or reaffirmed. The final line of the screenplay of *High Hopes* sums up the tone perfectly: 'Mrs Bender sits and contemplates the gasworks and the view beyond. Beside her, Cyril and Shirley stand together and enjoy life'.[13] Leigh will later strike the same note in the endings, both on screen and in the screenplays, of *Life Is Sweet* ('Natalie and Nicola sit together quietly at the end of their garden on a pleasant summer's evening'[14]) and *Secrets and Lies* ('And the three of them enjoy the afternoon together').[15]

As noted earlier, it is Cyril and Shirley's adaptability, their willingness to adjust to each other's needs and to other people's, that has brought them to this point. This is in contrast not only to the Burkes and the Booth-Braines, but also to Suzi, whose response to experience is entirely theoretical, and to Wayne, who is essentially passive and seems incapable of adapting very much to anything. The narrative 'journey', however, has obviously been Cyril's rather than Shirley's, since it is he who has realised the need to take greater care of his mother and has at least shown himself willing to consider changing his mind about the key issue of whether or not they should become parents.

Leigh has cited Cyril as one of 'a fraternity of male characters' who 'are outsiders in a way that is related to me, although not literally. That sort of character, that outsider position, that role is an important one that *does* come from something implicitly autobiographical'.[16] Characters up to this time whom he places in this category include Norman in *Bleak Moments*, Trevor in *The Kiss of Death* and Mark in *Meantime*, and they will turn up in most of his subsequent films: Andy in *Life Is Sweet*, Johnny in *Naked*, Maurice in *Secrets and Lies*, Hannah in *Career Girls*, both Gilbert and Sullivan in *Topsy-Turvy* and Phil in *All or Nothing* can all be described, in their various ways, as outsiders, not least because they are all disillusioned idealists. This character type is central to the way we read Leigh's films, each 'in some way an organic function of what the film is concerned with',[17] and therefore seems worth considering further. Even at his or her most extreme, as seen in *Naked*'s Johnny, the disillusioned idealist is very different from the cynic or the misanthropist, who never had any ideals in the first place.

It is nonetheless easy to categorise satire and the social commentators who use it as cynical, and indeed Leigh has often been accused of treating his characters unkindly, as we have seen in Geoff Brown's complaint about 'cruel satire, rather than compassion', or in Dennis Potter's strictures against *Abigail's Party* – or, for that matter, in Andy Medhurst's reservations about the treatment of Valerie in *High Hopes*. Critics at the time shared some of these reservations, though some of them differed as to whether he was being overly harsh in his depictions of the Burkes (the opinion, for example, of Derek Malcolm in *The Guardian*) or the Boothe-Braines (Victoria Mather in the *Daily Telegraph*). Most were agreed, however, that Cyril and Shirley represented the film's conscience. In *The Independent* Sheila Johnston found that the film 'eventually settles for a moral centre of gravity in Davis and Sheen',[18] Nigel Andrews in the *Financial Times* declared that 'the film's triumph is in the depiction, at once satirical and compassionate, of its two aging young Marxists'.[19] Even Suzanne Moore, in a negative review in the *New Statesman and Society*, made the same point when she complained that 'while Cyril and Shirley are portrayed naturalistically as "real people", the Booth-Braines are nothing more than a cluster of clichés';[20] and Michael Darvell, struggling in *What's On* to come to terms with Leigh's style, conceded that 'Cyril and Shirley are the most believable because they are the most ordinary'.[21]

The most sympathetic reviews offered a more considered analysis of such contentious issues as 'naturalism' and 'caricature' in character depiction. Derek Malcolm found the 'changes of gear between gentle and perceptive comedy and outright, almost Hogarthian farce, more than a little disconcerting', but went on to declare himself 'a firm believer that life is very much odder than most people appear to think, and so, often, are people'.[22] Alexander Walker, in the *Evening Standard*, said that 'the truth of each creation crosses the style change as well as the class divide',[23] while Philip French perceptively noted in *The Observer* that Cyril and Shirley possess 'a gift of self-mockery that the others lack', 'a questioning attitude towards society' and a 'generosity of spirit'.[24] *The Times*' David Robinson insisted that Leigh 'is in no way an off-shoot of the older kitchen-sink school of documentary realism' but rather belonged 'to the British satirical tradition', and that Valerie, Rupert and Laetitia were 'grotesques in the line of Gillray, Dickens and Tony Hancock'.[25] In an earlier *Observer* review, Sean French likewise identified 'a corrosive caricaturist's skill worthy of George Grosz'.[26]

Satirical or corrosive, maybe, but is Leigh unkind or even unfair to portray the Burkes and the Booth-Braines in the way he does? Is he guilty of, in Potter's stinging words, 'disdain', 'contempt' and, ultimately, 'snobbery'? Is his satire really 'cruel'? In suggesting that the opposite is in fact true, I would like to make a comparison with the comedies of John and Roy Boulting, the British cinema's most celebrated satirists of the 'New Wave' period. After an early career in film drama, ranging from 'social conscience' films to the prototype British gangster movie *Brighton Rock* (1947), they gained a reputation for satirical comedy in the late 1950s and early 1960s, lampooning such sacred cows as the Army (*Private's Progress*, 1956), the law (*Brothers in Law*, 1957), academia (*Lucky Jim*, 1957), international politics (*Carlton-Browne of the F.O.*, 1959), industrial relations (*I'm All Right Jack*, 1959), and the church (*Heavens Above!*, 1963).

Most of these were popular successes, and have consistently been recognised, even by unappreciative commentators, as significant British films (less subject to changes in critical fashion than, say, the *Carry On* series). Yet, both at the time of their release and afterwards, they have frequently been accused of being spiteful and cynical. Reviewing *I'm All Right Jack* for the *Financial Times*, for example, David Robinson felt that it 'ingeniously echoed the popular audience's narrowest and meanest fears and prejudices',[27] while the *Monthly Film Bulletin* criticised *Heavens Above!* for 'the nastiness of its view of people'.[28] Surveys of British cinema have, characteristically, tended to be equally hostile or dismissive. Gilbert Adair, in a book commemorating British Film Year in 1985, makes cursory reference to the Boulting Brothers' 'low-humour, mean-spirited, self-styled "satires" of Establishment institutions',[29] and in *The Great British Picture Show*, George Perry complains that in *I'm All Right Jack* 'their shafts often went wide, satire being supplanted by facetiousness' and that 'it is hard to find a properly defined point of view'.[30]

An honourable exception to this prevailing negativity was Raymond Durgnat, who offered an alternative perspective in his pioneering 1970 study *A Mirror for England*: 'Only disappointed idealism would dare, and know how to, parody the obstinate illusions of idealism with such sober inventiveness and such sympathetic venom'.[31] This comment was cited thirty years later by Julian Petley in an essay in the first full-length study of the Boulting Brothers. Making the case for a reading of the Boulting Brothers' satires as 'moral tales', Petley notes that *Private's Progress*, *I'm All Right Jack* and *Heavens Above!* are a threesome 'which, beneath their superficially modish cynicism and scatter-gun satire, can actually be read as the expressions of a profound disillusionment and a deeply disappointed idealism'.[32] As Petley cogently argues, rather than the films being cynical themselves, they are railing *against* cynical materialism and opportunism. The three films he groups together are possibly the most durable and potent of the Boulting Brothers' comedies; they virtually form a trilogy, in each of which an innocent central character is let loose in the world, discovers its frailties and imperfections, then promptly retreats from it in increasingly extreme fashion – respectively to the halls of academia, to the seclusion of a rural nudist camp, to isolation in outer space.

I do not wish to insist on too strong a comparison between Leigh and the Boulting Brothers; although of course he saw their comedies and admits that 'I was quite taken with them, mostly because of Peter Sellers, probably',[33] he does not consider them the equal of the Ealing comedies and regards them as 'sometimes politically suspect'.[34] In any case, there is a major difference in tone, in that the Boulting Brothers' protagonists start out idealistically but become disillusioned over the course of the narrative, whereas Leigh's have already had their idealism tarnished and are working out how to deal with the fact. Thus, crucially, the Boulting Brothers deal with the process of disenchantment, and Leigh with the process of resolution and salvation. Nevertheless, I believe that the fundamental distinction between frustrated disillusionment and misanthropic cynicism is vital to a proper appreciation of both, and I will return to a consideration of Leigh's satirical standpoint in relation to his next feature, *Life Is Sweet*.

Before that, however, let us consider one more example of a Leigh outsider who uses humour self-consciously, as a survival mechanism. Before making *High Hopes*, Leigh wrote and directed an eighteen-minute short film for Channel 4 called *The Short and Curlies* (1987). In this quirkily tender little tale, a gawky, nervy young man named Clive (David Thewlis) conducts a tentative courtship with Joy (Sylvestra Le Touzel), who works in his local chemist's shop. For Clive, whom Leigh describes as 'a compulsive joker, a kind of humorous motormouth',[35] constant gags and riddles are a way of hedging his bets, dodging and weaving his way through conversations by evading a subject with a joke one minute, then disclaiming it the next ('No, I'm joking'; 'No, no, seriously ... '). 'You've always got a joke, ain't you?' says Joy at one point, to which he replies: 'I wouldn't be joking if I wasn't being serious'. The satirist's mission – and dilemma – in a nutshell.

Notes

1 Quoted in Graham Fuller, 'Mike Leigh's Original Features', in *Naked and Other Screenplays* (London, Faber & Faber, 1995), p. xx
2 Mike Leigh, foreword to *High Hopes*, in *Naked and Other Screenplays*, p. 186
3 Mike Leigh, *High Hopes*, in *Naked and Other Screenplays*, p. 241
4 *Ibid.*, pp. 242–3
5 Interviewed on *The South Bank Show*, first broadcast ITV1, 13 October 2002
6 Quoted in Michael Coveney, *The World According to Mike Leigh* (London, Harper Collins, paperback edition, 1997), p. 195
7 Quoted in Susan Linfield, 'For Mike Leigh It's Rue Britannia', *New York Times*, 19 February 1989
8 Henri Bergson, *Le Rire* (1900), trans. Cloudesley Brereton and Fred Rothwell (London, MacMillan & Co., 1913), p. 10
9 Andy Medhurst, 'Mike Leigh: Beyond Embarrassment', *Sight and Sound*, 3: 11 (November 1993), p. 9
10 Ray Carney and Leonard Quart, *The Films of Mike Leigh: Embracing the World* (Cambridge, Cambridge University Press, 2000), p. 194
11 Mike Leigh, *High Hopes*, in *Naked and Other Screenplays*, p. 231
12 Ray Carney and Leonard Quart, *The Films of Mike Leigh*, p. 200

13 Mike Leigh, *High Hopes*, in *Naked and Other Screenplays*, p. 262
14 Mike Leigh, *Life Is Sweet*, in *Naked and Other Screenplays*, p. 183
15 Mike Leigh, *Secrets and Lies* (London, Faber & Faber, 1997), p. 103
16 Quoted in Graham Fuller, 'Mike Leigh's Original Features', p. xxii
17 Interview with the author, 5 April 2005
18 Sheila Johnston, *The Independent*, 12 January 1989
19 Nigel Andrews, *Financial Times*, 12 January 1989
20 Suzanne Moore, *New Statesman and Society*, 13 January 1989
21 Michael Darvell, *What's On*, 11 January 1989
22 Derek Malcolm, *The Guardian*, 12 January 1989
23 Alexander Walker, *Evening Standard*, 12 January 1989
24 Philip French, *The Observer*, 15 January 1989
25 David Robinson, *The Times*, 12 January 1989
26 Sean French, *The Observer*, 21 August 1988
27 David Robinson, *Financial Times*, 17 August 1959
28 T. M., *Monthly Film Bulletin*, 354: 30 (July 1963), p. 95
29 Gilbert Adair and Nick Roddick, *A Night at the Pictures: Ten Decades of British Film* (London, Columbus Books, 1985), p. 60
30 George Perry, *The Great British Picture Show* (London, Pavilion Books, 1985 edition), p. 201
31 Raymond Durgnat, *A Mirror for England: British Movies from Austerity to Affluence* (London, Faber & Faber, 1970), p. 101
32 Julian Petley, 'The Pilgrims' Regress: The Politics of the Boultings' Films', in Alan Burton, Tim O'Sullivan and Paul Wells (eds), *The Family Way: The Boulting Brothers and British Film Culture* (Trowbridge, Flicks Books, 2000), p. 26
33 Quoted in Graham Fuller, 'Mike Leigh's Original Features', p. xii
34 Lee Ellickson and Richard Porton, 'I Find the Tragi-Comic Things in Life: An Interview with Mike Leigh', *Cineaste*, 20: 3 (1994); reprinted in Howie Movshovitz (ed.), *Mike Leigh Interviews* (Jackson, University Press of Mississippi, 2000), p. 74
35 Director's commentary, 'The Short and Curlies', in *British Short Films* (Cinema 16, CIN16DVD001, 2003)

1 'Top of the world': Ruth Sheen, Edna Doré and Philip Davis in *High Hopes*

2 'We love you, you stupid girl!': Alison Steadman and Jane Horrocks in *Life Is Sweet*

3 'Aren't people pathetic?': Katrin Cartlidge, Gregg Cruttwell, Lesley Sharp and David Thewlis in *Naked*

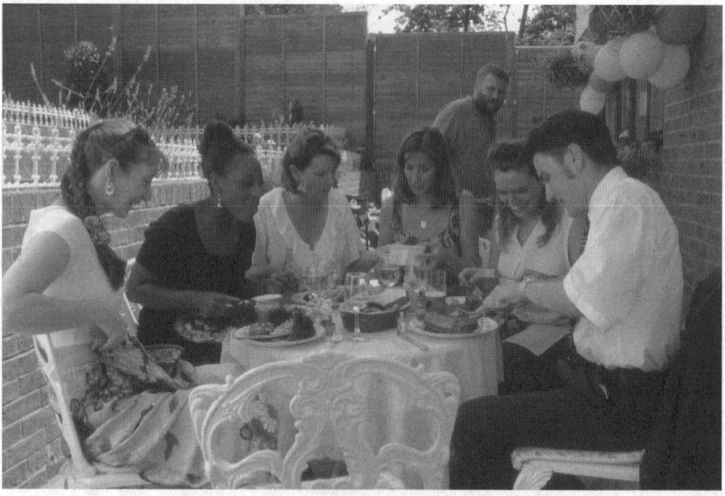

4 A bravura set piece: Elizabeth Berrington, Marianne Jean-Baptiste, Brenda Blethyn, Phyllis Logan, Timothy Spall, Claire Rushbrook and Lee Ross in *Secrets and Lies*

5 Younger selves: Katrin Cartlidge and Lynda Steadman in *Career Girls*

6 Rapport and chemistry: Lesley Manville and Timothy Spall in *All or Nothing*

7 Alone with her thoughts and fears: Alex Kelly, Imelda Staunton, Adrian Scarborough and Daniel Mays in *Vera Drake*

8 Mike Leigh during the filming of *All or Nothing*

'So long as you're happy': *Life Is Sweet*

5

An important development in Leigh's working life came in 1989 when he formed the production company Thin Man Films with Simon Channing-Williams, who had first worked with him on *Grown-Ups* as first assistant director and had co-produced *High Hopes*. For the company's first production, Leigh has said that he committed himself 'to making a comedy that would have a potentially larger audience appeal than *High Hopes*',[1] and this he achieved, as Graham Fuller notes: 'Lighter and sunnier in mood than *High Hopes*, but equally trenchant and moving in its depiction of ordinary people carrying on, doing what they can to survive and dream in the UK of enterprise culture, *Life Is Sweet* consolidated Leigh's international reputation as a man of cinema and as a great director of actors'.[2] The domestic setting and breezy tone may initially give the impression that this is going to be a feature-length pilot for, or spin-off from, a situation comedy (albeit a particularly good one). Ironically, it is after about half an hour (the standard length of a television sitcom) that the mood begins to change and darken.

As the film opens, the title *Life Is Sweet* appears on screen in big, bouncy, jaunty lettering of the type favoured by the publicists of the *Carry On* films. In what seems in retrospect an uncharacteristic opening for one of Leigh's films, the music is upbeat, indeed relentlessly cheerful. It is also diegetic: we are watching one of the principal characters, Wendy (Alison Steadman), teaching a Saturday-morning dance class, leading a group of young children in dancing to the tune 'Happy Holidays'. As we cut to a slightly later scene, in which she is helping them to put on their coats before leaving, a more wistful, rather melancholy (and non-diegetic) tune takes over. This bridges the cut to a medium shot of the North London house where Wendy lives with her husband Andy (Jim Broadbent) and their twin daughters, Nicola (Jane Horrocks) and Natalie (Claire Skinner).

Wendy is the hub of the family. She is also a good teacher: as the screenplay puts it, she is 'more concerned with getting the girls to express themselves and to enjoy the rhythm than with anything formal or rigorous'.[3] This ability to relate to children is intuitive; she has a strong maternal instinct. She works in a shop selling baby clothes and toys, and she admits to one customer that 'I get carried away, you know, cause mine are grown up'.

Indeed, Wendy has a tendency (not always unjustified, as we shall see) to talk down to people in general and to mother them. Like Beverly in *Abigail's Party*, she overuses the word 'little': 'Do you want a little sandwich?'; 'Is this your little coat ... Where's your little purse?'; 'Put your little cardigan on, Suzie ... put it on, cause you might get a little chill'. As usual in Leigh's work, this is more than just a mannerism, but rather reflects the way her adult life has been dominated by motherhood: she became pregnant at sixteen while doing her A levels – English and Business Studies – and put thoughts of a career on hold. In one of her more introspective moments, she will admit that she idealised what motherhood would be like: 'I used to think, oh, it'd be so nice to go to discos together and... bring their boyfriends home. Oh well, there you go!' Yet, around the family table she fantasises only half-jokingly about becoming pregnant again: 'I'd love another little baby!' Little babies are one thing; independent teenage girls are clearly a tougher proposition.

Andy's life too has been shaped by his having become a father at seventeen. He works as head chef in a large industrial kitchen, presiding over it efficiently – although, despite his professed obsession with health and safety, an accident at work puts him out of action for a while towards the end of the film. He works hard, as Wendy recognises, 'slogging his guts out in a job he hates', but still dreams of going into business for himself. However, his lack of realism and practical application are established early on, mainly manifested in his procrastinating on DIY jobs. 'Gonna get out there this afternoon, finish off that patio', he claims confidently on the Saturday lunchtime after the dance class. Wendy obviously does not know whether to laugh or cry at this: 'Oh, don't give me a heart attack, Andy, please!' By the next day she is reduced to pleading with him, 'How about having a little go at the patio today? Please'. But Andy's enthusiasm has rapidly faded; he is sure it will rain later, and when Wendy suggests that he could get on with tiling the bathroom as an alternative, he protests that he hasn't any grout.

Andy is in fact happier to spend his Sundays in the pub with his shady mate Patsy (Stephen Rea). On this particular Sunday, Patsy turns up at the house already the worse for wear, and somewhat overdressed with a sharp suit and bouffant, streaked hairstyle – both of which highly amuse Wendy and Natalie – despite the fact that he is unemployed. As he coaxes Andy away, we get a fair idea of the nature of their friendship from Andy's instant insistence that 'whatever it is, honest to God, I can't afford it'. He goes anyway, though, returning with a dilapidated caravan that has previously been used as a mobile café. Andy is confident that he can refurbish the van and use it to run his own burger and hot dog business: 'On a Bank Holiday weekend, I could make, what? Two, two and a half thousand quid'. It is the despairing Wendy who pragmatically points out that, the appalling state of the van notwithstanding, he has failed to take into account the need for a licence and the consequences of trespassing on another trader's patch.

On the whole, despite such disagreements and exasperations, Wendy and Andy have a better relationship with each other than with either of their two daughters. For their part, Nicola and Natalie have moments of shared embarrassment and exasperation at their parents, but still do not get on at all well, and are frequently critical of one another.

Nicola is accurately described by Michael Coveney as 'a reflex rebel',[4] and by Leigh as 'a receptacle of received ideas'.[5] Just as Suzi, in *High Hopes*, talks about issues so that she can get them clear and then talk about them to other people, Nicola reads about feminism and learns that 'I'm a feminist', rather than what this actually *means*. The depth of her real political awareness is summed up in her well-intentioned but ultimately ineffectual 'Bollocks to the Poll Tax' T-shirt. We learn that she gave up her A level studies, and now sits around the house all day, going nowhere and achieving nothing (she says that she is writing a novel, but we are not inclined to believe her).

Natalie, on the other hand, is working as a plumber. 'In her own quiet way', says Leigh, 'she's as much a non-conformist as Nicola. The difference is that the nature of her non-conformity doesn't preclude getting on with living and working and in some way fulfilling herself, within limited parameters'.[6] Whereas Nicola has no real friends and never goes out, Natalie does have a social life – we see her playing pool in the pub with a group of people. She is teased by her parents and her colleague Steve (David Neilson) because she buys men's clothes and eschews make-up, and responds to this resignedly but unemotionally ('Oh, very amusing!'); Nicola, in contrast, spits insults ('Capitalist!'; 'Sexist!'; 'Selfish pig!') at anyone who dares to criticise her – or who upsets her in any way, such as by asking her to join in a communal effort, or refusing to subsidise her smoking. While Nicola is of the opinion that all men are 'potential rapists', Natalie has no interest in boyfriends, but is not implacably opposed to the idea and assumes she will have children one day.

Nicola, however, does have a regular boyfriend (David Thewlis), whose name we never learn – an accurate enough reflection of his role in her life. She wants him to turn up when she chooses, to have sex with her the way she likes it (a fairly emotionless exercise, which includes his tying her up and smearing her with chocolate spread) and then leave immediately afterwards. Her family evidently know nothing of him and are merely bewildered as to why she needs to take so many baths.

The obsession with chocolate spread points to a darker secret: Nicola is bulimic. This is first revealed in a compact sequence of scenes set in the family bedrooms. As with the three scenes showing three couples going to bed in three different houses in *High Hopes*, these carry a special significance. In this most private of settings, the four characters reveal things about themselves that demonstrate all is not well in the household. Yet Wendy and Andy cuddle each other and laugh together just as Cyril and Shirley did in the earlier film, and work their disagreements out as they lie in bed chatting and joking together. Andy lies to Wendy about how much he paid Patsy for the caravan, and asks her, 'Do you want me to carry on doing my brain in at that bloody place for the rest of my life?' Wendy is sympathetic but remains practical: 'Andy, you can't jack in your day job without you got something definite to go to, right?' He argues that 'it's a risk, but it's a risk worth taking, ain't it?' Wendy does not disagree with this, merely joking that 'if the worse came to the worst, we could always go on our holidays in it!' They then make fun of their friend Aubrey (Timothy Spall), who is about to strike out in a catering venture of his own – a local restaurant – and whom Wendy has agreed to help out on his opening night. Andy warns her that 'you want to watch out for Aubrey in that kitchen. He'll come up behind you with a cucumber'. Wendy is aware of what she is taking on, acknowledging that 'I don't think it'll be a cucumber he'll be coming up behind me with!' – but she is obviously being sincere when she says that she doesn't fancy him: 'I'm not that desperate. Ah, bless him. I feel sorry for him, actually'.

They go on to discuss Nicola, which is the point at which Wendy admits that motherhood is not what she expected, and that 'she gets me in a right state, that girl. I heard myself shouting at her this morning, and I thought, "This isn't me". I don't recognise myself, you know, it's horrible'. However we see that theirs is a genuinely loving and mutually supportive relationship; we sense – and will see – that the family's problems are not fundamental, and can be overcome.

A few moments later, we cut to Nicola's bedroom, and see her open a locked suitcase full of chocolate bars and crisps. Gorging herself on these, she then uses a toothbrush to make herself vomit into a carrier bag. It is a shocking scene, not just because it is an unpleasant and disturbing sight, but also because we had not until now suspected the depth of Nicola's emotional problems. Indeed, as Ray Carney observes: 'The scene comes at precisely the point where we are about to write Nicola off. Five minutes more and she would have become a cartoon stick-figure of teenage whining and discontent'.[7] In the next room, we see Natalie, first reading an American travel brochure and then later lying awake and listening to Nicola's retching.

This sequence of private moments is thus revelatory in a number of ways. We learn that Nicola has a genuine problem, and that Natalie, while outwardly contented, nevertheless has her dreams and ambitions (the travel brochures have never been previously mentioned). We are also now aware that Natalie knows about her sister's bulimia, but has neither said so to Nicola nor told their parents about it. Andy, behind all his loafing and his *Goon Show* voices, is shown to be frustrated; his ambition to operate his own business is not just a pie-in-the-sky fantasy, but a genuine yearning for escape. And Wendy is revealed as a truly caring wife, mother and friend, who is both sympathetic and insightful. This too is something of a turnabout. Previously she may have seemed to belong to the category of characters (like Peter and Pat in *Bleak Moments* or Valerie and Martin in *High Hopes*) who are inflexible in their behaviour patterns and lack empathy with anyone else's perspective. Now, as Carney says, we revise our opinion of her: 'We had no idea that she was capable of getting outside herself in this way – that she was either this introspective or this self-critical'.[8]

Given the uncertainty up to this point about how we should respond to Wendy, it is appropriate that Alison Steadman's performance hovers on the edge of caricature without ever moving into it. This is, as ever, part of Leigh's method: 'Her giggle and so on suggest she's a bit soppy. In fact, as we find out, she's very much got her feet on the ground. The movie works against these kinds of preconceptions'.[9] Wendy's laugh certainly grates; in one scene in particular, she is looking in her wardrobe for something to wear on Aubrey's opening night and pulls out a pink angora top, provoking a machine gun burst of laughter from both her and Andy which is painful to listen to. Natalie is conspicuously unamused by their mirth, as she invariably is by one of Wendy's other mannerisms, a heavy-handed tendency to point out double meanings: 'I like mine nice and juicy', 'What, can't get it in the hole?' and so on. But the fact that she and Andy do laugh together is of course on the whole a positive trait, and their humour, however much it may irritate others, is genuine and unifying.

On occasions Wendy makes what seem like foolish comments; discussing Natalie's travel plans, she says, 'Fancy going to the States and not going to Disneyland' – although this could just as easily be taken as a sly comment on cultural colonisation, made credibly through a character rather than overtly through a political lecture. In any case, Wendy is certainly not ignorant; she it is who knows confidently that Prague is in Czechoslovakia when Andy and Aubrey are not sure. It is also an endearing touch that Wendy, whom we have seen leading the children's dance class very competently, on one occasion does a little dance for no audience, purely for her own enjoyment. Her propensity for mothering people at times seems overbearing, but at others an eminently reasonable method of coping with them. This is shown up in particularly sharp relief on the evening that Aubrey's restaurant opens, a sequence in which Wendy comes into her own as a genuinely capable and supportive wife and friend.

The omens for the opening night are not good. For one thing, Aubrey's menu is unappetising in the extreme. The starters include black pudding and Camembert soup, and saveloy on a bed of lychees. The main courses range from duck in chocolate sauce to liver in lager, or prune quiche ('the one for our vegetarian friends'). His bizarre culinary ideas aside, Aubrey has already been presented as a figure of fun. He is accident-prone, providing some moments of pure slapstick: in one scene Andy's caravan tips up with him inside it, and in another he tumbles spectacularly off his bed while bouncing on it to demonstrate the orthopaedic mattress to Andy and Wendy. It is no wonder that they spend most of their time laughing at him when they visit his restaurant. Carney aptly refers to Aubrey's 'off-the-peg sense of selfhood and just-add-water understanding of meaning';[10] in contrast to Wendy and Andy who can respond in human terms to people, Aubrey is another of those characters locked into received ideas and behaviour patterns designed to project his own image of himself. (It is Aubrey who in this film comes out with that recurrent line 'You've gotta laugh', although he never does laugh, exhibits no sense of humour, and in fact is furiously angry at the moment when he says it.)

On his first appearance in the film he arrives at Andy and Wendy's house wearing sunglasses, sneakers and a baseball cap, and driving a clapped-out red sports car, which he exits by ostentatiously stepping over the door rather than opening it. Nicola lets him in and perversely pretends that Wendy is out (she is actually in the back garden), leaving Aubrey sitting awkwardly in the living room nursing the pineapple that he has inexplicably brought for her – all of which rather undermines the trendy, mid-Atlantic persona that he is striving for. Aubrey's clothes, language and behaviour are all designed to keep up this image, and it is an image that will tragically fall apart amid the debacle of his opening night.

There is not a single customer that night, which is hardly surprising as, quite apart from the unattractive menu, Aubrey has done no advertising. As Wendy watches worriedly, he slowly gets drunk and eventually goes outside to harangue the world: 'You working-class morons! Go and eat your own shit!' The scene develops further into a hilarious, unbridled comic tour de force: Aubrey makes a crude and clumsy pass at Wendy ('I wanna fuck you'), starts to remove his clothes, wrecks the restaurant by upturning fully laden tables, then passes out trouserless on the floor. Leigh plays up the comic elements in his final collapse by shooting it so as to emphasise his bare legs and striped underpants. Faced with his unruly and petulant behaviour, Wendy's speaking to him like a child ('You're being a naughty boy!'; 'Behave yourself and leave your trousers on') does not actually seem out of place.

Nor does it when she returns home to Andy, who is also very drunk after an evening in the pub, talking football and putting the world to rights with Patsy. He is at first discovered asleep in the caravan, allegedly 'tidying up', and when she gets him inside she has to prevent him from raiding the fridge for more lager, bundle him upstairs and order him to 'get in that toilet and do a wee' as though he were a naughty boy. Just as her sense of humour may occasionally grate but is nevertheless obviously part of her survival mechanism, her addressing everyone as though they are children is clearly more than just an irritating mannerism. It is also a means of coping with men who insist on behaving like small boys, and of keeping the resulting situations under control.

Wendy, then, is perhaps the most triumphant example to date of a Mike Leigh character who is at all times individualistic, idiosyncratic, and *because* of this (rather than despite it) defies simplistic judgement. Again we recognise Leigh's pursuit of truth in his work: most people *are* complex, as are the interactions between them in real life, especially family life. Hence our reactions to his characters are not clear-cut; nor, for that matter, are Leigh's. Much comedy, as we have seen, is shot through with ambivalence, and satirical comedy is no exception.

The satirical commentator is in the first place aware that his or her characters have an ambivalent relationship to their wider social environment. We are all subject to social codes and dictates, but if society is the sum of its parts, we also have, to a greater or lesser extent, a responsibility for our own lives. Hence the satirist's occasional impatience, even anger, not just with society, but with those who acquiesce with its values (the assumption that 'America' equals 'Disneyland' for example) instead of thinking for themselves. Naturally, this applies to the satirist too – it could not be otherwise. This lends another layer of ambivalence: aware that his or her characters are both individual *and* social beings, the satirist is equally – and perhaps more painfully – aware of simultaneously standing apart *from* the subject matter and remaining inescapably a part *of* it. He or she is not only ambivalent about the characters' relationship to the world they live in, but about his or her own relationship to those characters, and to that world.

Given the complexity of the satirist's position, it is not surprising that, when commenting on his own standpoint, for example when talking to John Hind, Leigh can sometimes appear unsure, even a little evasive:

> *Hind:* Do you always think consciously, 'This character is someone I like, but this one isn't?'
> *Leigh:* It's very clear-cut I would have thought.
> *Hind:* Before you said you had sympathy for almost all your characters. Are you now taking sides?
> *Leigh:* Well, when I'm having a go at people it's really at 'us', not 'them'.
> *Hind:* Isn't that contradicting what you just said about it being clear-cut?
> *Leigh:* Mmmm. The point is, I'm getting at things, like upwardly-mobile bourgeois affectations, which in fact can be found in *all* of us – at least a bit. It's about ordinary lives. But I create a dialectic by setting varying types or styles of characters against each other.[11]

So if an occasional lack of sympathy towards characters goes with the territory, how are we to make critical value judgements about satire and satirists? Can we distinguish those who achieve a fundamental humanism, as I would insist that both Leigh and the Boulting Brothers do, from those who are merely misanthropic and cynical? This is clearly important in assessing Leigh's work, if we are to deal with the accusations that have been made about him of cruelty, condescension and lack of compassion.

I believe that the analysis conducted by John Cleese and Robin Skynner is the most helpful in this respect; it would certainly help Peter's colleague, in *Bleak Moments*, to demonstrate the difference between 'good jokes and bad jokes'. In their dialogue-based book *Life and How to Survive It*, Cleese and Skynner propose a model of analysing social interaction which they then apply to comedy:

> *Cleese:* You mean that the least healthy people are paranoid and need other people to blame and hate, but the most healthy people are affiliative?
> *Skynner:* Yes. Well, I'm suggesting that humour, like all other aspects of human behaviour, can be looked at in the same way. That is, any given piece of humour or laughter can be placed at some point on the spectrum between most paranoid and most affiliative. For example, take the nastiest kind of racial jokes. They'll be ways in which one

> group expresses its hostility towards another, so those jokes belong down the most paranoid end of the spectrum. Whereas the jokes you describe in which people acknowledge that they are laughing at failures which are common to all human beings, part of the human condition, would be right up at the healthiest end of the spectrum.[12]

The 'healthiest' model of satire would therefore clearly be affiliative, emphasising, as Cleese puts it, 'the similarities between people, not the differences'.[13] However, the awareness of the human condition that generates this sense of inclusion equally creates the ability to step back and take a long, hard, sometimes scathing look at the society of which one is nonetheless inescapably a part. Hence the ambivalence which can often be detected in the most biting of satires; Malcolm McDowell, for instance, has said of Lindsay Anderson that 'I think that only a man who loved his school and loved England could have made a film like *If ...*'.[14] Leigh's own next film, *Naked*, would prove as volatile and controversial as Anderson's great 1968 work.

Leigh's background perhaps engendered the kind of dual perspective characteristic of a born, or at any rate instinctive, satirist. 'Dad worked as a doctor, but I both went to school and lived in a middle-class home in the same building as his surgery *within* a working-class part of Salford', he has said. 'I didn't know where I stood. And that could explain the class clash in my work ... I suppose I was a big *observer* ... In the 1950s, which must have significance too, we moved surroundings to a more suburban middle-class area and I sampled *all that*'.[15]

Leigh seems to be making a connection here between his formative years and his perspective as defined by Ray Carney in his analysis of *Bleak Moments*, that of being 'half-inside and half-outside the experience, slightly above it yet still in touch with it, emotionally exposed and vulnerable to it but not overwhelmed by it'.[16] (He has elsewhere said that 'I suppose I was an insider and an outsider, all at once'.[17]) Hence, as Michael Coveney says, his relationship to his characters is characterised by 'an equal amount of detached affection and critical sympathy; that is how the quality, the timbre of the comedy is forged'.[18] Coveney cites Philip French's review of *Life Is Sweet* as passing definitive comment on the matter, and I see no reason to disagree:

> Leigh has been called patronising. The charge is false. The Noël Coward/David Lean film *This Happy Breed*, evoked by Leigh in several panning shots across suburban back gardens, is patronising. Coward and Lean pat their characters on the back, give them little medals in their own honours list. Leigh shakes them, hugs them, sometimes despairs over them, but never thinks that they are other than versions of ourselves.[19]

Nevertheless, Leigh has continued to be accused of being cruel or, at best, patronising towards his characters; some of the mud slung by Dennis Potter still sticks. Among those putting the counter-argument has been Andy Medhurst:

> There is a debilitating sentimentality surrounding the cultural representation of the 'working classes' in this country – as if the people lumped together under that label were an endangered species, proletarian pandas in need of protection – but Leigh doesn't toe this sanctimonious line, preferring to deliver up characters who unapologetically have tastes, manners and habits that middle-class audiences cannot help but find distressing.[20]

Medhurst goes on to quote Wendy's remark about Disneyland, and concludes that 'whether you find that patronising or accurate rather depends, I would suggest, on how many people like Wendy you meet in the course of your everyday life'.[21] The 'sentimentality' which Medhurst rightly identifies seems to have become bound up with the same critical orthodoxy's privileging of 'realism', however, so that this overly reverential approach has *itself* become accepted as 'realistic'.

As an illustration, compare Andy's purchase of the caravan in *Life Is Sweet* with the scene in Ken Loach's *Raining Stones* (1993) in which the unemployed central character Bob Williams (Bruce Jones) buys a rundown delivery van, clearly paying well over the odds in his desperation to acquire a vehicle which he believes will increase his chances of getting work. In contrast to Leigh's benign amusement at the antics of Andy and Patsy, Loach loads the dice in Bob's favour from the start: his need for a job is real and his desire for money motivated almost solely by the need to buy his daughter a communion dress, revealing him to be both a loving family man and a good Catholic.

I do not see why Leigh's stance should be regarded as the more patronising. Loach's tendency to accord his leading characters 'victim' status has surely no less potential for condescension, although in this case the boisterous, unsentimental humour of *Raining Stones* largely steers it away from left-of-centre hand-wringing over Bob's plight. Leigh, for whom unsentimental humour is rarely far away, appreciates that Andy's striving, however misguidedly, towards his dream makes him admirable *as well as* foolish and easily led. That, surely, is precisely the kind of humanism recognised by Philip French's review, and in its identification of the propensity within all of us for both commendable tenacity *and* irrational idealism, it is both unsentimental and, more importantly, realistic in more than a merely superficial, stylistic sense.

Leigh's humanism reaches what Graham Fuller calls 'something of a crescendo'[22] in *Life Is Sweet*'s climactic scene between Wendy and Nicola.

This occurs on the day after Aubrey's calamitous opening night. Nicola's lover comes round while she is alone in the house, but he refuses to go through their usual perfunctory sexual ritual. 'I don't want *it* ... ' he says. 'I want *you*'. Nicola accuses him of being a 'sentimentalist', but he persists: 'Come on, talk to me'. Challenging her to elucidate her political ideas, he eventually snaps. 'I'm trying to have an intelligent conversation with you. Are you capable of that?' he asks, before concluding, brutally, that 'You're a fake'. He leaves without them having sex, leaving Nicola shaken. But a bigger bombshell is to come.

Wendy returns home later. While she is cleaning the house, she sees Nicola sitting on the bed in her room, and expresses her worries: 'You're sitting there like there's a grey cloud over you, it's like the sun's gone in. You've got no energy cause you don't eat your dinners. And you've got no joy in your soul'. She cannot bear the fact that Nicola has 'given up', has no friends any more, and does nothing: 'I mean you say you want to change the world – you're supposed to be political, but I don't see you doing anything about it'. Nicola protests that she reads newspapers and watches the television; Wendy is typically pragmatic: 'You should be out there, helping the Old Age Pensioners or going on marches or whatever'. 'And you're so perfect!' counters Nicola. 'No', argues Wendy, 'I'm not perfect, but I haven't given up'. Her love for Andy, never seriously in doubt, comes to the fore as she tells Nicola that the 'rusty old caravan' is to her the sign of 'a man who's still out there, fighting, looking for his dream'. She admits that she didn't like Natalie working as a plumber at first, 'but I can see now that I was wrong, because she's happy'.

The revelations keep coming. Wendy and Andy struggled to make ends meet when she became pregnant, but they survived and 'came through, laughing'; as Leigh says, the film 'centres around a family that happened by accident, but who have gone through with it and have kept doing their best despite all their difficulties'.[23] Having given up her studies and got on with life as best she can, Wendy cannot bear the fact that Nicola has given up without ever having tried. Nicola has not until now realised that when she stopped eating at the age of seventeen, bringing her own A-level studies to a halt, she was hospitalised because the doctors gave her only two weeks to live. Deeply shocked, she falls back on the last, desperate cry of the 'misunderstood' adolescent: 'I didn't ask to be born!' Wendy makes one final appeal: 'I wouldn't care what blooming job you did, I wouldn't care how scruffy you looked, as long as you were happy. But you're not'. She practically begs Nicola to admit that she has problems, so that they can talk honestly about them (though she is still unaware of the full extent of these problems). 'If you hate me so much, why don't you throw me out?' whines Nicola, and

Wendy's reply is instant and from the heart: 'We don't hate you. We love you, right, you stupid girl!'

Wendy leaves, and each of them weeps alone. Domestic life does not allow Wendy much time for introspection: shortly after this incident she receives a call telling her that Andy has slipped on a spoon at work and injured himself. She goes off to collect him, and soon he is home with his leg in plaster and the family – even a reluctant Nicola, after some persuasion – closing ranks to look after him. In the final scene, Natalie and Nicola sit together in the garden; Natalie tells Nicola that she knows about her bulimia, and it seems that at least the two of them have reached an understanding and are prepared to act as support for each other. The family will survive. Like Wendy, none of them is perfect, but they have not given up.

The tone of the ending is familiar. But whereas *Bleak Moments* gained its sense of tragedy precisely from its lack of catharsis, and *High Hopes* built towards a comic set piece in Mrs Bender's birthday party, *Life Is Sweet* has powerfully and unforgettably taken us to a major emotional climax, and out the other side. As ever with Leigh, there is nothing artificial or melodramatic involved, nor has any contrived solution to the family's problems been found. But it is all perfectly credible in the context of these ordinary lives, and some kind of healing has unmistakably begun to take place. Life, love and laughter go on.

At the heart of the film's credibility is Leigh's – and his cast's – treatment of the characters. *Life Is Sweet* has its abstract themes, of course: Leigh has agreed that it is 'about food on one level. It's also about enterprise culture, via the character of Patsy'.[24] But that is the point. His films are only ever *about* anything via his characters. Food symbolises much in *Life Is Sweet*: the communal meals Wendy provides for the family; Nicola's solitary binge-eating and loveless sex games; both Andy's job and his dreams of something better; Aubrey's inflated ideas of running his own business. Andy and Aubrey, in particular, both struggling small businessmen, provide variations on that theme of enterprise culture. But consumption is never likely to become the in-your-face metaphor it had been, for example, in Peter Greenaway's *The Cook, the Thief, His Wife and Her Lover* (1989). Greenaway's characters are rarely more than pawns in his narrative design; Leigh's are the heart and soul of his work. And his satirist's compulsion to see and depict them in all their human complexity, for better and worse, only reinforces that. We are, in Robin Skynner's words, 'laughing at failures which are common to all human beings, part of the human condition', and for that reason we celebrate that humanity even as we laugh. Or cry, as the case may be. Wendy's tearful, exasperated comment to Nicola at the end of that scene – 'We love you, right, you stupid girl!' – could stand as a summation of Leigh's own ability simultaneously to care about and despair of his characters, and his talent for making us do the same.

Philip French, whose review is quoted above, also praised the film for the 'maturity of its vision and the depth of its feeling';[25] he was not the only critic to respond positively. Derek Malcolm said in *The Guardian*: 'Though one laughs at these people, the saving grace of the film is that, in doing so, one is frequently laughing at oneself ... But throughout the film there is a sense that laughter might at any moment break into tears'.[26] Malcolm also praised its visual style – 'Technically, it is the best of the three cinema films he has so far been graciously allowed to make' – noting Leigh's collaboration for the first time with cinematographer Dick Pope and production designer Alison Chitty, who both went on to work with Leigh again, Pope on all his subsequent features to date and Chitty on *Naked* and *Secrets and Lies*.

In the *Daily Telegraph*, Hugo Davenport detected a 'vigilant compassion' in *Life Is Sweet*;[27] Alan Stanbrook said in the *Sunday Telegraph* of Leigh's characters that 'he loves them all and is on their side';[28] and in the *Financial Times* Nigel Andrews, while feeling that the character of Aubrey 'left reality too far behind', thought that in the film's best moments 'we watch aghast with admiration, wondering when the thread will snap: when Steadman's cooing bonhomie and water-through-plughole laugh will tip into caricature (they never do); when Broadbent's asinine optimism will spring a leak (it never does); above all, when the terrifying Nicola will behave bizarrely enough for us to hang the placard 'unreal' around her neck and push her out of our minds. She never does'.[29]

This seems to me a more reasonable assessment of Nicola's portrayal than Anthony Lane's in the *Independent on Sunday* – his unsympathetic review declared that she 'complains of being misunderstood by everyone else, but frankly they treat her better than the film does' and detected none of the film's humanity: 'I shall never dispel a pang of unease in watching Leigh at work. We are made to feel better for his scrutiny of plain folk; yet that privilege puts us too far in the know. It shows them up for our pleasure'.[30] Other hostile reviews came from Sue Murphy in *Spare Rib*, who concluded that 'regrettably, accusations that Leigh patronises the working-classes are here – perhaps for the first time – justified',[31] and from Clive Hirschhorn in the *Sunday Express*, for whom Aubrey's opening night 'struck me as a patronising jibe at working-class yobs who venture into territory beyond their station ... As is often the case with Leigh, it is not always clear whether he embraces his characters' all-too-human imperfections and foibles, or secretly despises them'.[32]

Some other critics acknowledged doubts but finally came down in favour of the film. In *The Independent*, Adam Mars-Jones thought that its depiction of the family unit 'makes the film's politics seem sentimental and even reactionary', but conceded that 'the tone is warm, the twins are fascinating and the laughter is mainly humane'.[33] And in *The Times*, Geoff Brown put aside some earlier reservations: 'Previously, Leigh has caricatured without love; but in the bulk of *Life Is Sweet*, affection shines through the comic portrait of working-class suburbia on the march'.[34]

Audiences too were appreciative, although the film received only a limited British release, in what is sometimes (misleadingly) called the 'art house' circuit of independent subsidised cinemas; Leigh had not yet found his way into the multiplex cinemas which had begun to burgeon in the UK by this time. He had, as far as many people were concerned, succeeded in his aim of making a comedy with considerable popular appeal. True, some of the old charges, of caricaturing and patronising his characters, were still there, but such criticisms seemed to represent the minority viewpoint – for the moment at least. *Naked*, and greater controversy, were yet to come.

Notes

1 Quoted in David Robinson, 'Making Up Is Hard to Do', *The Times*, 18 March 1991
2 Graham Fuller, 'Mike Leigh's Original Features', in *Naked and Other Screenplays* (London, Faber & Faber, 1995), p. viii
3 Mike Leigh, *Life Is Sweet*, in *Naked and Other Screenplays*, p. 100
4 Michael Coveney, *The World According to Mike Leigh* (London, Harper Collins, paperback edition, 1997), p. 219
5 Quoted in Graham Fuller, 'Mike Leigh's Original Features', p. xxxii
6 *Ibid.*, p. xxxi
7 Ray Carney and Leonard Quart, *The Films of Mike Leigh: Embracing the World* (Cambridge, Cambridge University Press, 2000), p. 210
8 *Ibid.*
9 Quoted in Graham Fuller, 'Mike Leigh's Original Features', p. xxxii
10 Ray Carney and Leonard Quart, *The Films of Mike Leigh*, p. 221
11 John Hind, *The Comic Inquisition: Conversations with Great Comedians* (London, Virgin Books, 1991), pp. 82–3
12 Robin Skynner and John Cleese, *Life and How to Survive It* (London, Methuen, 1993), p. 86
13 *Ibid.*, p. 87
14 Malcolm McDowell, 'O Anderson!', *The Movie*, chapter 64 (1981), p. 1275
15 Quoted in John Hind, *The Comic Inquisition*, p. 84
16 Ray Carney and Leonard Quart, *The Films of Mike Leigh*, p. 49
17 Quoted in Graham Fuller, 'Mike Leigh's Original Features', p. xi
18 Michael Coveney, *The World According to Mike Leigh*, p. 222
19 Philip French, *The Observer*, 24 March 1991

20 Andy Medhurst, 'Mike Leigh: Beyond Embarrassment', *Sight and Sound*, 3: 11 (November 1993), p. 8
21 *Ibid.*, p. 9
22 Graham Fuller, 'Mike Leigh's Original Features', p. viii
23 *Ibid.*, p. xxvii
24 *Ibid.*, p. xxxi
25 Philip French, *The Observer*, 24 March 1991
26 Derek Malcolm, *The Guardian*, 21 March 1991
27 Hugo Davenport, *Daily Telegraph*, 21 March 1991
28 Alan Stanbrook, *Sunday Telegraph*, 13 September 1992
29 Nigel Andrews, *Financial Times*, 21 March 1991
30 Anthony Lane, *Independent on Sunday*, 24 March 1991
31 Sue Murphy, *Spare Rib*, April 1991, p. 23
32 Clive Hirschhorn, *Sunday Express*, 24 March 1991
33 Adam Mars-Jones, *The Independent*, 22 March 1991
34 Geoff Brown, *The Times*, 21 March 1991

'The future is now': *Naked* 6

Nothing in the bittersweet tone or the precisely observed domesticity of *Life Is Sweet* prepared audiences or critics for Leigh's next feature film, *Naked*, which remains his bleakest and angriest work, as well as his most controversial. It also marked his breakthrough to international recognition, and a shift in his career whereby each of his subsequent films would be radically different, in style or subject matter or both, from the one that had gone before. Indeed, in Leigh's own opinion, 'all of my work up to and including, and concluding with, *Life Is Sweet* is in one category, and from *Naked* onwards we move into a whole new chapter'.[1]

In any event, anyone who thought they had Leigh safely compartmentalised as a shrewd commentator on lower-middle-class suburban repressions and preoccupations would have been particularly taken aback by *Naked*. Its scope is much wider than anything Leigh had tackled before; for a Britain under a post-Thatcher Conservative government, and less than a decade from the new millennium, it offered trenchant comment on both where we were and where we were heading. 'It's about the impending apocalypse', Leigh has said. 'I felt in some way that I could make a film that could express the future through a bleak, urban landscape, by creating the world as it actually is now'.[2] This he certainly achieved: whatever the motive may have been for the naming of one of the film's female characters, there is a remarkable resonance in the memorable image of a homeless, hopeless, futureless and furious young man roaming that 'bleak, urban landscape' and impotently bellowing 'Maggie!' For all the issues the film raises, it is nonetheless recognisably the work of Leigh in that it is driven by its characters; they are never simply mouthpieces for political or philosophical comment. Rather *Naked*'s themes arise credibly from their lives and attitudes, which are treated with a complexity and ambiguity consistent with Leigh's other work and with the ways in which we react to people in life outside the movies.

Naked's principal character – its hero, up to a point, but we'll come to that later – is Johnny, blisteringly portrayed by David Thewlis. Through Johnny, *Naked* presents us with a furious, hyper-articulate, phenomenally well read, unstoppable tirade of abuse, nihilism and black humour which is liable to bludgeon the viewer as effectively as Johnny himself crushes just about every other character in the film into submission. It is the kind of film that leaves you feeling drained as much on its leading actor's behalf as by the verbal battering he has given you. For its admirers, though, it is exhilarating as well as exhausting.

The film runs a little over two hours – Leigh's longest feature up to that point – and the narrative more or less falls into four acts, lasting roughly half an hour each. The first begins with a hand-held forward tracking shot, drawing us into Johnny's world in much the same way as Hitchcock coaxes us into the opening scene of *Psycho* – a film to which Johnny will make ironic reference later. We are in a dark alley where Johnny is having rough sex with a woman. At first it seems to be a consensual act, but then he begins to hurt her, pushing her head back, and she attempts to fight him off. The sex, by this stage definitely non-consensual, continues, until he releases her and they run off in opposite directions, the woman threatening to 'tell my Bernard of you!' This is clearly no insignificant threat, for Johnny hastily packs a bag, steals a car and flees from Manchester to London.

The question of whether, from this point onwards, Johnny should be seen as a rapist is a matter of some dispute. Leigh thinks not: 'I don't think he's a rapist ... Whatever he's doing to that woman at the very beginning, it's somewhere along the line, by its context, consensual';[3] as does David Thewlis: 'He's not a rapist. At the beginning, that's not a rape. It's sex that gets out of hand. That's not to condone it. Obviously he's out of order'.[4] While ordinarily wishing to defer to the writer-director and the actor who after all conceived the character, and therefore know him better than anyone, I am personally less comfortable with the idea that a sexual act which *becomes* non-consensual does not *become* a rape. (That phrase 'gets out of hand', too, seems to me to be disclaiming male responsibility rather too easily.)

The next morning Johnny arrives at the house which his ex-girlfriend Louise (Lesley Sharp) shares with Sophie (Katrin Cartlidge), an unemployed, slightly spaced-out neo-Goth, and Sandra (Claire Skinner), a nurse who only returns from holiday near the end of the film, at which point we discover that she is meticulous to the point of neurosis. Louise is at work when Johnny arrives, so he and Sophie share a cup of tea and a joint, and he immediately regales her with both his jokes ('Have you got anything for a headache ... You know, like a monkey wrench or something?') and his bleak brand of philosophising ('You might already have had the happiest moment in your whole fucking life, and all you've got to look forward to is sickness and purgatory'). When Louise arrives, he is aggressive towards her, ridiculing her home and her job, then he and Sophie make love after Louise has gone to bed but not to sleep. The next day, Sophie irritates Johnny by following him around and then, back at the house, telling him that she both likes and understands him. Minutes later they again have sex, during which Johnny repeatedly and violently bangs her head on the arm of the sofa. Later that evening, he further antagonises both women, paces like a caged animal, and then storms off into the night leaving Louise angrily resigned and Sophie in tears.

In the second quarter of the film, Johnny, wandering the streets close to the West End of London, meets a Scottish youth named Archie (Ewen Bremner) who is looking for his lost girlfriend Maggie. While basically sympathetic and willing to help, Johnny scores verbal points off the aggressive and inarticulate Archie, taunting him with his bar-room-style philosophy ('What's it like being you?'), his references to Nostradamus and the Apocalypse, and his quick wit – his response to Archie's belligerent 'Are you taking the piss?' is 'You're fucking giving it away, aren't you?' After Archie has wandered off to continue his search, Maggie (Susan Vidler) appears and Johnny walks with her through the back streets and among derelict buildings, discoursing on the city as he goes ('You know that wherever you are in London, you're only thirty feet away from a rat?'). It is an unusually stylised scene for Leigh, the expressive lighting giving it the atmosphere of a modern film noir. Leigh has explained of the film's distinctive look that '*Naked* was shot using the bleach bypass process ... You miss out the bleaching in the lab and it gives you a saturated quality'.[5] When Archie turns up again, he and Maggie disappear into the night, energetically inflicting verbal and physical abuse on one another. Johnny is left alone in the middle of an urban wasteland: what Michael Coveney rightly calls 'the lingering image of a film about alienation, sexual violence and the city'.[6]

The way in which Archie and Maggie express their concern and their mutual dependency, through an instinctive aggression, looks like a kind of bizarre, distorted parody of a devoted couple. Johnny's next encounter, which takes place the following night, after a day on the streets, similarly seems to parody the notion of domesticity (concepts of 'home' run throughout the film and form one of its key themes). This pivotal sequence brings Johnny into a lengthy conversation with a security guard named Brian (Peter Wight), who allows Johnny to shelter in the unoccupied office block for which he is responsible – a role that

Johnny assesses as 'the most tedious fucking job in England'. Despite his apparently futile task, Brian doggedly maintains an essential optimism and faith in the future, despite Johnny's contention that 'nobody has a future. The party's over, man. Take a look around you. It's all breaking up'. In full apocalyptic flow, Johnny launches into his theories that the bar code and the Chernobyl disaster were both foretold in the Book of Revelation, by way of proving that 'the end of the world is nigh, Bri'. The scene lasts nearly twenty minutes, and is brilliantly sustained, perhaps the most exhilarating sequence in the film, the urgency and intensity of Thewlis's delivery excellently complemented by Wight's laconic earnestness. Like the previous sequence, featuring Archie and Maggie, it is strikingly shot in a more stylised fashion than we had by now come to expect from Leigh, notably in a long two-shot of Johnny and Brian silhouetted against the windows of the eerily empty building. If that previous sequence presented contemporary London in a manner reminiscent of film noir, this one, the expressionist shooting style notwithstanding, explores fin-de-siècle fears and concerns as Theatre of the Absurd, as, *Godot*-like, two men in a surreally empty environment conduct an insoluble debate by posing unanswerable questions about the nature of the universe.

Next, the two men look out of the window into a nearby flat, where they watch a woman on whom the sexually frustrated Brian regularly spies. Johnny leaves the office building and goes to the flat, where the woman (Deborah McLaren) invites him in for a drink. They appear to be on the point of having sex but, after seeing the skull-and-crossbones tattoo on her shoulder, Johnny becomes abusive, brutally telling her that 'you look like me mother'. While she is asleep, he steals some of her books and leaves. He meets Brian again and they go to a greasy-spoon café where Brian has breakfast and tells Johnny about his dream of retiring to a cottage in Ireland. After wandering about for a while, Johnny returns to the café and is taken home by the young waitress (Gina McKee), who offers him food, drink, a bath and the possibility of somewhere to spend the night. When he tells her that she has 'a very sad face', however, she begins to cry, turns on him and orders him out, provoking one of his more venomously bitter, if impotent, outbursts:

> I hope that when you're tucked up tonight, all snug and warm underneath your tear-sodden fucking duvet in your ankle-length Emily Brontë winding-sheet, that you spare a thought for me, with my head in a puddle of cold dog's piss. And I hope that you dream about me. And I hope that you wake up screaming. And I hope that all your fucking children are born blind, bow-legged, hare-lipped, homeless hunchbacks!

Meanwhile Jeremy (Greg Cruttwell), an odious yuppie who has appeared previously but has not until now been integrated into the main narrative, turns up at Sophie and Louise's house, claiming to be their landlord and intimidating them to the point where they retreat to the pub, hoping that he will have cleared off by the time they get home.

In the final quarter, Johnny is assaulted twice and loses the bag containing what seem to be all his worldly goods. The first attack is provoked by his pointless, aggressive goading of a bill poster ('Blank it all out till you die of apathy and fucking indifference!'); the second, when he is set upon by a gang, is unmotivated – unless the fact that it takes place in an alley is taken to suggest a retribution for the assault at the beginning of the film. (Johnny himself later suggests an ironic connection between the two events when he ruefully observes that 'I had to get out of Manchester cause I was going to get a beating. And I come down here and, er, get a beating'.) He returns to Louise's house, ill and raving, but regains enough of his old spirit by the morning to accept Louise's offer of a return to Manchester together. While she goes to work to hand in her notice, however, he takes some money left behind by Jeremy and, still injured, limps off down the road. In a reverse of the opening shot, the camera tracks away, leaving him behind, drawing us back out of his company and his life.

As Leigh tells it, the creation of the character Johnny came about because he wanted both to make a film with a man as the key protagonist, feeling that the women had been the focal points in *High Hopes* and *Life Is Sweet*, and to compensate Thewlis for having been 'short-changed' in the latter film when his screen time was cut back for dramatic reasons, by giving him 'a disproportionately good role' next time.[7] His concept was of 'a man of intelligence whose potential is being wasted';[8] he has said that 'a serious mistake is that Johnny never had a university or college education, a complete bloody waste, basically. When he was at school in Manchester, he plainly spent the entire time with people punishing him and throwing him out of the room rather than saying, "Here is a talent to be nurtured"'.[9] This character concept fed into another of Leigh's aims, cited at the beginning of this chapter, to make 'a millennium film', about 'the impending apocalypse'.

For his part, Thewlis embarked on a period of intensive research for the role, reading books that he thought Johnny would have read and 'putting an awful lot of learning together and coming up with the philosophy and attitude of the character'.[10] The actor recalls an eventual feeling of 'my brain being on fire, raging with ideas ... I felt I could confound and out-argue anybody'.[11] He concedes that this process of character development, however heady, made him difficult to be around:

'I don't think it's easy living with someone who's working with Mike at that kind of intensity. I don't expect to work that hard for the rest of my life'.[12] One incident also indicates how the nature of the film and the role took a characteristic risk of Leigh's working method to an extreme: rehearsing one of the confrontations between Johnny and Archie, the improvised fracas between Thewlis and Bremner became so convincing that an onlooker called the police – whereupon Leigh had to intervene and tell the two actors to come out of character. Thewlis reflects that anyone who witnessed the scene 'must have thought, "What did the little guy with the beard say? He should work for the UN"'.[13]

Leigh clearly gave Thewlis a considerable amount of freedom to develop his character: he describes him as 'the only actor in the world who could have played Johnny', while also observing that 'he hasn't been able to pull out all the stops in any other film to the level he was able to in *Naked*'.[14] The end result of their collaboration – Johnny – is a phenomenal creation. He is impossible to embrace, impossible to ignore, contemptuous of the world around him and even – or especially – of anyone who offers to help him or care for him. His position on the margins of society is perpetuated by the circumstances of his life and by his own determination to remain an outsider, a dissenting voice. He is the apotheosis of Leigh's disillusioned idealists, and in him the question of whether such characters are merely disaffected or actually misanthropic is seen at its starkest and most terrifying. As Leigh puts it, 'one of the most naïve things that has been said about him is that he's cynical. He's not cynical. He's sceptical about some things but he has a sense of values. At the same time he can't cope with actual relationships. These contradictions fascinated me'.[15]

At times Johnny's scepticism seems to be derived from the persona of the Shakespearean Fool, sitting on the fringe of society and commenting acerbically on what he sees; or from Hamlet, setting verbal traps to outflank people – like asking Louise if her work is 'everything you hoped it would be?' only to follow her affirmative reply with the unanswerable, 'What did you hope it would be?' There is also something about him of Raskolnikov, the protagonist of Dostoevsky's *Crime and Punishment* (1865–66), in his compelling complexity and his extreme capacity for both destructive *and* self-destructive behaviour. (Visually, too, he recalls Raskolnikov, with his generally shabby dress and voluminous overcoat.) Johnny's articulacy, and tendency to use classical or literary allusions to establish his power and superiority, equally give him the air of the discontented would-be intellectuals of the 1950s like Kingsley Amis's Jim Dixon (*Lucky Jim*, 1954), John Osborne's Jimmy Porter (*Look Back in Anger*, 1956), and John Braine's Joe Lampton (*Room at the Top*, 1957) – or, for that matter, their comic counterpart, Tony Hancock. (At one point, Johnny makes the claim – which could well be a serious one – that 'I could have been a doctor'; asked 'Are you a doctor, then?' in Galton and Simpson's *The Blood Donor* (BBC TV, 1961), Hancock's character replies airily: 'Well no, not really. I never really bothered'.)

Johnny brings this explosive cocktail of characteristics to bear on another literary and cinematic archetype: the interloper who appears, often apparently from nowhere, has a profound if unsettling effect on the lives of those he visits, and then disappears as suddenly as he arrived. This narrative structure defines texts as otherwise diverse as *I Lived With You* (by Ivor Novello, filmed by Maurice Elvey in 1933), *Shane* (by Jack Schaefer, filmed by George Stevens in 1953), *An Inspector Calls* (by J. B. Priestley, filmed by Guy Hamilton in 1954), and *Teorema* (by Pier Paolo Pasolini and filmed by him in 1968). The cinematic example of the archetype which corresponds most closely to Johnny, though, is surely Michel Simon's leading role in the 1932 adaptation of René Fauchois's play, *Boudu Sauvé des Eaux*, by one of Leigh's favourite directors, Jean Renoir. In his monograph on the film, Richard Boston notes that

> Boudu doesn't reject conventional values: he never had them in the first place. Michel Simon called Boudu a *pique-assiette*, which means something like a sponger or parasite, and he said that what he had learnt from Boudu was that one attitude to take to society is to loathe it ('*c'est de la vomir*'). Boudu may spew society out of his mouth: you wouldn't catch him doing anything as pussy-footing as 'rejecting conventional values'.[16]

Certainly not. Instead, he abuses the hospitality, home, family and servants of the man who has had the audacity to save him from his attempt at suicide by drowning. Like Johnny, Boudu at times resembles a particularly out-of-control Fool, a Lord of Misrule turned irredeemable rogue, as Boston goes on to note:

> Clown, trickster, joker, buffoon, jester, fool – in various forms this strange figure, laughing or laughed at, exists both outside the norms of society and at the same time somewhere very near the centre of human experience. He is an amalgam of gluttony, stupidity, sexuality, cunning, shiftlessness, malice, deceit and truth-telling. He breaks down distinctions between wisdom and folly, sanity and insanity, rule and disorder. He makes us laugh and he is often (like Socrates and Jesus) the scapegoat.[17]

No wonder, then, that the response provoked by Johnny, as such an extreme version of the type, is one of equally extreme ambivalence. Of course, the anarchy of the Fool was inherently constrained by his marginal role in society, and that of the Lord of Misrule by the context and duration of a carnival or other festive entertainment. The moment such figures seek to extend their licence into something more genuinely subversive, they must be suppressed or expelled. Both Boudu and Johnny, casting themselves as outsiders, deliberately push the people around them to the point where rejection is a certainty. So just as Boudu ultimately rejects the promise of a bourgeois lifestyle by – literally – jumping ship, just as Shane eventually rides off towards the far horizon from which he materialised, and just as a trio of Boulting Brothers' heroes retreated, as we have seen, to ever more isolated refuges – so Johnny eventually hobbles off to – who knows where? It seems, in fact, inconceivable that he will actually get anywhere, even assuming that he plausibly has somewhere to go.

Figuratively, of course, he's going absolutely nowhere. The woman he assaults at the beginning of the film shouts after him, 'You're fucking dead!', and he does seem to be in a state of limbo thereafter, perhaps even descending into a kind of hell. The title sequence which follows that scene certainly suggests it, with its compelling forward momentum and relentless music as Johnny heads down the motorway in a stolen car: if David Lynch ever shot a sequence on the M6, it would look like this. Johnny himself self-consciously reinforces the impression that he's undergoing a kind of living death: apart from his suggestion to Sophie, quoted above, that 'all you've got to look forward to is sickness and purgatory', he tells Brian that 'in my past life, I was dead', and when Maggie asks him if he's ever seen a dead body, he says, 'Only my own'. He may even think of himself as a Christ-like martyr: he looks up at one point after reading his pocket bible and mutters, 'Why hast thou forsaken me? Bastard!'

Johnny's particular state of limbo centres on that state of existential scepticism, or fin-de-siècle angst, already referred to. Incapable of complacency or of accepting anything on trust, he doubts and questions everything, even to the point of self-destructiveness. In one of his more articulate, almost endearing rants, he berates Louise:

> That's the trouble with everybody – you're all so bored. You've had nature explained to you and you're bored with it. You've had the living body explained to you and you're bored with it. You've had the universe explained to you and you're bored with it. So now you just want cheap thrills and plenty of 'em, and it doesn't matter how tawdry or vacuous they are as long as it's new, as long as it flashes, and fucking bleeps in forty fucking different colours. Well, whatever else you can say about me, I'm not fucking bored!

Not bored, no, but disillusioned. As noted above, it is a form of disillusionment we have seen before in some of Leigh's key characters, but taken in Johnny to an extreme which dramatically emphasises the ambivalence in both the character type and Leigh himself (as noted earlier, he acknowledges that such characters 'come from something implicitly autobiographical'). We have seen how Leigh retains a crucial sympathy for most of his characters at the same time as satirising them, even if in commenting on his approach he reveals a certain tension between the two standpoints. In the case of a compassionate social satire like *Life Is Sweet* or *Secrets and Lies*, this amounts to an ambivalence between barbed comedy on the one hand and rueful humanism on the other. A work like *Naked* is somewhat different. The satire here is of a Swiftian scope: the Dean Swift, that is, who wrote the swingeing *A Modest Proposal* (1729), in which he appeared to advocate the cooking and eating of one-year-olds as a solution to the problems of child poverty and overpopulation in Ireland. Satire of this kind does not deal wryly with social manners and mores, but dangerously with fundamental aspects of the human condition; not, here, with well-meaning if flawed middle-class suburbanites, but with a voluble, violent loose cannon like Johnny.

I have earlier cited the theories of comedy discussed by John Cleese and Robin Skynner. If we accept their contention that the best comedy is inclusive (what Skynner calls '"Isn't the human condition hilarious?" jokes'[18]) rather than exclusive, then good satirical comedy is unlikely to derive from the ridiculing of an 'out-group'. What it may derive from, however, is the satirist, and his principal character (in some cases his mouthpiece) casting *himself* as an 'out-group', as an outsider or lone voice railing against the rest of the world. Certainly Johnny's state of limbo, his chosen status as determined outsider, seems to stem from his need to question, to challenge, to gaze into the heart of the human condition. His reaction to what he sees is, like that of the satirist, complicated by the fact that he is inescapably a part of that condition. So, following Skynner's summation that jokes exist at a point on the scale between the extremes 'paranoid' and 'affiliative', Johnny's position is both paranoid *and* affiliative – in the sense not of finding a comfortable mid-point on the spectrum, but of simultaneously embracing the extremes of inclusivity and exclusivity, of belonging and standing apart. Hence, surely, his ambivalence as a character – his fluctuation between amusing and intelligent bar-room philosopher and anti-social aggressor – and the extreme difficulty of our reacting to him with any consistency.

Hence also Johnny's capacity for self-destruction, perhaps. He is somewhat reminiscent of Swift's Lemuel Gulliver on his return from his last voyage, to the land of the Yahoos. In her biography of Swift, Victoria Glendinning notes how Gulliver can now hardly bear to sit at the table with his wife, but observes: 'If she is a Yahoo, so is he. If there is disgust, there is also self-disgust ... A human being who had no Yahoo in him would not be fully human'.[19] Glendinning goes on to identify a similar ambivalence in Gulliver's creator, in terms which could equally well apply to Leigh or to Johnny:

> I think the capacity, or compulsion, to argue in any direction, or to play the devil's advocate, is not merely the opportunistic exercise of wit and ingenuity, in Swift's case or anyone else's. It is the result and the penalty of having a sharp intelligence, and the expression of an ambivalence produced by the knee-jerk certainties that end in ideological bigotry – even if those certainties reflect in exaggerated form what one quietly believes oneself.[20]

This combination of 'disgust' and 'self-disgust' need not be born of misanthropy; far from it. Spike Milligan, as combustible a mixture of idealism and misanthropy as you'd find in post-war British culture, once summed it up by saying that 'I would not detest the human race if I didn't love them so much'.[21] In this he surely echoed Swift's famous remark: 'I have ever hated all nations, professions and communities, and all my love is towards individuals ... But principally I hate and detest that animal called man: although I heartily love John, Peter, Thomas and so forth'.[22] I am also very taken with the description of a satirist a couple of generations after Milligan, Douglas Adams, laced with the familiar phraseology of his own *The Hitch Hiker's Guide to the Galaxy* (1979), which describes him as 'a gentle humanist whose anger and frustration at what we're doing to our insignificant blue-green planet was forever tempered by an optimistic belief in the unrealised potential of the primitive ape-descended life forms who inhabit it'.[23]

So if Leigh similarly both embraces and despairs of society, refusing to ignore the failings of humanity precisely because he is simultaneously so aware of its great potential, then he falls into a long tradition of satirists, from Swift onwards. The profound ambivalence at the heart of so much of his work, which informs the character of Johnny and fuels the relentless energy of *Naked*, comes from the instinct of the truly satirical social commentator.

The most widespread, and most potentially damning, criticism of *Naked* is that of misogyny. Does the film – does Leigh – condone Johnny's behaviour, or suggest that because most of the women he encounters allow him in various ways to walk all over them, they deserve the appalling treatment he dishes out? Leigh has characteristically preferred to let his film speak for itself and audiences to make up their own minds; yet, as Claire Monk observed in her review of *Naked* in *Sight and Sound*, 'silence is risky when you've invented a rapist/seer as your dominant mouthpiece'.[24] A later article enabled Monk to expand on her comments: '*Naked*'s attempt to show, but not comment on, misogyny and sexual violence is hugely problematic. Our distance as viewers from Johnny's position is never clearly delineated, producing a complicity with, rather than distance from, his perspective on the film's women – a perspective which is nastily interrogatory even when he is not dishing out violence or humiliation'.[25]

This 'problem', whereby our distance from Johnny is not clearly delineated, because he is a sufficiently contradictory character to appear quite engaging at times, is to a great extent endemic to the work of Leigh and of many other satirists, as we have seen. But, as Monk implies, the question of how far Leigh's attitudes can be conflated with Johnny's becomes especially contentious in this area. Nor has Leigh consistently chosen to clarify his stance. At times, his responses to the accusations of misogyny have seemed reasonable and considered: 'You don't make a film like *Naked*, with those kind of female roles and have dumb bimbos playing the parts', he has protested. 'The only kind of actresses who you're going to get to do that kind of work are highly intelligent, highly motivated, highly politicised feminists. No other kind of actress would be any good at it. And you don't make a film with those kind of actresses without their total commitment and collusion. Not to mention you don't make a film like that without an intelligent crew who wants to shoot it'.[26] At other times, however, his impatience with the persistence of such criticisms has shown itself in irritability and invective; he has complained of 'degrading crap of a quasi-feminist kind, which called the film misogynist and me misogynist, which is plainly ridiculous. It takes a serious misreading of the film to the point of naïve stupidity'.[27] His contention is that 'the film definitely and unashamedly deals with some unacceptable aspects of male heterosexual behaviour by showing two guys who manifest these traits in different ways',[28] and he points out that two of the film's most favourable reviews came from Georgia Brown and Amy Taubin of *The Village Voice*,[29] which he considers 'very on the ball ... You cannot meet more respectable feminists than that lot'.[30]

And indeed Johnny's behaviour is violently and repellently misogynistic on several occasions. We could, however, assume that the very fact that the film opens with him appearing to commit a rape is intended to make it shockingly obvious that Leigh intends to place male treatment of women in the foreground. It is also a strategy, says Leigh, 'to force you to come up with your own responses. The way I set Johnny up to start with is in the worst possible light, so that you've got to come to terms with the fact that he's actually a good guy'.[31] That statement – which, it should be emphasised, was an off-the-cuff comment, made during an interview at Cannes – might seem dubious if it were taken to suggest that the opening scene were justified purely in terms of narrative development (which would be to trivialise the inclusion of rape or near-rape in a drama by reducing it to a trope), or indeed of character development (which would let Johnny off lightly, suggesting that, as Andy Medhurst puts it, he 'is indulged by the film to a rather frightening degree – he might be a rapist but at least he's not posh'[32]). Fortunately, the structure of the narrative carries rather more thematic weight and reveals a more serious strategy.

Far from Leigh approving of Johnny's treatment of women, he seems deliberately to draw parallels between him and the loathsome Jeremy, sometimes designed to suggest connections, at others to hint at contrasts. As noted above, although Jeremy appears quite early on, we do not see him with the other principal characters, or in any way integrated into the main narrative, until over an hour into the film. The effect is to make him a rather abstract presence – the only character whom we get to know independently of an encounter with Johnny, he almost seems to exist purely as a point of comparison.

The timing of Jeremy's early, isolated appearances is very specific. We first cut to him during the conversation between Johnny and Sophie while they are waiting for Louise to get home. Johnny has launched into one of his diatribes, on this occasion about space travel: 'What do they think they're going to find up there that they can't find down here? They think if they piss high enough, they're going to come across the monkey with the beard and the crap ideas ... '. When he asks Sophie, 'Are you with me?', she attempts to join in, with her theory that space rockets are 'big metal pricks – you know, I mean, the bastards aren't satisfied with fucking the earth up, they've got to fuck space and all'. Both the interruption to his flow and the reference to aggressive phallic symbolism appear to antagonise Johnny, who quickly changes tack to reassert his verbal and sexual dominance: 'Will you tell me something, love? Are you aware of the effect you have on the average mammalian, Mancunian, x-y-ly-chromosome, slavering, lusty male member of the species?' Seconds later, the scene changes to a gymnasium where Jeremy is seen working out, then attempting to chat up a masseuse (Carolina Giammetta) with the less than charming gambit, 'Do you think women like being raped?' The abrupt switch to an unrelated scene implies a comparison: Johnny's sexual aggression towards Sophie; Jeremy's towards the masseuse. This is reinforced by her response: 'You talk a lot, don't you?' – which is presumably what we have just been thinking about Johnny. While it is true that, even at this early stage, Jeremy's attitude seems the more offensively aggressive and cynical, Johnny's exchange with Sophie cannot fail to be coloured by our memory of the opening scene and our knowledge of his potential for sexual violence.

We next see Jeremy a little later, by which time Louise has returned home and Johnny has angrily reminded her of the postcard that she sent him with her address, which he regards as an insult (but which he nevertheless kept and used to find her when he needed somewhere to go). He sneers at her 'posh job in the big shitty' and, even more cruelly, at her bedroom: 'I see you've got a ceiling at the top with a floor on the lower level, and a wall at either side. And only a single bed. Sad, really'. From this unpleasant jibe we cut back to Jeremy who is now dining out with the masseuse, questioning her about the size of her breasts, and asking her, 'Are you a feminist?' when she accuses him of being sexually frustrated. Back to Johnny and Sophie, kissing and embracing. Johnny begins to undress her, and at this stage she is co-operating enthusiastically, guiding him to the zip on her bodice rather than the tassels ('You've tried the stairs, I think we should take the escalator'). Back, briefly, to the restaurant, where Jeremy has failed to seduce the masseuse. 'This is terribly disappointing', he says; 'You don't like rejection, do you, Jeremy?' she replies. We cut again, to Johnny and Sophie making love. This is presented in accordance with the screenplay's description of it as 'passionate and loving. No aggression from Johnny',[33] although again our attitude to Johnny's behaviour is influenced by the fact that we see Louise in the next room, wide awake and presumably listening to them. Back again to Jeremy, who has now gone back to his flat, not alone but with the waitress who served them in the restaurant (Elizabeth Berrington). He bites her painfully as they kiss and, by way of foreplay, frightens her with a stuffed lizard, pins her roughly to the bed and asks her if she has ever thought of committing suicide.

Clearly neither Johnny nor Jeremy is being presented as likeable in their dealings with women, both seeming to use aggression as a cover for a degree of insecurity. Leigh's cutting between the two men is teasingly ambiguous, though. Jeremy seems to take predatory, hostile male behaviour to a repulsive extreme; yet our reaction to Johnny can hardly be one of even qualified approval, particularly since we *may* regard him as having committed the rape (albeit not a premeditated one) that we have only heard Jeremy talk about.

There is another interesting, almost subliminal, juxtaposition immediately after we have seen Johnny viciously banging Sophie's head on the sofa while they have sex. We cut to Louise's boss, Mr Halpern (Peter Whitman) – his only appearance in the film – leaving work and nearly forgetting to take a bunch of flowers with him. Could this be a further universalisation of male behaviour, hinting at a casual, neglectful sexism regarding relationships? Or an intimation that he is hen-pecked, which is the inevitable long-term result of a relationship? Or are the flowers not for his wife or long-term partner at all? It is an incidental detail, but a rich one.

The first time we see Jeremy integrated with the other main characters is comparatively late in the narrative, when he descends upon the house (calling himself Sebastian Hawks). He coerces and eventually rapes Sophie, and she is all but traumatised by the time Louise gets home. Thoroughly intimidated by him, and reluctant to call the police for fear they would believe him not them, the two women are eventually forced to retreat to the pub and wonder when they dare go back home. This sequence of events is again intercut with what's happening to Johnny: his encounter with the waitress who allows him into the flat she is minding, looks after him, but then becomes distressed and throws him out. There is a neat cut at one point from Jeremy, reclining on the sofa, having driven Louise and Sophie from the room, to Johnny, reclining on the waitress's living room floor, anticipating a warm night indoors which is ultimately to be denied him. The comparisons continue to tease us. At this stage nothing we know about Jeremy encourages us to feel anything but contempt for the way he treats people, in his professional or private life (a brief earlier scene showed him in his Porsche, bellowing savagely at a business associate down his mobile, to the barely suppressed terror of the young woman in the passenger seat). We have, however, seen enough of Johnny to know that, while he is capable of treating people abominably, he has real if undirected intelligence and is capable of acts of kindness (he is willing to help Archie and Maggie, and even his patronising treatment of them is to a great extent triggered by Archie's aggression). On the other hand, while we cannot help feeling a little sorry for him when the waitress changes her mind and tells him to leave the flat, his haranguing of her, cursing her future children, is manifestly out of all proportion; Jeremy's methods are more insidious, reclaiming 'his' territory as landlord and thus making Louise and Sophie refugees from, later prisoners in, what they, as tenants, regard as their home.

That notion of home is an important one, and another key distinction between Jeremy and Johnny – in fact, between Jeremy and every other major character in the film. We do not know what Johnny's domestic status was up in Manchester – he may have been renting, or living with his mother, whom he professes to despise – but by putting himself in the position of having to flee to London, he has made himself disenfranchised, a drifter without a roof over his head. It seems like a sore point at times; at any rate, Louise actually manages to shut him up at one point when, after spending his first night in the house, he is trying to bully her and she simply says, 'I live here'. When Brian asks him, 'Have you got nowhere to go then?', he says, 'Yeah, I've got an infinite number of fucking places to go. The problem is, where you stay'. Even when Johnny thinks he has snatched a few minutes' comfort in the passenger seat of a Rolls-Royce, the chauffeur, who has initially assumed him to be someone else – a rock musician, perhaps – quickly realises his mistake and orders Johnny out. Archie and Maggie are likewise homeless and on the run, Archie having seriously assaulted his father. The waitress is minding the flat for a gay couple whom she does not know. The woman opposite the office block seems not to own that flat either: she has 'never noticed' the map of Ireland on the wall. Brian dreams of moving to a cottage in Ireland where he thinks he lived in a previous life – it may well be a futile dream designed to give him some purchase on the future by which he sets so much store (when he says, 'Don't waste your life', it seems addressed as much to himself as to Johnny). Louise, Sophie and Sandra rent from Jeremy who, as we have seen, is only too happy to remind them of the power that this gives him over them: basically, he is able to intimidate them as he does because he has a key and can let himself in. Property is power. When Brian allows Johnny into the empty office block to shelter on the condition that 'You must be invisible. I must be seen', the comment has resonances outside its immediate context, concerning the social and political status of the employed (however menial and pointless the job) compared to the homeless.

To some extent, then, Jeremy's role in the film is clearly to make Johnny appear more sympathetic. The intercutting of scenes involving each of them at crucial moments creates comparisons pointed enough to highlight common aspects of aggressive male behaviour. But Johnny is less cold, callous or calculating than Jeremy, and anyway he has qualities Jeremy does not. The similarities having been established, the crucial differences between the two men are thrown into sharp relief towards the end of the film, when they briefly appear together. Johnny, beaten, demoralised, sick and delirious, returns to the house, where the women take him in, and where Jeremy is still lording it over them.

Johnny's rather self-conscious obsession with death has been alluded to above; we already know that Jeremy also claims to have a death wish. 'I'm going to commit suicide', he tells the terrified waitress as he pushes her onto the bed near the beginning of the film. 'On my fortieth birthday ... I don't want to be old'. His pessimism, we note, is entirely personal, entirely self-centred, in a way that Johnny's despairing world-view, however self-indulgent and self-dramatising, is not. Nor can one imagine Johnny, even at his most provocatively nihilistic, coming out with Jeremy's cynical comment that 'I think AIDS is rather healthy, in its way ... I realise that's not the fashionable thing to say, of course ... But the world is over-crowded, isn't it? It could do with a bit of pruning'. And near the end of the film, Jeremy looks down at Louise and Sophie, huddled on the floor with the battered, bleeding, weeping Johnny, and says, 'Aren't people pathetic?' This again is a far cry from the Swiftian self-loathing that is always very evident at the heart of Johnny's own aggression. No ambivalence to be found here; Jeremy clearly does not include himself among the 'people' he judges so unfeelingly. The appearance of the two men – Johnny collapsed in a heap, enveloped in his voluminous coat; Jeremy still strutting around in his skimpy underpants – couldn't be in starker contrast, and nor could their perspectives. We have indeed seen Johnny at something like his worst, but we have recognised in him a fundamental humanism which is alien to Jeremy, a distinction encapsulated in the gulf between Johnny's serious joking and Jeremy's mirthless snigger.

The implication that Johnny may indulge in some appalling, indefensible behaviour but that Jeremy is far worse, more powerful and more dangerous, is of course reinforced by Leigh's treatment of the two characters. It has been claimed with some justification that 'if a character in a Mike Leigh film wears a suit or drives a BMW, he won't be allowed anything approaching the degree of depth or complexity the other characters have'.[34] Leigh is fairly unrepentant about this: 'If a character is really drawn unsympathetically – like Jeremy in *Naked* – then it's because he *is* unsympathetic, that's what he's about'.[35] Obviously, and as we saw in relation to *High Hopes*, this privileges certain characters over others; seeing no obligation to be even-handed in the matter, Leigh presents Jeremy as a less detailed character than Johnny precisely to suggest that we need not waste time looking for redeeming features in a man who exploits his tenants, the women he encounters, and God knows who else in advancing his own interests. Johnny, on the other hand, is presented in all his facets: vulnerable and bullying, amusing and frightening, intelligent and maddening. This, I would submit, may be unabashed subjectivity on Leigh's part, but it does not make for a lack of realism. Indeed, the very subjectivity may in one sense be a more truthful way of viewing the characters than a balanced approach: for all of us, being human and therefore imperfect, are not the people we like the ones in whom the positives outweigh the negatives, and the people we dislike the ones in whom we see only the faults?

The very idea that Johnny exhibits any positive, even agreeable characteristics, may itself be unthinkable to some viewers. But if we compare him, for example, to Trevor (Tim Roth), the unremittingly unpleasant leading character in Alan Clarke and David Leland's *Made in Britain* (1982), we can see the light and shade in Johnny's personality more clearly. Both he and Trevor are intelligent and articulate, but guilty of terrible anti-social behaviour (sexist in Johnny's case, racist in Trevor's), which leads them to commit acts of unforgivable violence. But the differences are there: Johnny's aggression is, sometimes at least, verbal rather than physical, and he has real, if bleak, perspectives on society and the human condition, whereas Trevor is not noticeably more insightful than anyone else around him – insofar as he chooses to articulate the motives for his aggressively anarchic attitudes, he does so solely in racist terms, and his views on authority are not much more profound than Pink Floyd's 'We don't need no education'. (The shallowness of his opinions is highlighted by the ease with which his black companion can be persuaded to join in his racist attacks.) Likewise, while Johnny's dark humour, however rebarbative, is evidence of an active, searching, challenging mind, on the very rare occasions when Trevor makes jokes, they too are inextricably linked to his racism ('I speak fluent Punjabi and chapatti', he obnoxiously tells the clerk at the job centre).

Jeremy, then, both mirrors unacceptable aspects of Johnny's behaviour, while exhibiting sufficiently crucial differences to highlight Johnny's more acceptable, occasionally endearing traits. But what of the women characters themselves? Even some critics like John Hill, who accept that *Naked* 'does not endorse the misogyny of the film's character', may regard it as 'weak in giving a satisfactory expression to an alternative ethos of independence', so that it ends up 'more successful in giving voice to Johnny's rage than embodying the experiences of the women characters'.[36] Hill is of course correct in saying that Johnny's is certainly, and by some distance, the dominant presence and the dominant viewpoint; and I think his comments carry more weight than Suzanne Moore's diatribe against the film in *The Guardian*:

> Even if we accept *Naked* as another of Leigh's 'Life is Shit' type pieces of social realism, how come all the female characters are pathetic drips with silly voices? Women to whom men do things but who appear to do nothing for themselves? What sort of realism is this? To show a misogynist and surround him with such walking doormats has the effect, intentional or not, of justifying such behaviour.[37]

In fact, the women in the film are by no means such a homogeneous bunch as Moore suggests – even if they are nowhere near as closely delineated as Johnny (one or two of them are not even given names) and are largely defined by their reactions to him. (In an earlier piece, Moore lumped the women in *High Hopes* together in similarly cavalier fashion, arguing that 'Leigh is not particularly kind to his female characters who always seem either crudely drawn or shallower than the men. Even Shirley comes across as a bit thick and while Cyril gets to make speeches by Marx's grave, she twitters on about "emotional" matters'.[38] As I hope my reading of *High Hopes* made clear, in my opinion Shirley is certainly not 'a bit thick' and she never 'twitters on'; for my money, in the Highgate Cemetery sequence she comes over slightly more sympathetically than Cyril.)

We see both Johnny and Jeremy, at different stages in the film, in passing encounters with two anonymous women in succession: Jeremy at the beginning, with the masseuse and the restaurant waitress; Johnny later, with the 'woman in the window' and the café waitress. As we have seen, the masseuse is a match for Jeremy in their conversation, and she declines to go home with him. The waitress does go back to his place, where he treats her shockingly – our last sight of her is as 'she screams out loud in pain and fear',[39] to quote the screenplay. Of the two women encountered by Johnny, he treats the woman whom Brian watches most cruelly – indeed his motive for going there and making a rough attempt at seduction seems to be as much to taunt Brian as to find somewhere to spend the night. He is gradually repelled by her demand that he should bite her, by her skull-and-crossbones tattoo and by her tempting him with what she intends as sexy poses. He callously informs her that she reminds him of the mother whom he hates (and variously claims is dead and/or a model for porn magazines), steals from her as she sleeps and goes on his way. A similar insult is dealt out when the café waitress takes him to the flat she is minding and offers him a shower. 'You're not going to creep up on me with a big knife dressed up as your mother, are you?' he asks, before adding, 'it looks like you already are dressed up as your mother'. She seems intimidated by this gratuitous verbal bullying, and by Johnny's classical allusions ('I don't mean that to sound homophobic. I mean, I like *The Iliad*'), but is finally driven to send him away, standing up to him and not giving in when he protests. We might be surprised by the arbitrary nature of the comment that triggers her decision: 'You've got a very sad face' is not the worst of insults, and Thewlis's inflection as he delivers the line is subtle and ambiguous, so that it is difficult to tell whether Johnny is mocking her again or making a genuinely sympathetic comment. However, while we may feel some pity for him for being thrown out just as it seemed that he had found somewhere to stay, we recognise the scenario as part of his recurrent behaviour pattern of challenging people to reject him, even if they treat him kindly.

Of the three flatmates, Sandra appears for the least screen time, and is the least complex, though no less credible for that. Despite John Hill's view that 'whatever validity her remarks [to Johnny] may have are undermined by Claire Skinner's clever but heavily mannered performance',[40] I would argue that the element of exaggeration in characterisation here is a valid and effective means of creating an instantly recognisable 'type', and that Skinner's staccato hand gestures and unfinished sentences are genuinely evocative of Sandra's obsession with an orderliness that she cannot actually articulate but clings to nonetheless in the face of a chaotic world. Her challenging of Johnny is undermined not so much by Skinner's performance, as by the character's narrowness of outlook, which in fact the performance effectively conveys. When Sandra is reduced to dismissing Johnny's philosophising as 'silly questions' and a tendency merely to 'take the piss', we sense that he has been straying into areas which her own worldview leaves out, or ignores as being too difficult to deal with.

In the case of Sophie, we do indeed see a character terminally unable to motivate herself to take control of her own life. Of all the women in the film, Sophie most closely matches Suzanne Moore's definition of a 'walking doormat' – with the possible exception of Maggie who, while feisty, seems locked into an inescapably violent relationship with Archie. Sophie's vulnerability is well established, but so is the abject helplessness and submission to humiliation that it brings. Johnny is clearly threatened by her emotional neediness and claims to fellow-feeling: as noted above, his vicious banging of her head on the sofa as they have sex comes directly after she says that 'I'm in love with you, Johnny ... I understand you'. Worse is to come for Sophie when Jeremy turns up: she simply sighs, 'Oh God, here we go', as he makes advances on her, and then submits to coercion and violent, painful sex. She is aware of the iniquitous nature of such oppressive male behaviour, but seems frustratingly resigned to it: in the pub with Louise while they are avoiding Jeremy, she says: 'I don't know what they want from you half the time. What they start off liking you for they end up hating you for. Don't like you if you're strong, don't like you if you're weak; hate you if you're clever, hate you if you're stupid. They don't know what they want'. John Hill contends that this is an isolated instance of a contemplative conversation between two female characters in *Naked*,[41] yet it is not necessarily any less memorable for that; in fact it probably stands out more notably. In giving the above speech to Sophie, Leigh also makes it seem less like the sermon it could have been in other hands; instead it again enriches the characterisation, Sophie's awareness of the problem being paralysed by her professed inability to do anything about it. Her passivity undoubtedly makes her complicit in the ordeal she undergoes; indeed it is made to seem like one of her recognisable character traits when the not unsympathetic Louise returns home and just assumes that the whole thing has been nothing more than 'one of your orgies'. This, however, suggests neither that it is how the majority of women respond, nor that it is in any way desirable. On the contrary, most of the other characters are frequently exasperated with Sophie, up to and including our last sight of her, when, as Ray Carney puts it, 'she sadly stumbles away in tears to face new bouts of humiliation'.[42] Katrin Cartlidge and Lesley Sharp have both, unsurprisingly, defended the portrayal of Sophie and some of the other women in the film on the grounds of depicting the truth rather than an ideal. 'There are a lot of people like that going around', said Cartlidge, while Sharp has argued that 'there are a lot of women in abusive relationships who find it very hard to get out of them'.[43]

If Sandra is the epitome of ineffectual order and Sophie of self-destructive chaos, then Louise occupies a pragmatic position somewhere between the two. She is the nearest we see in the film to a stable character (of either gender) simply coping with the vagaries of ordinary life. She seems more in charge of her own destiny than any of the other characters, and while we may regard her as misguided in her continuing affection for Johnny, she is by no means in thrall to him. She knows him well, and is often able to give as good as she gets in their verbal exchanges, especially at the end of the film, when they trade insults which seem almost good-natured compared to some of their previous exchanges ('I only got 'em [a pair of shorts] to piss you off', she taunts him; 'Mission accomplished', he replies). In contrast to her genuine concern for Johnny – and to Sophie's passivity – she appears to play along with Jeremy's sledgehammer-subtle chat-up lines ('Nice tits'), but once she's goaded him into opening his trousers, she grabs a kitchen knife and threatens to cut off his penis. Her decision to quit her dull job and return to Manchester is on the whole a positive one, even if it was Johnny's presence that pushed her into it. There is real affection between them as they sing the song 'Take Me Back to Manchester When It's Raining', but the semi-delirious Johnny immediately undercuts the tenderness of the moment by saying, 'I've got a hard on'. In the same way, he will deny the sentiments expressed in the song in the cold light of morning, by turning his back both on Louise and a return 'home'. It is a betrayal, without question, even if Louise seems to want to go back to Manchester anyway, with or without him. For Johnny's part, the practical consideration that he is still presumably in danger of a beating back home hardly seems to matter any more. There is no going back. As Andy Medhurst notes, Louise 'is prepared to take him on, self-effacingly to offer him healing and comfort, until he scents the closing trap and bolts for the closing credits'.[44] We have seen sufficient evidence of men behaving very, very badly to feel that, up to a point, this reaction may typify male responses to relationships and commitment. Yet we have also seen – and heard – enough of Johnny to understand that the bolt is wholly characteristic of him as an individual. Genuine love and compassion would penetrate his defences, threaten his independence, challenge his more antipathetic instincts about himself and the people around him.

The critical response to Johnny, and to the film, was mixed, to put it mildly. Suzanne Moore was far from alone in reacting so angrily: 'All the women are drab victims who are begging to be humiliated',[45] said Anne Billson in the *Sunday Telegraph*, while in *The Times* Geoff Brown acknowledged that 'Leigh's heart plainly goes out to lost, insecure souls', but found the film misogynistic, raising a familiar objection in the process: 'The women, seen mostly as punchbags or pitstops for passing males, bear the brunt of Leigh's fondness for caricature'.[46] In *The Independent* Adam Mars-Jones detected a 'gloating emotional ugliness',[47] and in the *Daily Mail* Christopher Tookey declared that Johnny 'comes across, not as the publicity blurb's "ultimate anti-hero of the Nineties", but as an arrogant, half-educated nitwit with nothing more to recommend him than an acid tongue'.[48] Jonathan Romney, writing in the *New Statesman and Society*, also had reservations about Johnny and was consequently unconvinced by the film's claims to state-of-the-nation satire, finding it 'hard to feel that the cruel world its characters inhabit is more than simply a shabby, bleak backdrop for one startling solipsistic character turn'.[49] The most extreme negative criticism came from Julie Burchill, who reckoned the film was inviting her to laugh at the homeless or at rape victims: 'Why is laughing any better than turning a blind eye? Surely, it's worse: the government may be callous swine – but they're not using these issues to get, or to give, a cheap laugh'.[50] Having so drastically, and perversely, misinterpreted the film, and thrown in her objections to the 'Beaujolais' moment in *Abigail's Party* for good measure, Burchill went on to accuse Leigh, quite erroneously, of concealing his middle-class roots and his Jewishness; all in all, an extraordinary attack.

Other critics were more torn between being appalled at the film and admiring its achievements. In the *Evening Standard* Alexander Walker seemed genuinely shocked as he recounted the way in which *Naked* 'freezes the blood with its eloquent endorsement of nihilism',[51] and in the *Financial Times* Nigel Andrews found it 'maddening: part good, part bad, part ugly'.[52] Hugo Davenport in the *Daily Telegraph* thought it 'a harsh, gruelling film, but an unforgettable one',[53] Sheridan Morley in the *Sunday Express* judged it Leigh's 'best and bleakest work to date ... a terrifying journey into the underworld of contemporary Britain',[54] and Derek Malcolm said in *The Guardian* that it 'may be an uneasy film to sit through, but is still able to weave considerable comic entertainment into the process of drawing blood'.[55] In *Time Out*, Geoff Andrew noted that 'it explores a peculiarly male form of cynical self-loathing which manifests itself in misogynist insults and violence' before going on to give perhaps the most accurate summary of the film: 'Alternately hilarious and hard to stomach (there's one, maybe even two rape scenes), Leigh's picaresque fable is his most troubling, complex and intriguing work since *Meantime*; it's also his most cinematic by far'.[56] Whether for its cinematic achievements or the boldness of its vision, or both, *Naked* won the Best Director award at Cannes (alongside a Best Actor award for Thewlis), bringing Leigh his greatest international recognition to date.

The sound and fury may have died away, but the arguments are not likely to be resolved any time soon. It is irrefutably provocative to place at the centre of a film a character of such contradictions, complexities, awesome intelligence and culpable failings; even more so to make him a protagonist in whom the shocking treatment of women is such a dominant trait. But *Naked* is a film designed to provoke on many levels. It is a film of great scope and ambition, setting out to do many things. But what Leigh never sets out to do is make things easy – not for his characters, not for his audience and not for himself.

Notes

1 Interview with the author, 5 April 2005
2 Quoted in Graham Fuller, 'Mike Leigh's Original Features', in *Naked and Other Screenplays* (London, Faber & Faber, 1995), p. xxxviii
3 Interview with the author, 5 April 2005
4 Quoted in Amy Taubin, 'Heir to the Anger', *Village Voice*, 14 December 1993, p. 70
5 Quoted in Graham Fuller, 'Mike Leigh's Original Features', p. xxxix
6 Michael Coveney, *The World According to Mike Leigh* (London, Harper Collins, paperback edition, 1997), caption to photograph between pages 168 and 169
7 Lee Ellickson and Richard Porton, 'I Find the Tragi-Comic Things in Life: An Interview with Mike Leigh', *Cineaste*, 20: 3 (1994); reprinted in Howie Movshovitz (ed.), *Mike Leigh Interviews* (Jackson, University Press of Mississippi, 2000), p. 72
8 Leigh quoted in Graham Fuller, 'Mike Leigh's Original Features', p. xxxix
9 Quoted in John Naughton, 'There's No Face Like Gnome', *Empire*, 100 (October 1997); reprinted in Howie Movshovitz (ed.), *Mike Leigh Interviews*, p. 128
10 Thewlis quoted in David Sterritt, 'Mike Leigh Calls It as He Sees It', *Christian Science Monitor*, 7 September 1993; reprinted in Howie Movshovitz (ed.), *Mike Leigh Interviews*, p. 43

11 *Ibid.*
12 Thewlis quoted in Desson Howe, *Washington Post*, 30 January 1994; reprinted in Howie Movshovitz (ed.), *Mike Leigh Interviews*, p. 49
13 *Ibid.*, p. 50
14 Online discussion, 10 March 2000; edited transcript on the website *Film Unlimited*, www.film.guardian.co.uk, 17 March 2000
15 Quoted in Graham Fuller, 'Mike Leigh's Original Features', p. xxxv
16 Richard Boston, *Boudu Saved From Drowning* (London, BFI Publishing, 1994), p. 42
17 *Ibid.*, p. 44
18 Robin Skynner and John Cleese, *Life and How to Survive It* (London, Methuen, 1993), p. 87
19 Victoria Glendinning, *Jonathan Swift* (London, Hutchinson, 1998), p. 185
20 *Ibid.*, p. 280
21 Quoted in Alfred Draper, *The Story of the Goons* (London, Everest Books, 1976), p. 72
22 Jonathan Swift, letter to Alexander Pope, 29 September 1725
23 Philip MacDonald, 'Life, the Universe and Douglas Adams', *Doctor Who Magazine*, 306 (25 July 2001), p. 42
24 Claire Monk, *Sight and Sound*, 3: 11 (November 1993), p. 48
25 Claire Monk, 'Men in the 90s', in Robert Murphy (ed.), *British Cinema of the 90s* (London, BFI Publishing, 2000), p. 163
26 Quoted in Lee Ellickson and Richard Porton, 'I Find the Tragi-Comic Things in Life: An Interview with Mike Leigh', *Cineaste*, 20: 3 (1994); reprinted in Howie Movshovitz (ed.), *Mike Leigh Interviews*, pp. 70–1
27 Quoted in Howie Movshovitz, 'Rehearsals Hold Key to Mike Leigh Films', *Denver Post*, 3 November 1996; reprinted in Howie Movshovitz (ed.), *Mike Leigh Interviews*, p. 107
28 Quoted in Graham Fuller, 'Mike Leigh's Original Features', p. xxxvi
29 Georgia Brown, *Village Voice*, 20 December 1993, p. 70; and Amy Taubin, 'Heir to the Anger', p. 70
30 Quoted in Lee Ellickson and Richard Porton, 'I Find the Tragi-Comic Things in Life: An Interview with Mike Leigh', p. 70
31 Quoted in Howie Movshovitz, 'Mike Leigh's Grim Optimism', *Denver Post*, 22 February 1994; reprinted in Howie Movshovitz (ed.), *Mike Leigh Interviews*, p. 52
32 Andy Medhurst, 'Mike Leigh: Beyond Embarrassment', *Sight and Sound*, 3: 11 (November 1993), p. 10
33 Mike Leigh, *Naked*, in *Naked and Other Screenplays* (London, Faber & Faber, 1995), p. 17
34 Online discussion, 10 March 2000; edited transcript on the website *Film Unlimited*, www.film.guardian.co.uk, 17 March 2000
35 Quoted in Graham Fuller, 'Mike Leigh's Original Features', p. xxiii
36 John Hill, *British Cinema in the 1980s* (Oxford, Oxford University Press, 1999), p. 173
37 Suzanne Moore, 'Reel Men Don't Eat Quiche', *The Guardian*, 12 November 1993
38 Suzanne Moore, *New Statesman and Society*, 13 January 1989, p. 44
39 Mike Leigh, *Naked*, in *Naked and Other Screenplays*, p. 20
40 John Hill, *British Cinema in the 1980s*, p. 173
41 *Ibid.*
42 Ray Carney and Leonard Quart, *The Films of Mike Leigh: Embracing the World* (Cambridge, Cambridge University Press, 2000), p. 235
43 Quoted in Michael Coveney, *The World According to Mike Leigh*, p. 34
44 Andy Medhurst, 'Mike Leigh: Beyond Embarrassment', p. 10

45 Anne Billson, *Sunday Telegraph*, 7 November 1993
46 Geoff Brown, *The Times*, 4 November 1993
47 Adam Mars-Jones, *The Independent*, 5 November 1993
48 Christopher Tookey, *Daily Mail*, 5 November 1993
49 Jonathan Romney, *New Statesman and Society*, 5 November 1993, pp. 34–5
50 Julie Burchill, *Sunday Times*, 7 November 1993
51 Alexander Walker, *Evening Standard*, 4 November 1993
52 Nigel Andrews, *Financial Times*, 4 November 1993
53 Hugo Davenport, *Daily Telegraph*, 5 November 1993
54 Sheridan Morley, *Sunday Express*, 7 November 1993
55 Derek Malcolm, *The Guardian*, 4 November 1993
56 Geoff Andrew, *Time Out*, 3–10 November 1993, p. 68

'Welcome to the family': *Secrets and Lies*

7

After the controversy of *Naked* came one of Leigh's best loved and most highly acclaimed films. Applying the epic thematic and structural scale of *Naked* to the intimate domestic environment of his earlier work, *Secrets and Lies* proved to be his most popular film up to that time, winning the Palme d'Or and the International Critics' Prize at Cannes (as well as a Best Actress award for Brenda Blethyn) and receiving five Oscar nominations in the major categories of Best Film, Best Director, Best Screenplay, Best Actress and Best Supporting Actress. In the event, however, it didn't win in any of these categories, and Leigh proved characteristically unwilling to brush off the disappointment with the usual platitudes about 'stiff competition' or 'an honour just to be nominated': 'It was a total piss-off to go home with nothing. To say otherwise would be bullshit. It was not, as they say, a nice night out ... Maybe I'd be a better sport if it had been a straight, clean fight. But we all know it's politics'.[1]

Oscar night frustrations aside, Leigh must have been pleased with the film's success: it received a wider UK release than any of his previous work and 'made more at the box office than his last three films combined';[2] it also 'took $50 million worldwide, propelling Leigh into the directorial front rank'.[3] As evidence of its continuing popularity it was voted fortieth in the 1999 'BFI 100' industry poll. (*Life Is Sweet* also made it in, at number 95, although *Naked*, astonishingly, was nowhere to be seen.) The film had also marked a turning point in that it moved Thin Man Films into the European co-production market, funding from the French company CiBY 2000 affording Leigh around twice the budget he had had for *Naked*.

Secrets and Lies deals with big issues – among them love, death, marriage, race, adoption, estrangement and the inability to conceive children. Yet it is still a character-based, rather than issue-based, work. The characters remain real and recognisable, never mere mouthpieces through which the themes can be dealt with; and, as ever, Leigh and his actors treat their human frailties with rare perception and sympathy.

As the film opens, a funeral is taking place and the music is appropriately melancholy. It gives way almost immediately to the mourners singing the hymn 'How Great Thou Art', and as the camera pans round at a respectful distance, we see that most of those present are West Indian. Eventually we close in on one particular young woman, Hortense (Marianne Jean-Baptiste), who is composed but tearful. A floral tribute in the form of the word 'Mum' is placed on the grave, and we instinctively form the connection between Hortense and the deceased.

Other connections between characters are made early on. From the funeral, we cut to a wedding, establishing the recurring social rituals that will reappear through the film, culminating in a dramatic and eventful birthday party. In a neo-classical mansion, a nervous, unhappy-looking bride is being photographed on her wedding day, while her father hovers intimidatingly in the background. The photographer is Maurice (Timothy Spall), whose amiable professional patter ('you're under no obligation to, but you can if you want to give me a tiny little twinkle') eventually coaxes a smile out of her.

Next time we see Maurice he is with his wife Monica (Phyllis Logan) in their immaculate detached home. They discuss Maurice's niece Roxanne (Claire Rushbrook), who will soon be twenty-one, and whose photo Maurice keeps on the mantelpiece. He is proud of the portrait, which he took himself, but tellingly says of Roxanne that 'I reckon that's the last time she ever smiled'. Maurice's professional life is of course based on constantly persuading people to look happy – and before long the film will present us with nineteen brief vignettes showing a variety of groups, couples and individuals being photographed by him with varying degrees of co-operation. (These vignettes are mostly presented in two groups, followed by one final, isolated, scene featuring a particularly sour Greek Cypriot couple.) His comment about Roxanne, however, alerts us to the fact that putting a smile on other people's faces is not such a simple matter away from the lights and the camera. In this scene, for example, there is clearly friction between him and Monica about Roxanne's mother, Maurice's sister Cynthia (Brenda Blethyn). They have not seen Roxanne for two and a half years, and Cynthia has never been invited to visit the house in which they have lived for almost a year. 'I suppose we'd have to invite Cynthia as well', says Monica as they discuss the possibility of having Roxanne round to celebrate her birthday, adding waspishly, 'There's no show without Punch'. Maurice responds evenly that he is sure Cynthia would like to see their home. 'Oh, I'm sure she would!' replies Monica meaningfully, to which Maurice merely replies,

'She can't help it'. Tactfully he compliments Monica on the way she has decorated the house and says that 'It's about time you showed it off'. Again, his professional role in keeping everyone superficially happy is carried over into his domestic life, but the cumulative strain that this is causing him is not yet apparent.

Certainly Maurice seems to be right in his guess that Roxanne does not smile much. After a couple of brief scenes showing Roxanne and Cynthia working, respectively as a road sweeper and in a box factory, we see them for the first time having a conversation. Cynthia complains that Roxanne has 'been sitting there for a month with a face like a slapped arse' and gets the angry reply, 'Well, what's there to smile about?' Cynthia changes the subject, complaining that Maurice has not phoned her recently and that it is Monica who is putting the blocks on her being invited to see their new home ('Toffee-nosed cow ... what's he want with six bedrooms, anyway?').

In contrast to Maurice and Monica's house, with its many bedrooms and intricate stencilled decorations, Cynthia still lives in the rented terrace house where she and Maurice grew up, and which is full of their father's possessions ('Some of it hasn't been touched since Mum died'). She became the hub of the family at the age of ten following her mother's death, and became pregnant with Roxanne when she was twenty-one; she has always had people dependent on her, and now that she has nobody to 'mother' – although Roxanne still lives at home, she is fiercely and understandably independent – there seems to be a loneliness and lack of purpose in her life. Maurice is four years younger, so was only six when his mother died. In a later scene he reveals to Monica that his father 'never said a word about my mum after she'd died' and that he is still not sure exactly how he felt himself. It seems that Monica suffered a similar loss, her father dying when she was young, but she resists Maurice's attempts to discuss it ('Too young to remember'), and when he asks her if she had to look after her own brother, her response is another dig at Cynthia: 'What, you mean like your big sister looked after you? No, I did not'.

After the initial conversations between Maurice and Monica, then Cynthia and Roxanne, establishing their relationships and feelings for one another, we return to Hortense, who has previously been glimpsed only at the funeral. She is an optometrist, and is seen giving a little girl an eye test. She deals with the girl with an easy, reassuring manner that is practised but entirely natural and unforced. This is already a significant contrast to Maurice: whereas his job relies on working hard to put people at their ease – and even then he is not always successful – Hortense makes the little girl smile quite effortlessly, even though this ability is not crucial to her professional role, but merely makes her that much better at it.

That weekend Hortense goes to her late mother's house to sort through her possessions. As she does so, her two brothers (Brian Bovell and Trevor Laird) and sister-in-law (Claire Perkins) are downstairs, arguing. The married brother clearly has designs on the house and is badgering the other accordingly ('You could split this into two flats, and it'd still be bigger than our place'), though he is taken aback in his turn when his wife interjects with the argument that they need space because they may yet have more children than their present two. Brief though the scene is, it wonderfully encapsulates how the grief of the funeral ritual can so easily give way to pragmatism and selfish bickering. Leigh is also adept at structuring his films to remind us that every family has its own story; this one, fleetingly hinted at, relates on at least one level to the issue of having children, which runs throughout *Secrets and Lies*. The narrative could equally well develop by exploring the relationships between the brothers or between the husband and wife – or, for that matter, by entering the lives of the various groups and individuals who are seen posing for Maurice – but, of all the possible stories, the one we are going to go with is Hortense's. Rather than exploring the relationships within her existing family, the film will follow her as she discovers a new one.

The woman whose funeral we saw at the start of the film was, it transpires, Hortense's adoptive mother. Now she has decided to set the necessary procedures in motion to seek out her birth mother. This narrative strand, in fact, had been a key point of departure for Leigh: 'The actual specific jumping-off point for me was the fact that there are people very close to me who have had adoption-related experiences, which I obviously can't talk about'.[4]

An initial exchange of letters leads Hortense to a meeting with a social worker named Jenny (Lesley Manville), who shows her a folder full of the papers relating to her adoption, and does her best to explain the possible pitfalls and problems which may lie ahead if she decides to take matters further. Jenny is a wonderful supporting character: a professional doing her best under various institutional constraints, clearly well intentioned but somewhat awkward in her attempts at conversation. Discussing the time when Hortense was told that she was adopted, for example, she clumsily asks, 'And do you remember how you felt about that?' – though she is relaxed and open enough to join in Hortense's amusement as she replies, 'Well, it's not exactly something you forget, is it?' Jenny sometimes gets things wrong – she distractedly looks at her watch and glances through the door panel in the middle of telling Hortense that 'we're a professional service, and we know how to handle these things' – but she is sincere in her efforts to relax Hortense and to apply human touches to a bureaucratic process that unavoidably impinges on a situation in which emotions should take precedence. Her good intentions *and* limitations are signalled by Leigh and Manville with marvellous economy.

Under the provision of the 1976 Act of Parliament that permitted adopted children to trace their birth parents, Hortense is allowed to take the folder away with her, having learned that her birth name was 'Elizabeth' and her mother's name was Cynthia Purley. As it happens, it still is. At this stage, we have of course met a Cynthia, but have only heard her named once, by Monica – and, if we have been sharp-eyed, we may have noticed the sign outside Maurice's photographic studio, giving his surname as 'Purley'. Although Hortense is perturbed by the section of the form which refers to her mother as being white, Jenny points out that 'it's perfectly feasible that your mother was white, isn't it?' and insists that this could not be an administrative error. The different groups in the narrative are gradually coming together.

The next move for Hortense is to request a copy of her birth certificate, which is duly sent to her. Among the information it contains is Cynthia's address – the same house that she still lives in – which, after consulting her London *A to Z*, Hortense drives to and looks at, before driving away again.

Maurice also drives to the house on the same day, and visits Cynthia, much to her surprise. Cynthia makes tea while Maurice uses the outside lavatory; Cynthia produces a toilet roll for him almost as soon as he arrives, so either this is something of a ritual, or her mothering instincts are almost telepathically attuned to his needs. They discuss Monica's stencilling, Roxanne's boyfriend Paul (Lee Ross), whom Cynthia has yet to meet properly ('Shifty looking bleeder – walks like a crab'), and the idea of a barbecue to celebrate Roxanne's forthcoming birthday. They also reminisce about the times when Maurice used to bring his girlfriends back to the house ('You didn't mind me sitting there, did you?' says Cynthia, to which Maurice merely chuckles reflectively) and, at the age of seventeen, to help her with Roxanne's nappies. While they talk, we cut to Hortense, now back in her flat, almost phoning Cynthia, but not quite able to do so.

Meanwhile, Maurice offers Cynthia money to pay for some necessary repairs to the house and asks her what she is going to do with 'all this junk' in their father's old room. She does not answer, but begs him to 'give us a cuddle', flings her arms around him and bursts into tears, telling him that 'you're the only one I've got' and pleading for confirmation that he loves her. Cynthia's lonely despair and Maurice's awkwardness at her outburst are beautifully conveyed by Blethyn and Spall, the two characters even just about managing to share a tiny moment of laughter as they embrace ('My little brother! ... When are you going to shave, eh? Slap your arse!'). A few moments later, however, she asks him, apropos of a tatty old artificial Christmas tree, 'You ain't going to make me an auntie now, are you?' and he is suddenly speechless. He seems on the verge of telling her something, but instead leaves rather abruptly, giving her the money he earlier promised (or maybe which he regularly gives her on his infrequent visits?) and reminding her to tell Roxanne about the barbecue.

Between visiting Cynthia and going home, Maurice repairs to a pub, where we see him sitting pensive and alone with a pint of lager. Above him is what the screenplay describes as 'a huge antique portrait of a forgotten dignitary',[5] which dominates the otherwise empty pub and seems to dwarf Maurice, emphasising his inner loneliness and the strain of his role – familial and professional – of keeping everyone smiling. Later still, after he has returned home and following his failed attempt to discuss bereavement with Monica, we learn a couple of family secrets. Firstly, both Maurice and Monica know about Cynthia's adopted child; they assume that she has told Roxanne, but cannot be certain. Secondly, they too have a secret ('What's there to know about us?' – 'You know what I mean'), which Monica is anxious to keep from others, especially Cynthia. We are not made aware of what this is, but might assume it is connected to the severe period pains which we have earlier seen Monica suffering and, especially after Maurice's being genuinely overcome when Cynthia mentioned his making her 'an auntie', speculate that it relates to the overall theme of having children. The conversation ends when Monica is once more scathing about 'Saint Cynthia' and Maurice, emotional now, says, 'She tried her best ... she gave me a lot of love', and wanders out into the garden to be alone with his thoughts.

After a further tetchy exchange between Cynthia and Roxanne, there is another brief but telling shot of Maurice alone, this time at the back of a congregation as a wedding takes place. Leigh then cuts to Monica, 'at the same moment' according to the screenplay,[6] also sitting alone, on their staircase. Poignantly, at the very moment when a new union is taking place, their isolation from each other is emphasised; Maurice taking refuge in his job, Monica in her immaculate domestic surroundings.

Contact is finally made between Cynthia and Hortense just after a particularly fraught conversation has led to Roxanne storming out of the house. Cynthia's persistent questioning about her daughter's contraceptive arrangements – in the garden, of all places, and culminating in the wonderful line: 'I've got a Dutch cap floating around somewhere upstairs, you could have that' – infuriates Roxanne to the point of telling her, 'You make me sick, you stupid bitch'. She marches round to Paul's flat, where the two of them undress rapidly and joyously, leaping all over his bed, while back home Cynthia collapses in floods of tears.

It is at this inopportune moment that Hortense phones. Cynthia is at first incredulous, believing the name 'Elizabeth Purley' to be a reference to her dead mother rather than her first child. When the truth finally dawns, she slams the phone down and rushes to the kitchen, where she is sick into the sink. After a few moments' hesitation, Hortense rings again and Cynthia, very frightened, answers and tells her that 'you can't come round here, cause no one knows about you, see?' However, she reluctantly agrees to the possibility of their meeting, and takes down Hortense's number. It appears to be later the same day when Cynthia, after much agonising, rings her back and they arrange to meet. 'What are you doing this Saturday coming?' asks Hortense; 'Nothing', replies Cynthia bitterly, 'I'm never bloody doing anything'. Yet this is a small turning point for her; she suddenly brightens a little, buying steak and beer for Roxanne, and determining to have 'a few early nights'. Later she will be able to be as secretive as Roxanne has been, going out for the evening without saying where or with whom. There will be a few more emotional switchbacks on the way, but her situation is gradually beginning to improve.

The sequence in which Cynthia and Hortense finally meet, outside Holborn tube station, and then go to a nearby café to talk, is justly one of the best remembered in the film. Most of the scene is shot in just one take, lasting around nine minutes, with the two women sitting in the café on the same side of a table. In fact, says Leigh of this scene, 'we did shoot mid-shot singles and close-ups, but when we looked at the dailies the following day – and we only did two takes – the second take was so totally, utterly perfect that we knew straightway without a shadow of a doubt that this was it'.[7] By keeping the scene as a sustained two-shot, Leigh gives Brenda Blethyn and Marianne Jean-Baptiste a huge amount of control over its pace and rhythm, and they repay him handsomely; their timing and interaction could not be bettered. To carp, as Adam Mars-Jones's *Independent* review did, that they would surely have sat opposite each other rather than side by side, is therefore to miss the point.[8] As usual with Leigh, the effect has little to do with *surface* realism (where people may or may not be likely to sit in a café) and everything to do with a *deeper* realism (the emotional truth of the characters).

Cynthia is as sceptical about their relationship as Hortense originally was but, after initially protesting that 'I don't mean nothing by it, darling, but I've never been with a black man in my life', she pauses and thinks. And remembers something. 'Oh, bloody hell!' she exclaims, and bursts into tears again, sobbing that 'I'm so ashamed'. Exactly why she should be 'ashamed' is never fully explained. Was the conception the result of a quick fling, or a one-night-stand, or brief sex with someone she never even knew? Could it, even, have been a rape? Whatever, the memory is obviously traumatic, painful and long-suppressed. She does tell Hortense that she never knew her baby was black, being too upset to see her at the time of her birth, and had thought that the birth was premature. Now, as the memory returns, she realises that she in fact had had sex with someone else, six weeks before the man she assumed was the father.

They talk about themselves, and Hortense drives Cynthia home, reassuring her that 'I don't want to disrupt your family or anything ... I just had to see you. I had to know who you were'. Cynthia is not fully convinced that she was not a major disappointment to Hortense, but wishes her well and, next day, phones to say 'how nice it was to meet you yesterday'. Rather to Cynthia's surprise, Hortense suggests a meal out together. By the end of the conversation, both of them are smiling.

After the growing warmth of their reunion comes one of the film's most uncomfortable sequences, set in Maurice's studio and shop. He is taking photographs of an attractive young woman (Emma Amos) whose face has been severely scarred in a car accident, and who now needs the pictures for her insurance claim. She is very bitter; the accident was not her fault, but has led to her losing her job as a beauty consultant. 'She's so lovely', says Maurice's assistant Jane (Elizabeth Berrington) as the woman leaves. 'Not any more, she isn't', replies Maurice, in an introspective moment of fatalistic realism that contrasts with his usual please-everyone public face.

On her way back to her car, the woman appears to be bothered by a scruffy little man with long, unkempt hair, who has been sitting on a bench outside. Just as Monica arrives, on her way home after a shopping trip, Maurice recognises the man as Stuart Christian (Ron Cook), from whom he bought the photography business. Stuart had gone to Australia to make a career there, a plan that has clearly not worked out. Entering the shop, he tells them that he and his wife split up when he went to Australia, and his mother died while he was there. He appears to have a drink problem, and is very obviously angling for Maurice to cut him back in, challenging him that 'you've done very well out of my business, haven't you?' Maurice is reasonable but firm: 'No, Stuart, no – it used to be your business – I bought it from you, it's my business'. He points out that he got no response from the client list he inherited from Stuart, and that he has built a successful reputation by staying small, preferring to cover a limited number of weddings himself rather than contracting them out. When he explains that 'it's not in my interest to get some tosser in – I mean, I'll have no control – it could fuck up my reputation', Stuart takes it personally ('I'm not a tosser!') in a way Maurice had never intended, since in his view Stuart is not a candidate for employment. He promises to bear him in mind, and says goodbye. As they watch him go, Maurice's humane side reasserts itself in what one suspects is his broad outlook on life: 'There but for the grace of God'.

During their conversation, Stuart has said bitterly that 'you try and make people happy – and what d'you get back? Nothing!' As we have seen, this comment on the fate of the professional photographer applies to Maurice's personal life too, because of the family loyalties he is having to juggle and the rifts he is having to deal with. Matters come to a head at the birthday barbecue he and Monica host for Roxanne. Cynthia is also invited, of course, as are Paul and Jane. On an impulse, Cynthia has also asked Maurice if Hortense can come; they have by now been out together on a number of occasions, to restaurants, bars and the cinema. Although her request is motivated by her conviction that Hortense is now 'family', Cynthia passes her off as a friend from work, and Maurice agrees that she can come along.

The entire party sequence is a technical and dramatic tour de force, bringing the narrative to a climax in an escalating set piece that, on the way to delivering its emotional catharsis, leaves the spectator frequently not knowing whether to laugh or cry. Lee Ross comes splendidly into his own here as Paul, virtually a one-man surrogate audience, repeatedly glimpsed in the background, teeth clenched in uncertainty about how to react and apprehension as to what could possibly be coming next.

One can hardly blame him. The party starts tensely enough, friction between Cynthia and Monica evident from the outset. Initially Maurice is not even there to mediate since he is away picking Jane up from the station when Cynthia, Roxanne and Paul arrive by minicab; fortunately he returns not long afterwards. Nevertheless, Cynthia manages to rattle Monica with her over-enthusiastic hugs and kisses, and her lack of subtlety in giving their house the once-over: 'you've landed on your feet here' is her less than fair or tactful assessment. When she asks for an ashtray, Monica pointedly replies, 'There's one on the coffee table, Cynthia. I didn't think you would've given up'. Even Maurice and Roxanne, who have a genuinely affectionate rapport with each other, argue over whether or not she should go to college, Maurice insisting that 'you've got a good brain' and Roxanne countering that 'I don't want to use it, though'. Paul works as a scaffolder. 'Bet that's hard work', says Maurice; 'Can be, mate', replies Paul, in one of those classic lines in Leigh's films that make us laugh out loud just because they are so right for the character and the moment, rather than because they are funny on paper.

Meanwhile, Monica shows Cynthia and Jane around the house, extolling the 'Mediterranean feel' and the tranquillity of the 'peach tones', and embarrassedly rushing to put down the lids on the toilets in her and Maurice's separate bathrooms. Jane gazes admiringly, making all the right comments, while Cynthia repeatedly blurts out the wrong ones: 'What was the matter with your other one?' when looking at Monica's new car, and 'I can see Maurice thrashing about in there!' on being shown their brass four-poster bed.

Shortly afterwards, Hortense arrives, and Cynthia behaves just a little too over-protectively as she is introduced to everyone and they make small talk. As they all sit down to eat, Leigh and the cast treat us to another bravura set piece: for six and a half minutes, the camera remains still, positioned just behind Maurice's empty chair – he is in the rear of the frame, cooking the meat on the other side of the patio – and the seven characters variously sit, move back and forth, help themselves and each other to food, and talk to, at and over one another. It is immaculately orchestrated and full of beautifully observed touches: Cynthia's continued fussing, especially over Hortense; Monica's irritation with Cynthia's fussing and mild discomfiture when her offers of mustard are twice ignored by people ('Can't get rid of it, can you?' says Cynthia helpfully); Hortense's hesitation when trying to reconcile the details she is giving out about her life and background with Cynthia's story that they work in the same factory. Most importantly, the whole scene rings absolutely true to this kind of not-quite-informal social occasion. Both action and dialogue are enacted with an effortless spontaneity that could only be arrived at through intense and intricate preparation; if any single scene is testament to the value and effectiveness of Leigh's working methods, it could well be this one.

Later, as they all go inside and the sequence begins to move to its climax, the visual style changes: 'Leigh cuts between big close-ups and shots in which a foreground figure is in focus and a second person behind them slightly out of focus', noted Philip French, describing this as 'masterly movie-making that never draws attention to itself'.[9] They have come in out of the rain and, signalling the imminent change of mood and the recriminations and revelations to come, there is an ominous thunderclap outside as the scene begins. As everyone gathers to watch Roxanne cut her birthday cake, and to give her presents,

Cynthia is looking distressed. Her acute insecurity has been near the surface throughout the party. When Maurice arrives and kisses Roxanne before her, she asks him rather pathetically, 'Ain't you got one for me, then?' Being shown around the house by Monica, she could almost have been entering another world, with such unimaginable luxuries as large bedrooms and new carpets; later she takes pride in revealing, presumably by way of compensation, that Hortense has a car and 'a mortgage and everything'. Now, after a few glasses of wine, she is clearly upset and feeling bested, especially when Maurice gives Roxanne a birthday card with a wad of notes in it – 'Wish I'd brought *my* present with me now', she grumbles.

Out of this complex cocktail of emotions, accentuated by drink, comes Cynthia's compulsion to admit that Hortense is her daughter. This she does while Hortense is in the bathroom, and in her absence Maurice, Monica and Roxanne casually remark on how nice she seems. Cynthia can no longer keep her feelings buttoned up: 'She takes after her mother', she says and, when they ask how she knows, reveals that 'she's my daughter'. No wonder that when Hortense returns, it is to a stunned silence broken only by Cynthia's weeping. Told what has been said, Hortense keeps her dignity – 'It wasn't supposed to happen like this' – and admits that it is true. Not surprisingly, Roxanne's reaction is the most extreme: the revelation has come as enough of a bombshell to the rest of the group; Roxanne has discovered, in one fell swoop, both that she has a half-sister she never knew about, and that Maurice and Monica have long been aware of the fact. She first flees to the bathroom, then orders Paul to get her coat and rushes out with him nervously in tow.

After a moment's hesitation, Maurice runs after Roxanne and Paul. He finds them sitting at a nearby bus stop and tries to persuade Roxanne to return. In the fraught atmosphere back at the house, other recriminations are flying. Cynthia accuses Monica of successively turning her father, Maurice and now Roxanne against her. She is still bitter that Maurice took a share of their father's insurance money, which he clearly would not have done but for Monica's influence. 'He was entitled to it!' insists Monica, and as the two of them argue, our sympathies fly back and forth until we are lost in the morass of old grudges and resentments. Cynthia protests that she was struggling at the time, working as a cleaner as well as her day job in order to care for Roxanne; 'And didn't we know it!' snaps Monica uncharitably. At this point, despite all of Cynthia's foibles, we are taking against Monica: she has never done anything but spend Maurice's money, says Cynthia; what else is money for, asks Monica, apparently not having considered the possibility of helping anyone else with it. Then Cynthia tells her, 'You want to try bringing up a kid on your own!' and we realise that this has hit Monica hard. Bearing in mind the hints we have been given, we by now suspect that all of Monica's material possessions are a compensation for what she would dearly like but cannot have; just as we think we know whose side we are on, we are reminded that taking sides in a situation involving such complex human emotion is really not the point.

Maurice persuades Roxanne to come back with him, enlisting Paul's support, and repeating and clarifying his earlier assessment of Cynthia: 'She can't help it – she's never had enough love'. As they march off in single file, as if into battle, we feel for them, but also find them irresistibly comical: Maurice's bulky figure clad in his voluminous summer shirt and baggy shorts; Roxanne sullen and tearful; Paul bringing up the rear, clenched and apprehensive.

When they return, Cynthia tells Roxanne the truth: that she had Hortense when she was sixteen, never thought that she would come looking for her, but is glad she did. Resentful that Maurice told Monica her secret, she will not let things lie, and when Monica asks, 'Why shouldn't he? I am his wife after all', Cynthia pushes things too far, demanding, 'Then why don't you behave like his wife? ... Why don't you give him no kids?' At first Maurice tries to make her be quiet but then, having bottled things up long enough, suggests that Monica 'tell her'. Monica cannot bring herself to do so, and it is left to Maurice to take the initiative and break the silence himself: 'She can't have kids. Simple as that. She's physically incapable of having children. We've had every test known to medical science. She's been pushed around, prodded, poked, had operations – we've had fifteen years of it and she can't have a baby'. To the distraught Monica, he says, 'I love you to bits ... but it's almost destroyed our relationship ... you know it has' and, the floodgates open now, launches into a long, heartfelt expression of his frustration and pain: 'There. I've said it. So where's the bolt of lightning? Secrets and lies! We're all in pain. Why can't we share our pain? I've spent my entire life trying to make people happy, and the three people I love most in the world hate each other's guts, I'm in the middle and I can't take it any more!'

It is, to be sure, a speech that would normally seem more at home in the theatre than in the cinema (what critic Nigel Andrews dismissively called 'a here-comes-the-message speech'[10]), and the use in it of the film's title may especially strike some as a contrivance. Yet, in stopping the film in its tracks after all the previous ensemble action, it is undeniably true to the character and the context. Maurice's outburst *does* stop proceedings and bring the other characters up sharply; it *is* uncharacteristic of him, just as it is untypical of the film as a whole, which is precisely why everyone shuts up and listens to him. Just as the summer storm came out of nowhere, so does Maurice's pained tirade, and it has the same beneficial effect of clearing the air. This is the point towards which the narrative has been leading; what started as Hortense's journey of discovery has turned into a similar journey of discovery and self-discovery for all the characters. As if to acknowledge her role as catalyst, it is to Hortense that Maurice now turns, rather than to his wife, sister or niece: 'I'm sorry, Hortense. But you are a very brave person ... you wanted to find the truth, and you were prepared to suffer the consequences'. Cynthia embraces Monica; Monica tells her, 'You're so lucky, Cynthia'. Paul puts his arm round Roxanne. Maurice asks Hortense whether she really works at the factory, and is told that she's actually an optometrist. Ruefully, he chuckles and welcomes her to the family. Jane, now in tears, bursts out, 'Oh, Maurice, I wish I'd had a dad like you – you're lovely' – a line which, whenever I have seen the film with an audience, invariably gets *either* a big laugh *or* a big, sympathetic 'aaaahhhh'. Either way, the response consolidates the relief of the tension that has been building since the start of the scene, and arguably since the start of the party itself.

There are a few more details still to emerge. Cynthia now tells Roxanne for the first time that her father was an American student whom she met in Benidorm; though he walked out on her abruptly and without telling her, Cynthia remembers him as a nice man. However, she cannot answer Hortense's question as to whether her own father was also nice, and can only reply, 'Oh, don't break my heart, darling!' Amid the general air of souls being purged, there is no relief to be found in the unburdening of secrets this time, only in more tears.

Two brief scenes remain, both seeming to confirm that, all these revelations having come to light, renewal is possible. Maurice and Monica are seen cuddling up in bed – always the sign of a good relationship in Leigh's films, as we have seen – and they seem to accept that children are not the be-all and end-all in a marriage, that 'we've got each other, haven't we?' and can move on from there.

The very final scene is of Hortense visiting Cynthia and Roxanne. She and Roxanne talk in the back garden, finding common ground in memories of loneliness when they were children, and resolving to go for a drink together. Roxanne would introduce Hortense, she insists, as her half-sister. 'Yeah', says Hortense after a moment's thought. 'Best to tell the truth, isn't it ... That way no one gets hurt'. Cynthia now comes out with tea and biscuits, and the three of them sit together. 'This is the life, ain't it?' says Cynthia, and although she is sitting on an old sunbed in the small, cluttered back garden of a rather rundown terrace house, we can see her point. For the first time she has both her daughters around her and, more importantly, has the opportunity to build a new relationship with them both, so that the three of them can function as a mutually supportive group.

Hortense's integration into the family group is not, within the narrative, ever made problematic by the fact that she is black and they are white. This has antagonised some critics, including Geoffrey Macnab who, reviewing the film for *Sight and Sound*, felt that the film says too little about her background and 'skims over the black experience of "Englishness"'.[11] Margaret Walters, in the *New Statesman and Society*, also thought that Hortense 'remains a cipher summoned up to provoke white reactions'.[12] Leonard Quart, interviewing Leigh for *Cineaste*, asked him whether racism was less of a problem in Britain than America, which Leigh categorically denied: 'For me to pretend that racism is absent from English working class or lower middle class life would be a deeply irresponsible action'.[13] Yet he does play down 'the black experience', in the sense that we see little of Hortense's personal life, apart from that brief glimpse of her family, and a warm, affectionate sequence in which she talks insightfully to her friend Dionne (Michele Austin).

Yet that does not mean that Leigh is ignoring the wider social issue of ethnicity, or simply reducing it to the level of a dramatic contrivance (the fact that Hortense is black and Cynthia is white providing a solid dramatic pretext for the initial scepticism from both that they are related). His concern here is plausibly to depict 'the generation of young black people in the world who are growing up, moving on, getting away from their ghetto stereotypes, being positive, and exploring avenues of possibility'.[14] And it is wholly possible that if he *had* raised the issue of racial conflict he would have been subjected to the perfectly valid converse criticism: that characters (and thus actors) from ethnic minorities should not *only* be included in a drama when their ethnic background is specifically relevant, and that to make an automatic correlation between black characters and social problems is to perpetuate negative images.

Leigh does not shy away from such issues when it would be true to the character relationships in a particular piece of work; in Act Two of his play *Ecstasy* (1979) there is a debate between four of the characters in which various racist myths are raised and debunked without any sense of didacticism or narrative strain.[15] However, in *Secrets and Lies* there is no logical reason why any of the characters *would* necessarily be racist. That said, there is a neatly observed moment when Hortense arrives at Maurice and Monica's house for the party. Even though Monica knows

Cynthia's 'friend' is expected – and has earlier asked Maurice when she will arrive – she immediately says, 'No, I'm sorry ... ' and tries to close the door. As Leigh has said, 'Her response to Hortense is based on the fact that it's a Sunday, and she's black and dressed in black. She simply thinks that Hortense is a Jehovah's Witness'. Monica's racist assumption that this person could not possibly be Cynthia's friend is highly revealing of a more insidious form of prejudice, which is totally plausible in the context of her character and environment.

Monica is one of the two characters in the film who most lean towards being portrayed through quirks and mannerisms, the other of course being Cynthia – although, as ever, the idiosyncrasies are absolutely true to the characters and the situations they find themselves in. In Monica's case the mannerisms take the form of her obsessive tidiness, the way she bustles about cleaning and minutely adjusting ornaments – her paranoia about the toilet lids being left up is a wonderfully funny touch – and her flared-nostrils, pursed-lips disapproval of Maurice, his family and his habits ('You're not having any steak in this house'). Cynthia's idiosyncrasies are verbal as well as behavioural: her plaintive voice and habitual use of 'sweetheart' and 'darling' in almost every sentence, alongside her fidgety, angular movements, her permanent frown and air of being perpetually on the verge of tears.

As elsewhere in Leigh's work, the mannered portrayals reflect the fact that Cynthia and Monica are also the characters with the least purchase on reality. Both are deeply vulnerable beneath their brittle, nervy exteriors, insecure about themselves and their roles in life. Cynthia, now that she has nobody to look after, is depressed and lonely, and in danger of driving Roxanne away with her over-possessive behaviour (we see how uncomfortable Maurice also is when she demands that he cuddle her). Monica too is, in her own way, distressed that she has nobody to 'mother'; in denial about the fact that she cannot have children, she represses her feelings and channels all her emotional energy into keeping her house spotless. Yet while we sometimes laugh at both of them, we do not feel unkindly towards either of them. Monica is often abrasive, but Leigh and Phyllis Logan make us aware of her emotional and physical pain so that, even though we do not learn the real cause of her unhappiness until the very end of the film, the characterisation never becomes merely dislikeable. I could not disagree more with Ray Carney's opinion, expressed in a footnote, that Monica is another in a line of Leigh's female characters whose 'childlessness functions as a shorthand indication of a larger emotional deficiency'.[16] As with Michael Coveney's similar comments about Beverly in *Abigail's Party*, I think that the reverse is true: Monica's inability to have children is one of the reasons *for* her emotional repressions and hang-ups, not crudely representative *of* them. Leigh, it seems to me, is in no way blaming her for her childlessness, as Carney's approach implies, but only, and gently, for failing to recognise that a childless marriage need not be an unfulfilled one and to focus instead on the relationship between her and Maurice, rather than on their home. (Maybe one of the questions Leigh intends us to take away from this film is whether, having got to know Hortense better, she and Maurice will decide to adopt a child.)

Cynthia, in Brenda Blethyn's unforgettable performance, is an even more pronounced combination of the endearing and the exasperating. We laugh at her and cry for her practically in the same breath; her repetition of 'sweetheart' and 'darling', for instance, is not just a silly mannerism, but an expression of her desperate need for reassurance that she is loved. The same can be true of the most apparently trivial detail: when Hortense tells Cynthia her full name, Hortense Cumberbatch, over the phone, and Cynthia ridiculously mispronounces it – 'Clumberbunch?' – her error is both risible in its clumsiness *and* completely understandable in view of the shock she has just received. Even more than Monica, she never totally loses our sympathy. Think, for example, of the scene in the café when, after it has dawned on her that Hortense really is her daughter, her near-hysterical laugh turns into sobbing, and compare it to a similar moment, played for broad comic effect, involving Valerie in *High Hopes*. Whereas Valerie merely appeared ludicrous and inadequate, we fully understand the roller coaster of feelings that Cynthia is going through, and her breakdown from laughter to tears movingly reminds us of the fine line between the two emotions in everyday life. In *Secrets and Lies* it is Cynthia who utters that familiar line, 'Gotta laugh, ain't you, sweetheart? Else you'd cry' – and Cynthia who precisely embodies the tragicomic ethos that informs so much of Leigh's work.

Seeking to define this tone, Leigh, although understandably wary of being pigeon-holed, has admitted that 'it would be quite dishonest if I were to deny my films are Jewish in their way. The tragicomic view of life, the melancholy, if you know what you're talking about, there is a Jewish flavour to it, a Jewishness in the spirit of it. I could deny it, but it would be stupid'.[17] This seems as good a cue as any to consider some fascinating comparisons between Leigh's work and Woody Allen's. Both are film-makers who seem unwilling, indeed unable, to be other than defiantly themselves, and who resolutely avoid corporate conditions of production which would compromise their working methods. While achieving an admirable consistency of quality and vision, they have both tended to receive greater recognition as important artists in continental

Europe than in Britain or America. Like Leigh, Allen frequently has that ambiguous, 'half-inside and half-outside' relationship to his characters. In the extended interview published by Faber, Stig Björkman points out how, in films like *Annie Hall* and *Manhattan*, 'you make ironical remarks about left-wing intellectuals, a group of people of which I presume you count yourself as a member'. 'Yes, and which I observe', replies Allen.[18] Finally, there is – up to a point – a certain similarity in their working methods: Allen, with rare exceptions, is not given to letting actors see sections of the script in which their characters do not appear.[19] Conversely, since both create meaning at least as much by the way they cut *between* scenes as *within* them, they allow actors a great deal of control through a fondness for sustained scenes – one- or two-shots, or static shots in which characters move in and out of the frame.

There are of course major differences between the two, most obviously the fact that Allen often appears in his own films, whereas Leigh never does. Allen also claims never to watch his films when they have been completed; Leigh is very happy to view his own work ('If you don't like it, how in hell's name can you expect anyone else to?'[20]) – which is one of the reasons why his commentaries on the DVD releases of his films are so entertaining. And, most fundamentally, Leigh famously works extremely closely with his actors, both individually and collectively, whereas Allen is generally far less communicative; actor Alan Alda has said of him: 'He has a unique style of directing that doesn't involve talking to you ... If you don't do it the way he likes, he rewrites it so that you have to do it a little bit more like what he had in mind. And then he gives you another chance, rewrites it again, and at the third or fourth time, then he fires you'.[21]

Nevertheless I think it is especially interesting to compare *Secrets and Lies* to Allen's *Crimes and Misdemeanors* (1989). Both are major cinematic works, richly textured and combining serious and comic themes to hugely satisfying effect, via two narrative strands which interlock and eventually converge at a family's social occasion. Quite coincidentally, each has an optometrist/ophthalmologist at the core of one strand and a film-maker/photographer central to the other.

The ophthalmologist in *Crimes and Misdemeanors* is Judah Rosenthal (Martin Landau), who was brought up to believe that 'the eyes of God are on us always', but resorts to using the murderous associates of his shady brother Jack (Jerry Orbach) to dispose of his suddenly inconvenient mistress Dolores (Anjelica Huston). In *Secrets and Lies*, Hortense's profession reflects her own clear-sightedness and self-awareness, as well as her role as the catalyst through which others will come to see themselves and each other more clearly. Judah's 'moral vision is not good', in direct contrast to *his* professional expertise, and yet in taking the action he does, he is in one sense acknowledging 'the real world' as represented by his brother. One of his patients is a rabbi named Ben (Sam Waterston), who goes blind over the course of the narrative; Allen describes this as symbolic of his blindness 'to other things, to the realities of life'[22] – whereas Judah's pragmatic approach allows him literally to get away with murder.

Allen himself plays the film-maker in *Crimes and Misdemeanors* – Cliff Stern, a principled but financially unsuccessful director of documentaries who, like Maurice in *Secrets and Lies*, has a troubled marriage and a lonely sister. More crucially, just as Maurice's professional efforts to put smiles on faces mirror the losing battle to keep everyone happy in his private life, Cliff unsuccessfully tries to control life – both his own and other people's – through film-making, and frequently seeks refuge from the world in daytime visits to the movies. Cliff seeks reassurance of a moral structure through the teachings of Louis Levy, a philosophy professor – but, significantly, we only ever see Professor Levy on film, not in the real world; the assurance he offers turns out to be illusory when Cliff hears that he has inexplicably committed suicide.

As these brief comparisons suggest, metaphors of vision and seeing are central to *Crimes and Misdemeanors* and *Secrets and Lies*. 'Didn't someone say the eyes are the windows of the soul?' asks Professor Marcus of his prospective landlady Mrs Wilberforce in Alexander Mackendrick's *The Ladykillers* (1955); 'I don't really know', she replies, 'but it's such a charming thought, I do hope someone expressed it'. Indeed they did, and they do again in both Allen's film and Leigh's – although the different contexts are revealing. In *Secrets and Lies*, it occurs during the barbecue: optometrist Hortense says that 'you can tell a lot about people from looking at their eyes' and photographer Maurice agrees, 'That's true', to which his assistant Jane adds: 'Windows to your soul'. In *Crimes and Misdemeanors*, Dolores asks Judah, 'Do you agree the eyes are the windows of the soul?' 'Well, I believe they're windows', he replies, evading the moral implications of her question, 'I'm not sure it's the soul they see'.

Thus Allen's worldview is bleaker, more pessimistic than Leigh's, with less certainty about the salvation to be found in human relationships. By the end of *Crimes and Misdemeanors*, for example, Cliff and his wife are about to get a divorce, whereas the ending of *Secrets and Lies* suggests renewed hope for Maurice and Monica's marriage. Yet although Allen's final scene, where Judah and Cliff meet for the first time, has Judah insist 'this is reality' and tell Cliff that 'if you want a happy ending, you should go see a Hollywood movie', the coda suggests a more optimistic possibility. As the now-blind Ben waltzes with his daughter at her wedding reception, the last word goes to the unseen Professor Levy: 'It is only we, with our capacity to love, that give meaning to the indifferent universe – and yet, most human beings seem to have the ability to keep trying, and even to find joy from simple things like the family, the work, and from the hope that future generations might understand more'.

Leigh's characters, too, will keep trying and will find joy in 'simple' things like families, and the coda to *Secrets and Lies* is typical of his work. Nobody has had his or her life changed by any implausible coincidences, unlikely revelations or any kind of *deus ex machina* intervention. But paths have crossed, revelations have been made and lives have changed. The changes have been brought about by events that have forced the characters not to achieve feats of dramatic heroism, but simply to find strength within themselves and their relationships with each other.

Most critics responded enthusiastically to the film, its characters and its humanism, even those who had previously qualified their enthusiasm for Leigh's work. In *The Guardian*, Jonathan Romney declared himself a convert and the film 'nothing short of miraculous', working towards a telling point when he described it as 'the first Leigh film in which all the performances absolutely gel with the world portrayed ... they're self-evidently tour-de-force performances and yet you believe in them as real people. The characters in this film are all acting anyway, all trying to keep their world functioning, to cover up its cracks and lacks'.[23] Geoff Brown said in *The Times* that 'Leigh is a master at choreographing scenes of social embarrassment, and he can do so now with a humane touch he never allowed himself before',[24] and Geoff Andrew, in *Time Out*, thought the film 'funny, perceptive and very moving' with 'none of the caricature or sentimentality that tainted much of his earlier work'.[25] Adam Mars-Jones, in *The Independent*, thought it 'a wonderful film ... but it isn't very much like a Mike Leigh film',[26] though Anne Billson remained unmoved in the *Sunday Telegraph*: 'Small-scale domestic drama isn't automatically uncinematic, but Leigh's long takes, rambling pace and emphasis on dialogue help make it so'.[27] The *Daily Telegraph*'s Quentin Curtis found *Secrets and Lies* rather more enjoyable and successful in what it set out to do: 'Leigh has made a humane comedy that not only laughs at the agonies of class and racial differences, but also helps to heal them'.[28] Important aspects of Leigh's place in British cinema were also highlighted by the *Daily Mail*'s Christopher Tookey, who found *Secrets and Lies* 'as uplifting as any American feelgood comedy, but with the truthfulness of great documentary ... These are the kind of people who don't normally appear on a cinema screen',[29] and by Tom Shone in the *Sunday Times*, who said that 'among British directors, Leigh is pretty much alone in being the only one whose talents don't seem limited by a sense of who his films are made for'.[30]

Professionally, Leigh was on a high after *Secrets and Lies*: awards in Europe, Oscar nominations in America and, in Britain, great popular success in both the mainstream and subsidised cinema exhibition sectors, with a critical reaction which at last declared – not unanimously, not without caveats, but more loudly than ever before – that his refusal to compromise and his flair for the compassionate chronicling of ordinary lives marked him out as a unique and formidable talent.

Notes

1 Quoted in Larry Worth, '*Lies* Director Shows True Colors', *New York Post*, 5 August 1997; reprinted in Howie Movshovitz (ed.), *Mike Leigh Interviews* (Jackson, University Press of Mississippi, 2000), p. 122
2 Kenneth Turan, 'The Case for Mike Leigh', *Los Angeles Times*, 22 September 1996; reprinted in Howie Movshovitz (ed.), *Mike Leigh Interviews*, p. 86
3 John O'Mahony, 'Acts of Faith', *The Guardian*, 19 October 2002
4 Quoted in Graham Fuller, 'Mike Leigh's Original Features', in *Naked and Other Screenplays* (London, Faber & Faber, 1995), p. xlii
5 Mike Leigh, *Secrets and Lies* (London, Faber & Faber, 1997), p. 40
6 *Ibid.*, p. 43
7 Quoted in Ray Pride, 'The Leigh Way', *New City*, 7 November 1996; reprinted in Howie Movshovitz (ed.), *Mike Leigh Interviews*, p. 111
8 Adam Mars-Jones, *The Independent*, 23 May 1996
9 Philip French, *The Observer*, 26 May 1996
10 Nigel Andrews, *Financial Times*, 23 May 1996
11 Geoffrey Macnab, *Sight and Sound*, 6: 6 (June 1996), p. 51
12 Margaret Walters, *New Statesman and Society*, 24 May 1996, p. 15
13 Quoted in Leonard Quart, 'Raising Questions and Positing Possibilities: An Interview with Mike Leigh', *Cineaste*, 22: 4 (1997); reprinted in Howie Movshovitz (ed.), *Mike Leigh Interviews*, p. 131
14 Graham Fuller, 'Mike Leigh's Original Features', p. xlii
15 Mike Leigh, *Ecstasy* (London, Nick Hern Books, 1999), pp. 95–6
16 Ray Carney and Leonard Quart, *The Films of Mike Leigh: Embracing the World* (Cambridge, Cambridge University Press, 2000), p. 267
17 Quoted in Kenneth Turan, 'The Case for Mike Leigh'; reprinted in Howie Movshovitz (ed.), *Mike Leigh Interviews*, p. 90
18 Stig Björkman, *Woody Allen on Woody Allen* (London, Faber & Faber, 1995), p. 39
19 See, for example, Eric Lax, *Woody Allen* (New York, Vintage Books, 1992), p. 46
20 Quoted in John Naughton, 'There's No Face Like Gnome', *Empire*, 100 (October 1997); reprinted in Howie Movshovitz (ed.), *Mike Leigh Interviews*, p. 128
21 Interviewed on *Desert Island Discs*, first broadcast on BBC Radio 4, 27 October 1991
22 Stig Björkman, *Woody Allen on Woody Allen*, p. 213
23 Jonathan Romney, *The Guardian*, 23 May 1996
24 Geoff Brown, *The Times*, 23 May 1996
25 Geoff Andrew, *Time Out*, 22–29 May 1996, p. 72

26 Adam Mars-Jones, *The Independent*, 23 May 1996
27 Anne Billson, *Sunday Telegraph*, 26 May 1996
28 Quentin Curtis, *Daily Telegraph*, 24 May 1996
29 Christopher Tookey, *Daily Mail*, 24 May 1996
30 Tom Shone, *Sunday Times*, 26 May 1996

'All these memories': *Career Girls*

8

Still keeping us on our toes, Leigh followed the ensemble playing and emotional sweep of *Secrets and Lies* with a carefully crafted miniature. *Career Girls* focuses on just two young women, Hannah (Katrin Cartlidge) and Annie (Lynda Steadman), who used to be flatmates when they were students in the mid-80s and, having not seen each other for six years, spend a weekend together at Hannah's London home. It turns out to be a weekend full of coincidences and unexpected blasts from the past.

Leigh makes no attempt to obscure these coincidences, which the characters point out and discuss, as Stella Bruzzi noted in her review of the film in *Sight and Sound*: '*Career Girls* flaunts its own artifice, deliberately announcing itself as a deeply implausible tale'.[1] Similarly unrealistic is the use for the first time in Leigh's films of flashbacks – a familiar enough cinematic device, but an overtly non-naturalistic one, deployed extensively here to make explicit contrasts. While the heart of the narrative concerns the progress of the two women on what Leigh calls 'the long trek from twenty to thirty',[2] the presence on the periphery of estate agents and yuppie landlords hints at wider changes in the decade between the film's past and present.

The film starts as Annie travels down to London on the train for her weekend with Hannah, and we see a series of flashbacks, punctuated by brief shots of her in the present, remembering. Not all the flashbacks in the film are flagged up as 'subjective' memory in this way, by the standard cinematic method of showing a character deep in thought, then cutting to the flashback, but when they are, the memories are usually Annie's. However, we are invited to take them as an accurate representation, since there are no explicit discrepancies between Annie's memories, Hannah's or the unattributed flashbacks.

We see their first meeting, when they were both students at North London Polytechnic. Hannah is already sharing a house with a girl named Claire (Kate Byers), and Annie has come to enquire about a vacant room there. Very unsure of herself, Annie has difficulty making eye contact with people, is inclined to twitch nervously, and has asthma and a facial skin complaint. Hannah is equally full of mannerisms; nervy and brittle, she is hardly still for a moment and compulsively cracks jokes, which she punctuates by slapping herself on the forehead, or generally makes comments designed to wrong-foot the newcomer. When Annie asks at the front door, 'Are you Hannah?' she replies, 'It's Hann-*ah*, actually'. As they go inside, a cassette by The Cure is playing; Annie says they are her favourite band and Hannah immediately tells her they are Claire's favourite too, presumably knowing that they aren't so that Claire will deny it when Annie asks 'Really?'

Annie is worried that Hannah and Claire's advertisement for a housemate specifies 'must have G.S.O.H'. She does not know what this means, and worries because 'I don't know if I've got one, you see'. Hannah again takes the opportunity to lead her on, claiming that the initials stand for 'good sense of housekeeping'; it is Claire who tells her the truth, that 'it means "good sense of humour"'. Already we realise that Hannah's own sense of humour is based on an apparent desire to amuse herself at other people's expense (except that she does not seem noticeably amused) and a need to stay one step ahead of everyone. She is genuinely quick-witted – when Annie tells them her skin complaint is dermatitis, she replies, 'Well, it's better than determinitis, which is what I've got, let's face it' – but there is nothing endearing about her joking. She is in fact deeply insecure, attacking through wisecracks as a form of defence. Later in this initial sequence of flashbacks, as Annie is actually moving into the house, we see Hannah returning from a visit to her mother, and realise that this relationship may be part of her problem: she storms in and shuts herself in her room, shouting 'Bitch! Pervert!' and vowing that 'I'm never fucking going there again!'

We return to the present, as Hannah meets Annie at King's Cross station. They are genuinely pleased to see one another, if a little anxious about meeting again after so long apart. Leigh, Cartlidge and Steadman wonderfully capture the slight awkwardness of the situation, and we are curious as to how a friendship which seems to mean quite a lot to both of them could have developed from the unpromising beginning we have just seen.

As they drive to Hannah's flat, the film cuts to another flashback in which Hannah, an English student, introduces Annie to a ritual involving a copy of *Wuthering Heights*. This entails chanting 'Ms Brontë, Ms Brontë', then asking a question and opening the novel at a random page to supply the answer. Although Hannah, the expert at wrong-footing people, is momentarily disconcerted herself when Annie, who is from Yorkshire, says that Emily Brontë's house 'is near my house ... I've been there', she quickly recovers by insisting that Annie has a go. Annie asks the question, 'will I find a fella soon?' and is answered by the quote 'must come'. 'Wow!' says Hannah triumphantly, but then abruptly changes the subject to Annie's skin complaint, reducing her to tears by commenting that 'you do look as though you've done the tango with a cheese grater'. As Annie runs out and shuts herself in the bathroom, we see Hannah looking sad and angry with herself; the unkind humour seems to be a compulsion she can barely control. Moments later she speaks to Annie through the closed door, saying, 'I was only pissing about' by way of apology, followed by the familiar refrain, 'you gotta laugh, though, ain't you?' Needless to say, nobody laughs.

In the present, they arrive at Hannah's flat. Annie compliments the colour scheme: 'Primrose'. 'Looks like piss', replies Hannah, 'I've gone off it now'. We note that her brusque manner is still capable of disconcerting Annie, who is doing her best to obey the social niceties involved in visiting someone's home. When she sees Hannah's fax machine, she says admiringly, 'Oh, you've got everything'. Hannah's response, 'I wouldn't say that', introduces an overtone of scepticism about material possessions which will run throughout the film (and we might recall the dramatic irony of Jane's similar comment about Maurice and Monica's home in *Secrets and Lies*).

The next few sequences continue to move between past and present, neatly contrasting their lives then and now through the issue of where they live. In the past, they are seen getting to grips with the politics of student accommodation, whether dividing up books and mugs as they move out of another flat, above a Chinese takeaway, or the dilemma of choosing housemates, as they work out how best to let Claire know that they want to share with each other, not her (which they later do by each lying to her). In the present, however, they discuss the relative merits of buying or renting property and consider house prices, as well as comparing niggles about their jobs and colleagues. But it is clear that their contemporary, more mature selves have retained their sense of fun: instead of traipsing around the usual London landmarks, Hannah plans for them to spend some time going round to look at properties that she cannot actually afford because 'it'll be a giggle'.

Their conversation about house prices also throws up an exchange that neatly encapsulates one of the key differences between them: 'I couldn't buy on my own', says Annie; 'I couldn't buy with anyone else', replies Hannah. Both of them lack confidence, but Hannah is nervous of dependency, Annie of loneliness. They elaborate on this later, as they eat the dinner that Hannah has prepared and afterwards discuss their relationships with their respective mothers. Hannah's mother is, according to her, 'still the model of maternity ... swigging two bottles of gin a day and puking up my Sunday lunches every week'; Annie's is 'still baking her own bread'. Annie's mother 'fancies somebody at work'; 'Last time my mother had a lover', says Hannah, 'I had to call the police'. Annie is living back with her mother, but wants to move out again: 'I need my independence', she says, 'cause I've never really had it, you see'. 'I've had independence rammed down my throat ever since I can remember', counters Hannah. 'And I wouldn't exactly call having to look after your alcoholic mother independent'.

In the next flashback to their student days – and the first to be cued by a shot of Hannah thinking rather than Annie – their conversation reveals that when both of them were eight their fathers walked out on them, leaving their mothers for other women. This appears to have had a traumatic effect on both of them: Annie does not remember anything before the age of eight; Hannah claims not to have cried since she was nine. The scene also introduces another key theme – that of coincidence, which will loom large over their weekend together.

While Hannah is lying in bed recalling this conversation, Annie is remembering Ricky (Mark Benton), one of their fellow students. Ricky is overweight, with long greasy hair, and about as nervy as the younger versions of Hannah and Annie put together, every hesitant, disjointed statement he makes accompanied by vague, jabbing hand gestures and jerky head movements, his half-closed eyes never quite making contact. After a brief scene showing him arriving late at a psychology lecture, we see him moving into their flat above the takeaway. He has had some kind of altercation with his landlord ('I was going to smack him one, but, um ... ') and obviously has nowhere else to go. Although needy and helpless, he is also capable of being terribly tactless. When Annie asks what he thinks of the flat, he replies, 'I don't like the brown', and the sofa on which he will be sleeping 'might be a bit small, but ... '

We next see the three of them in the pub, where Hannah feels vaguely patronised and intimidated as Annie and Ricky expound on what they have learned as psychology students. Ricky's tactlessness is again evident, demonstrating that he has some insight into psychological theory but no practical social skills; in his own opinion, honesty is simply his 'cardinal trait' ('I, er, tell it like it, er ... '). Although he resists discussion of his own personality, he tells Annie bluntly that she always seems 'stressed' and that this might be a cause of her 'scabby skin and that'. Hannah leaps at once to Annie's defence: 'Excuse me! Do you think your ample form is anything to do with the fact that you stuff your face? Or is it just that you're not getting enough sex, maybe?' If Ricky is at all crushed by this, he doesn't show it, but turns the conversation back to Annie, asking her about a dream that she described in a seminar, about a 'dark figure' in her bedroom, carrying a stick. This is clearly something she does not wish to talk about outside the seminar room – it is, as she later tells Hannah, 'a real private thing' – and Hannah is again forced to defend her.

Hannah having stormed out of the pub, Annie goes back to join her at the flat while Ricky heads to the takeaway, where we see his lack of social graces once more making him inadvertently rude: 'Can you put a lot of curry sauce on, because last time you didn't put enough on'. Meanwhile Hannah and Annie talk. 'Sometimes I get the devil in me', says Hannah. 'I was scared. Ricky's so tactless', says Annie. Hannah admits that 'I quite like him actually. He's sussed isn't he?' and tells the incredulous Annie that 'he fancies you'.

The next evening, the three of them, all apparently quite drunk, are dancing together in the flat – Ricky reluctantly joining in after some cajoling. Hannah goes to bed, leaving the other two together, and Annie performs the 'Ms Brontë' ritual, asking 'will I have a fuck soon?' The word 'death' comes up as a result, and she bemoans 'the bloody death of my sex life'. After Ricky asks 'Ms Brontë' the same question and gets a blank page by way of reply, he plucks up the courage to tell her, in his hesitant way, that 'I like you', then 'I fancy you ... I, I love you'. Caught off guard, Annie is forced to backtrack clumsily on her earlier statement about the 'death' of her sex life, claiming unconvincingly that 'I'm in love ... with someone else'. Ricky, under the pretence of going for curry and chips, leaves, and does not return to the flat or to college. After a while Hannah and Annie go in search of him to the northeast seaside town where he lives with his nan (Margo Stanley). They have a conversation with her, and she tells them that he has 'gone out'. Asking her to pass on a message, they leave, and the film returns to the present. During this long series of flashbacks, unbroken except for a few brief shots of Annie lying awake and remembering, Ricky has entered the film and apparently departed again, and the question of what happens to him will not be answered until much later.

We now stay in the present for a while, as Hannah and Annie visit the first of the properties they have arranged to see, an opulent modern waterside flat; the screenplay describes them approaching 'a block of up-market vulgar luxury penthouse apartments'.[3] The flat is owned by Mr Evans (Andy Serkis), a man in his mid-thirties. Unaware of the appointment (he dismisses the agent as a 'fucking plonker'), he greets them unshaven and wearing only a dressing gown and slippers, but invites them in anyway. Hannah and Annie can hardly conceal their amusement as he shows them around, unabashed by the porn magazine left lying open in his bedroom, reciting 'microwave, oven, hob' like a mantra in the kitchen, and proudly showing them the status-symbol view over the River Thames; 'I suppose on a clear day you can see the class struggle from here', says Hannah. Asked what the neighbours are like, Evans says 'dunno', but proudly points out nearby Canary Wharf. 'It's a shame they couldn't afford an architect', comments Hannah.

Evans, whom Hannah judges to be 'coked out of his head', offers them wine, champagne, beer, cognac, a cigarette or 'a whiff of spliff', and asks them, 'What are you doing later on?' 'Nothing that involves you, that's for sure', Hannah tells him. When they make their excuses to leave, he asks if they are 'looking for a place together', unsubtly insinuating that they might be a lesbian couple, and then becomes aggressive, pursuing them to the lift and in the process locking himself out of the flat in his dressing gown and slippers, clutching a bottle of champagne and three glasses. Hannah and Annie laugh uproariously and helplessly as they descend in the lift and drive away, and we see how their friendship is confirmed by the bond of shared laughter.

Their next appointment is at a converted Victorian house, where they are shown around by an estate agent called Adrian Spinks (Joe Tucker). If Hannah's brittle wit came to the fore in dealing with Evans, here it is the more sensitive and perceptive Annie who assesses the situation more quickly, recognising Adrian as a former college friend. He plainly does not recognise either of them, and is merely preoccupied with showing them around in a fairly desultory fashion. His smooth professional persona is yoked to the same consumer-society values as the uncouth yuppie Evans, revealed by his mechanical recitation of a similar list of domestic desirables: 'Fridge-freezer, washer-drier, dishwasher'; and, again like Evans, he asks them if they are 'looking for a place together' – although his response to learning that they aren't is a disinterested 'thought you might be', as opposed to Evans's obnoxious 'I thought you was geezer birds'.

When Annie asks him to repeat his name, Hannah too recognises Adrian, and her realisation cues the next flashback. Hannah meets Adrian at a party, during the time that she and Annie were still living with Claire, and they become lovers. From what we see, it is a fairly volatile relationship, not helped by Adrian's tendency to utter pleasantries like 'when I fuck a woman, she stays fucked!' and to flirt with Annie. Eventually he leaves Hannah and begins a relationship with Annie, although we never learn the exact circumstances; it would appear that they do not discuss it much at the time, as when, later and in the film's present, Hannah admits that 'I was really quite hurt by all that, you know', Annie replies, 'I knew it – deep down inside I knew that, but why didn't you ever tell me?' We see Annie and Adrian together in a single scene, during which Annie confesses to a 'recurring fantasy' in which she is forced to have sex while 'a lot of men' watch. For the second time in the film, her tentative confiding of a dream is trampled over by an insensitive male response, when Adrian offers to 'bring my mates back after five-a-side to watch, if you want', leaving her devastated.

After a brief scene in the present, in which Adrian concedes that the two women are 'vaguely familiar', we see a further flashback in which he walks away from Annie when she talks about 'commitment', saying crudely and unfeelingly, 'Vagina. Nice place. Wouldn't want to live there'. Judging by Annie's shocked reaction, this incident marks the end of their relationship. There is an immediate, and ironic, cut back to the present, where Adrian reveals that he is now married, and proudly shows off photos of his daughter. Unimpressed, Hannah and Annie leave, Hannah informing him that the house is 'a load of crap'; he off-handedly replies, 'No, not my cup of tea, neither'.

That evening, Hannah and Annie go for a Chinese meal, and discuss the differences between themselves. Annie is thinking about the memories that the weekend has brought back, and reminds Hannah that 'I don't remember my childhood'. 'Who wants a crap memory, though?' counters Hannah. As they both acknowledge, each envies the other. 'I'm not strong enough to be as vulnerable as you', says Hannah; 'But I see that vulnerability as a weakness', replies Annie. 'You're the strong one'. 'If we could be a combination, we'd be the perfect woman, wouldn't we?' observes Hannah. 'Unfortunately, we can't'. But what they can do, each seeing the other as the stronger, is to complement each other by gaining strength from their friendship.

They go on to discuss Ricky, and when Hannah says, 'I wonder what happened to him', we are reminded that we still do not know whether they ever met up with him on their journey north, or indeed whether they ever saw him again. They speculate that he could by now be 'a rock star' or 'a company manager' or 'as thin as a beanpole', all of which supposition will very soon acquire a tragic irony. Before this, however, there are other narrative incidents for us to take in. First, we see a brief but significant flashback in which Hannah and Annie are seen preparing to leave the flat above the takeaway. Of course, we have already had a glimpse of this occasion, but this time the logistics of dividing up their possessions have given way to a focus on the emotional wrench it clearly represents for them. They both find themselves in tears, which in Hannah's case is presumably the first time she has cried since the age of nine, consolidating the healing effect that Annie's friendship is capable of having on her. Indeed, we realise – and just after we have seen their present selves discussing the emotional needs they look to men to fulfil – that each is probably the most important person in the other's life, the one to whom there is the closest emotional bond. Back in the present, in the restaurant, Hannah recalls a trip to Yorkshire to stay with Annie's family: 'It was quite a revelation, actually ... you know, everyone being nice to one another. I wasn't used to it'. We learn that she has a sister, Francesca, who is her alcoholic mother's favourite, despite the fact that, as Annie points out, 'you have always been the one to look after her'. 'Oh, I know', says Hannah. 'You're the only person who's ever really appreciated me'.

The day after their encounter with Adrian, there are further coincidences, which they both comment on explicitly: 'What's going on, eh?'; 'This is really weird now'. First they see Claire, who jogs past them in a park without noticing them; a fair reflection, presumably, of how their friendship with her ended. Then, on their way back to the station, they pay a return visit to their old flat, where they are disappointed to find that the takeaway is boarded up and neglected, and their old Georgian front door has been replaced by, in the screenplay's words, 'a crude modern flushed one'.[4] But there is one final coincidence, and one final shock, to come. They are astonished and upset to find Ricky, sitting outside the boarded-up takeaway incongruously clutching a large cuddly elephant. 'I wanted curry and chips', he says pathetically. Despite the fact that he is wearing a dishevelled suit and tie, and in direct contrast to their frivolous speculation the previous night about how he might have changed, Ricky has clearly not developed or moved on at all. If anything, he has degenerated, not only stumbling inarticulately in getting his words out, but only semi-coherent. He is making his way to Hastings: it appears that he has had some kind of failed relationship – 'she says I'm not the dad, but I am' – and the elephant is for the child that he wants to see. It is unclear how much of all this is in his imagination, since the only evidence of 'his' son is a torn photograph. As before, Ricky is not without insight – 'I'm like a idiot savant. Just haven't found any savant yet' – but his failure to change or develop is reflected in his assumption that Hannah and Annie still live above the shop, and will invite him in for a cup of tea. He is also more aggressive, telling them, 'don't patronise me' and snapping, 'Mind your business! What do you care?' when asked if he lives alone. Shaken and tearful both at his sorry state and at his rejection of them, Hannah and Annie get back in the car, Ricky's final abusive shout of 'Lesbos!' ironically reminding us of Evans's and Adrian's assumptions about them.

Ricky's outburst and their retreat cue in the film's final flashback, to their visit to his seaside hometown. Only now do we discover that they did find him after their conversation with his nan, but that he was too embittered even then for any reconciliation to be possible. 'Come to have a laugh, have you?' he asks. 'Take the piss? ... Come to lead us on a bit more, have you?' He then tells them to 'fuck off back where you came from!' and yells, 'Rancid! Rancid!' after them like a drunk on a park bench. The question of 'what happens to Ricky?' has lingered over the film ever since he disappeared, and it is now answered almost simultaneously and identically in past *and* present, again emphasising how he has not changed, how his life has not moved on.

And now Annie and Hannah part, though clearly not for the last time, as both of them are keen to meet up again soon. 'I don't like stations', says Annie as she prepares to leave. 'I like trains though'. For her, it seems, as for the film, the journey is important, not the destination. Typically of a Mike Leigh film, no magical transformation has taken place between past and present. They are still recognisably themselves, Annie still nervous and unsure of herself, Hannah still brittle and self-conscious; but they are more mature and a little more equipped to deal with whatever life throws their way, not least now that they have rediscovered their bond of friendship. Neither is settled, neither has yet reached her final destination, but having made the same journey has given them an unbreakable bond. The process of development is more important than the idea of becoming a 'different person'.

The characters' development is strikingly reflected in the writing and performance. Leigh surely demonstrates here, once and for all, that the stylised acting and the idiosyncratic characterisation in his films are a deliberate strategy, rather than something he simply does because it is an instinct he cannot or will not fight against. The highly mannered dialogue and performances in the flashbacks reflect the way the two women were – nervy and unsure of their identities and relationships with others as their younger selves – whereas the more low-key portrayals in the present demonstrate the mature, more stable people they have now become.

This was recognised by Geoff Brown who, reviewing the film for *The Times*, noted how Leigh 'paints with broad strokes to chart the difference between then and now', concluding: 'By the end of this wayward yet touching film, Leigh's caricatures have become living people, mirrors for ourselves, and you want the best for these career girls as they make the best of their faults and foibles'.[5] Some critics found the reduced scale of *Career Girls* a let-down after *Naked* and *Secrets and Lies*: in *Time Out*, Tom Charity called it a 'thin, disappointing film',[6] and

Philip French thought it 'a step backward' due to 'the treatment of the men and the over-emphasis on that old Leigh device of discovering a character through a weird voice'.[7] Reservations about the characterisations were also expressed by the *Evening Standard*'s Alexander Walker, who felt that the film 'makes accomplices of its cast and twists humanity into shapes freakish yet identifiable',[8] by *The Independent*'s Adam Mars-Jones, who saw 'acting exercises, not acts of insight',[9] and, most strongly, by John Diamond in the *New Statesman and Society*, who found the actors 'constrained by the phoney liberty of those improvised scripts'.[10] Nigel Andrews's review in the *Financial Times* was more favourable, declaring that '*Secrets and Lies* was a richer movie, but *Career Girls* is precise, mischievous, almost forensic',[11] while *The Guardian*'s Richard Williams seemed to be alone in not only praising 'the remarkable work of Cartlidge and Steadman' but also preferring *Career Girls* to *Secrets and Lies* because 'the people in it feel more real'.[12]

The most extreme critical reaction came from Gilbert Adair, writing not a review but an article in *The Guardian* in which he drew a tenuous comparison between his reaction to *Career Girls* ('To say I hated it would be putting it mildly') and the then recent case of a thirteen-year-old schoolgirl named Kelly Yeomans, who had tragically committed suicide after suffering appalling bullying at school:

> In any event, it was after reading about Kelly's suicide that I knew why I so abominated *Career Girls.* Leigh picks on his characters. He ridicules them. He bullies them. He jeers at them as fat and smelly and bristling with tics. And it makes scant difference that, in the film's present tense sequences, the same characters (with one exception, however) are shown to have matured into reasonably stable, functioning adults, since Leigh cavalierly elects not to reveal how the transformation has occurred.[13]

As Adair was at pains to point out, he had previously been a supporter of Leigh's work ('which I once rashly compared in *Sight and Sound* to Yasujiro Ozu's'), so his excessive vilification requires some unpicking. Does Leigh really bully or ridicule his characters? And should we really regret the lack of any glib explanation for what are perfectly natural changes and developments? Far from being cavalier, it seems to me that the changes ring so true precisely because they do not *need* explanation, because Annie and Hannah are still so recognisably – and plausibly – themselves. We *all* change; we have all (surely?) looked back at our younger selves and cringed or groaned at the recollection. 'What if a spectator with acute dermatitis sees *Career Girls*?' asks Adair. 'What is he or she supposed to think? So this is how others perceive me?'[14] Well, conceivably. But that would be an unfortunate, knee-jerk reaction, which would completely miss (as Adair appears to) the point of the film's flashback structure. More realistically, might the spectator in question not think: this accurately captures the way I feel about myself now, but there is hope. People can and do change. Change, in fact, is not merely possible, it is inevitable.

Other characters in the film point up the natural, gradual nature of the way in which Hannah and Annie have developed. Adrian, for example, has changed greatly on the surface – it is almost possible, on a first viewing of the film, to wonder whether he is being played by the same actor in past and present – yet his manner and his approach to his chosen profession, not to mention his reaction to meeting Hannah and Annie again, demonstrate that he is still, fundamentally, the selfish, callous person we have seen in flashback.

And then there is Ricky, who is presumably the 'one exception' to which Adair refers, and whom he describes as 'an obese, tic-ridden, practically autistic slob'.[15] Leigh and Mark Benton certainly present us with a fairly unsparing portrait of a recognisably dysfunctional young man, but am I alone in finding an underlying compassion in the characterisation which Adair's harsh description completely fails to acknowledge? Bullied and ridiculed? It is ironic that a character who is only ever actively antagonistic when he fails to take other people's feelings into account should be written off as being unfeelingly portrayed. Jeered at for being 'fat and smelly and bristling with tics'? As opposed to something we are encouraged to mock, Ricky's overall appearance is surely a pointer to his crucial lack of self-image and self-awareness; the fact that he is overweight, for example, is at least partly attributable to his habit of eating curry and chips late at night. And if, occasionally, his mannerisms make us laugh, then at least that unashamedly avoids the risk of treating a basically pitiable character with patronising sentimentality. Adair does admit to finding 'politically correct mawkishness' unacceptable (even calling it 'the bane of Ken Loach's work'[16]), yet he sees the characterisations in *Career Girls* as 'snuffing out all genuine emotion and empathy'. Interestingly, he does not suggest anywhere that Adrian and Evans are ridiculed – which they most assuredly are, for their attitudes and shallow materialistic values – presumably because they are portrayed quite naturalistically (which, in the context of Leigh's work, reflects the way they never doubt their own smug images of themselves). Admitting that he finds it 'impossible' to see beyond the 'external behavioural idiosyncrasies' in the characters, Adair erroneously correlates the comic stylisation with contempt.

All that notwithstanding, we do of course ultimately recognise that Ricky is a flawed character who is likely to carry on heading nowhere and never quite realising why or being able to do much about it. In a film which deals so much with change, he acts as a reminder that not to move on at all is to risk actually moving backwards. 'Time moves forward and yet stands still simultaneously', wrote Leigh in his introduction to the published screenplay of *Career Girls*;[17] the film shows us, through the warmth of their characterisation and the acute observation of those around them, how Hannah and Annie have developed as people while staying true to themselves and to each other.

Notes

1 Stella Bruzzi, *Sight and Sound*, 7: 9 (September 1997), p. 38
2 Mike Leigh, *Career Girls* (London, Faber & Faber, 1997), foreword
3 *Ibid.*, p. 40
4 *Ibid.*, p. 72
5 Geoff Brown, *The Times*, 18 September 1997
6 Tom Charity, *Time Out*, 17–24 September 1997, p. 78
7 Philip French, *The Observer*, 21 September 1997
8 Alexander Walker, *Evening Standard*, 18 September 1997
9 Adam Mars-Jones, *The Independent*, 19 September 1997
10 John Diamond, *New Statesman and Society*, 19 September 1997, pp. 40–2
11 Nigel Andrews, *Financial Times*, 18 September 1997
12 Richard Williams, *The Guardian*, 19 September 1997
13 Gilbert Adair, 'See Me After School, Leigh', *The Guardian*, 11 October 1997
14 *Ibid.*
15 *Ibid.*
16 *Ibid.*
17 Mike Leigh, *Career Girls*, foreword

'Laughter – tears – curtain': *Topsy-Turvy*

9

Prior to 1999, Leigh described himself as 'a closet Gilbert and Sullivan freak'.[1] With *Topsy-Turvy* he emerged from the closet, firmly declaring his long-standing delight in the comic operas of librettist William Schwenck Gilbert and composer Arthur Sullivan, whose intermittently stormy collaboration began in 1871 and continued for two and a half decades, mostly under the management of Richard D'Oyly Carte at London's Savoy Theatre. The emergence was a spectacular one, given both the film's unusually (for Leigh) lavish production values and the highly positive reaction to it. It also marked a breakthrough for Leigh in that it was 'the first film I made that had no television money in it at all, in any shape or form'.[2]

Given the radical departure suggested by its period setting and necessarily substantial musical content, *Topsy-Turvy* was always going to attract attention. Way in advance of its UK release, the film had already gained Jim Broadbent a Best Actor award at the Venice Film Festival for his performance as W. S. Gilbert, while in America *Topsy-Turvy* was named the year's Best Picture by both the New York Film Critics Circle (who also cited Leigh as Best Director) and the National Society of Film Critics. Speculation that this was to be a harbinger of Oscar-night success proved inaccurate, however: the film was nominated in the four categories of original screenplay, art direction, costume design and make-up – and won only the last two. Its sole BAFTA award was again for make-up, despite nominations in four other categories, including the Alexander Korda Award for Best British Film. *Evening Standard* Awards for Best Film and Best Actor (Broadbent again) may well have seemed small consolation.

Nevertheless, the critical reaction was on the whole extremely favourable. Richard Schickel found it 'one of the year's more beguiling surprises',[3] while Philip French applauded the look of the film, the 'wonderful ensemble cast' and the 'consistently elegant and funny' dialogue.[4] Reviewing the film for *Sight and Sound*, Andy Medhurst admired the 'rich and complex' staging, the 'typically judicious balance of heartbreak and farce' and 'several diamond-sharp moments when an apparently casual observation illuminates a whole architecture of social assumptions' – although he also thought that there were 'too many indulgent performances of their songs'.[5]

That last point must, perhaps, remain more than usually a matter of personal taste, but the generous musical extracts certainly bear unmistakeable witness to Leigh's passion for Gilbert and Sullivan. (Passion is scarcely too strong a word; his favourite descriptions of their songs are 'sexy' and 'succulent', at least if his commentary on the DVD of the film is anything to go by.[6]) The enthusiasm was developed early in his life; there were recordings of their work in the Leigh household, and he listened to them keenly. The D'Oyly Carte Opera Company also made regular visits to Manchester's Opera House.

Further explaining the genesis of *Topsy-Turvy*, Leigh recalled growing up in 'that great Victorian city' of Manchester, and 'wanted to do a period piece that interested me with believable characters in a Victorian setting'.[7] He also wanted to reclaim Gilbert and Sullivan from a certain manner of presentation: 'They've been done a disservice, because there's a whole subculture, particularly in the amateur arena, of fat middle-aged people acting and singing these parts badly, which were very wittily and sexily created for young performers'.[8] Likewise, he was keen to apply his usual practice of striving for truth, rather than superficial 'realism', to a historical drama, to get under the skin of the period as opposed to the slavish reconstructions which have given rise to the dismissive term 'Heritage cinema': 'It seemed so utterly unlikely for me to do something like this that I obviously wanted to try it. I suppose I wanted to make a period film just for the wheeze of it, and I just liked the idea of taking this chocolate-box subject matter and subverting it by doing it for real'.[9] In addition, the film is a tribute to all those involved in the production of art, and especially comic art. Interviewed on stage at the 1999 London Film Festival, Leigh was asked what the film was about, and replied: 'Us. What we do. Why we suffer'. He went on to say that this encompassed anyone who takes seriously the job of contributing to other people's leisure time, such as 'people who make chocolates and beer'.[10]

These aims came together with a long-standing idea of Leigh's to cast Jim Broadbent as Gilbert, dating from 1992 when they had made the short film *A Sense of History* together for Channel 4. Broadbent himself wrote the screenplay of *A Sense of History*, as well as playing the lead role of the fictional twenty-third Earl of Leete, who gives the viewer a conducted tour of his estate and recounts its history. Languid, supercilious and possessed of an unquestioned sense of entitlement, the Earl is a callous monster, motivated solely by his determination to conserve what he considers to be his family's rightful heritage. Yet there is increasingly a wistful sadness in his eyes as, for example, he recalls his mother ('She was stupid, vain, lazy and craven – we adored her, but she paid us scant attention'), or the bullying he and his brother suffered at the hands of his brutal father. Even the murders he reveals himself to have committed are tinged with a dreadful melancholy: his elder brother, whom he killed to ensure his own inheritance, having judged him unfit for the position – an opinion later disproved by his discovery of the brother's private diaries; or his first wife, inconveniently in the way of an affair with a woman he then lost anyway; and his two young sons, who possibly witnessed the killing of their mother. Bombastic and vulnerable by turns, the Earl is a masterly comic creation, and it is easy to see why Leigh should have seen the foundations of a fine W. S. Gilbert in Broadbent's conception and portrayal.

In assembling the rest of the cast, Leigh's usual commitment to authenticity (as opposed to realism) led him towards actors who could do their own singing and play the various instruments themselves as required. Allan Corduner proved 'a terrific discovery',[11] being an actor who could both offer skilled musicianship and bring Arthur Sullivan to life in a way vividly enough to prevent the film being unduly skewed towards Broadbent's imposing portrayal of Gilbert. Shirley Henderson, auditioning for the role of soprano Leonora Braham, recalled her early career as a club singer in Fife, and reasoned that if she could pull off a credible performance in that demanding environment, she ought to be able to convince Leigh.[12] And Timothy Spall would, by this stage in his career, have surprised few people with his splendid, full-blooded portrayal of actor and baritone Richard Temple, but perhaps rather more by displaying a most respectable singing voice. The cast also includes some enjoyable cameos from familiar faces, including Alison Steadman, by now Leigh's ex-wife, as a theatrical costumier, Andy Serkis, in scene-stealing form as the flamboyant choreographer John D'Auban, and Katrin Cartlidge, working with Leigh for the last time before her untimely death in 2003, as a brothel Madame.

The period is wonderfully evoked; among the British cinema's historical dramas of the time, only Terence Davies' 2000 adaptation of *The House of Mirth* rivalled *Topsy-Turvy* in capturing the textures and nuances of a period, rather than merely pointing a camera at an immaculate reconstruction of it. The work of Eve Stewart, Lindy Hemming and Christine Blundell as, respectively, production designer, costume designer, and make-up and hair designer, is exemplary in its meticulous research and realisation, and Dick Pope's cinematography does them, and the film, proud. Noting that the Savoy 'was the first public building in the world to be lit by electricity', Pope even commissioned hundreds of hand-blown bulbs to give an authentic look to the theatre scenes.[13]

The historical reference points are carefully chosen both to anchor the narrative and to offer revealing insights into the attitudes and mores of the period. The key scene in this respect takes place in February 1884, when, as a caption tells us, 'news reaches London of the killing of General Gordon by the Mahdi's troops at Khartoum'. Actors George Grossmith (Martin Savage), Rutland Barrington (Vincent Franklin) and Durward Lely (Kevin McKidd) discuss this shocking incident over lunch in a busy restaurant, ludicrously assuming that codes of sportsmanship somehow apply ('It just isn't cricket'; 'It's completely contrary to all the rules of engagement') and revealing an unquestioned, patronising racism. Lely responds somewhat acerbically to Barrington's comment that 'We strive to bring them civilization and this is their gratitude' with a reminder that only a few years ago the English militia massacred fifty-six families on the Isle of Skye. A further reminder of colonialism close to home comes in a scene set that evening, as Temple and Lely discuss the day's events in their dressing room. Asked if he has heard 'the real news of the day', Temple assumes this to be a reference to 'the Fenian bomb – oh, dreadful!' – although Lely is actually talking about the indisposition of Grossmith and Barrington, who have over-indulged on oysters during their lunch.

These are deadly serious overtones, handled deftly and with scalpel sharpness. Elsewhere, there is much fun to be had at the expense of the characters' reactions to then new technology such as doorbells and fountain pens. In one early scene Gilbert conducts a hilarious telephone conversation with the D'Oyly Carte company manager Mr Barker (Sam Kelly), the two men announcing themselves with uneasy formality as they are forced to shout down the unfamiliar device ('Hello?' – 'Is that you, Mr Gilbert?' – 'Hello?' – 'Hello?' – 'Good morning, Barker' – 'This is Barker speaking' – 'Gilbert here'). It is hard to imagine any actors getting richer comedy out of the scene than Broadbent and Kelly. One wonders if some of Leigh's critics would regard all this as patronising if it felt slightly closer to home; maybe the historical distance affords him a certain exemption.

Given the fine contributions made to the film on both sides of the camera, it is not surprising that Leigh regards *Topsy-Turvy* as a great ensemble achievement. It is, just as he wished, much more than just another 'chocolate-box' version of history, and is further enriched by

Carl Davis's judicious and inventive orchestrations of Sullivan's music on the soundtrack.

The departure from contemporary characters and settings notwithstanding, it comes as a relief in *Topsy-Turvy* to find that the essence of Leigh's familiar style is never far away. As Medhurst concluded, 'despite its initially disorienting costume trappings, it's very much "a Mike Leigh film" after all';[14] and it is certainly hard to conceive of any other writer or director creating a scene in which the Savoy's proprietor Richard D'Oyly Carte (Ron Cook) utters the immortal line, 'I don't know about you, but, speaking for myself, I could murder a pork chop'. Thematically, the key here as elsewhere in Leigh's work is the contrast between public faces and private selves, which is obviously heightened by the theatrical setting. One of the joys of the film, indeed, is that Leigh's insights into the lives of Gilbert and Sullivan and their theatrical troupe are inseparable from his sensitivity to the pleasures and pains of the creative process, and the ways in which repressed emotion can be channelled into art. Gilbert in particular seems a typical Leigh protagonist in this respect, placing Jim Broadbent's touching portrayal at the heart of the movie.

The lives of Gilbert and Sullivan had been dealt with before by the British cinema, in Frank Launder and Sidney Gilliat's *The Story of Gilbert and Sullivan* (Gilliat, 1953). Unlike that film, *Topsy-Turvy* does not attempt comprehensively to cover the men's entire careers, beginning instead at a point where their relationship is already becoming strained. Gilbert, though happy enough to continue writing their successful series of Savoy operas, has been rattled by a critic's description of him as 'the legitimate monarch of the realm of topsy-turvydom', while Sullivan is ambitious to compose something more weighty than whimsical, and is finding Gilbert a difficult collaborator ('Working with Gilbert would kill anyone', agrees D'Oyly Carte).

The contrasts between the two men are clearly delineated right from the beginning of the film, which takes place on 5 January 1884, the opening night of their eighth collaboration, *Princess Ida*. Sullivan, whom we see first, is ill, only making it to the theatre with the assistance of his disapproving manservant Louis (Dexter Fletcher), not to mention an injection of morphine, several cups of strong coffee and a lot of determination ('I've never missed one yet'). However, he conspicuously comes to life when he is finally in front of the orchestra conducting the overture (what Leigh calls 'the medicine of theatre'[15]); immediately the show is over, he collapses backstage in a corridor.

Whereas Sullivan clearly thrives on the atmosphere of the theatre and the audience's rapturous applause, Gilbert cannot bring himself to be in the auditorium during the performance, and sits alone in the Green Room within earshot of the stage, puffing on his cigar and frowning grimly. Immediately after the performance, he seems to leave the theatre, passing the collapsed Sullivan on the way. 'What happened?' he enquires, presumably about his collaborator's health, although he could conceivably be fishing for information as to how the play has gone; we will soon discover that he is deeply insecure and incapable of accepting a compliment.

After this briefest of glimpses of the two men together, their first proper meeting comes a little over half an hour into the narrative. This is the cue for what Leigh calls 'one of our favourite things'[16] – that is, the static, uninterrupted two-shot, held in this case for about three minutes as they sit on the sofa in Sullivan's study, and emphasising theirs as the film's central relationship. (Interestingly, an earlier sustained two-shot, of Gilbert and his wife Lucy (Lesley Manville), known as Kitty, at breakfast, was interrupted by the arrival of their butler. The fact that no such interruption happens during the conservation between Gilbert and Sullivan perhaps privileges their partnership as collaborators over Gilbert's marriage; this would certainly be symptomatic of his own neglect of Kitty because of his obsession with his work. A later, shorter sustained shot frames actors Temple and Lely through the door to their dressing room, privileging their status as leading actors, although again it is not an unbroken two-shot, their conversation being topped and tailed by the interventions of the dresser and call-boy.)

Although the scene of this first conversation evolved through Leigh's usual process of improvisation with his cast, it incorporates genuine quotes from letters exchanged between Gilbert and Sullivan. Each, we learn, believes that he subordinates his own talent to the other's to maintain the success of their partnership; also Sullivan wants to break away, feeling limited by Gilbert's repetitious propensity for whimsical comic fantasy or 'topsy-turvydom' – which has reared its head again in his latest proposal. 'In 1881, it was a magic coin; and before that it was a magic lozenge; and in 1877 it was an elixir', Sullivan complains. 'In this instance', replies Gilbert, as if it were to make all the difference in the world, 'it is a magic potion'.

By the time of a later conversation in Carte's office, they are no nearer to an agreement. A heat wave has brought the run of *Princess Ida* to a premature end, and it has been replaced by a revival of their earlier *The Sorcerer*. Gilbert has submitted several revised drafts of his scenario, but Sullivan remains unable to find inspiration for a musical setting in any of them, and continues to object to the idea of a magic potion, a device he considers not only over-familiar but 'utterly contrived'. 'Every theatrical performance is a contrivance, by its very nature', argues Gilbert, adding: 'If you wish to write a grand opera about a prostitute dying of consumption in a garret, I suggest you contact Mr Ibsen in Oslo. I am sure he will be able to furnish you with something suitably dull'. They part at an apparent impasse. Helen Lenoir (Wendy Nottingham), Carte's secretary and later his wife, concludes: 'This will be a very sad day for many thousands of people'.

The disagreement on this occasion is only temporary, however – more serious rifts were to come later in their careers – and over the course of the film they do get back together again to create what many regard as their masterpiece, *The Mikado*. The genesis and preparation of *The Mikado* form the rest of the narrative, incorporating what Leigh calls 'flash-forwards' to extracts from the eventual production,[17] and intercut with sections from their other work. Throughout the process, the contrasts between Gilbert and Sullivan continue to be highlighted. In the months that have elapsed between the opening night of *Princess Ida* and their conversation in Sullivan's study, for example, Sullivan has been to Europe, enjoying himself by cavorting with prostitutes and dining in high-class restaurants. Gilbert has been back at home in England, suffering the heat wave, fretting over the reviews and box-office returns for *Princess Ida*. Their residences likewise reflect their dissimilar lifestyles: Gilbert's town house is opulent but austere; Sullivan's apartment is more Bohemian and exotic.

As they prepare for *The Mikado*, we see consecutive scenes of Gilbert and Sullivan rehearsing with, respectively, the actors and the orchestra. Sullivan makes criticisms of the musicians affably but firmly: 'I really don't mind whose mistake it was, Mr Plank, as long as it doesn't happen again'. He has an easy but incontestable authority, and exhibits no false modesty when his musical director Cellier (Stefan Bednarczyk) admonishes a hapless bassoonist by reminding him that 'Dr Sullivan is dead. Long live Sir Arthur'. (Sullivan was indeed knighted in 1884; Gilbert had to wait until 1907 to be similarly honoured.) Gilbert is more brusque in rehearsal, irritably dismissing as 'rubbish' Grossmith's attempt to suggest his character's lowly origins on the line 'A terrible thing 'as 'appened': 'A terrible thing *has* just happened, Grossmith – you've become a cockney ... we're in Japan for heaven's sake, not Stepney or Bow. Do it properly!' (Earlier in the same scene, Grossmith says: 'Well, another fine mess you've got us into', and is corrected by Gilbert: 'My line is, a *nice* mess you've got us into ... ' – a homage to Laurel and Hardy's endlessly misquoted catchphrase, by way of recompense, perhaps, for Johnny's erroneous assertion in *Naked* that 'apparently they didn't get on in real life'.)

Later, on *The Mikado*'s opening night in March 1885, Sullivan visits the nervous, morphine-addicted Grossmith in his dressing room, and sensitively tries to put him at his ease – 'We shall have a great triumph, you know' – while Gilbert, who is not actually allowed in to see Grossmith, only succeeds in passing on his own nervousness, blurting, 'Good luck ... and be careful with the sword' as a parting shot. As before, Sullivan enjoys the experience of being in the theatre, whereas Gilbert cannot even bear to remain in the building, returning only at the end of the performance. When they both take an enthusiastically received curtain call, Gilbert is stiff and uncomfortable, in contrast to Sullivan's ease in front of an audience.

The neuroses which make Gilbert so unable to enjoy the success of his work are equally detrimental to his private life, in particular through his emotional neglect of Kitty. The morning after the opening of *Princess Ida*, breakfast in their house is dominated by his irritation with the *Times* review, which, while noting that the opera 'will probably run for a year', also contains that infuriating reference to him as 'the legitimate monarch of the realm of topsy-turvydom'. That night, he is still brooding on this 'humiliating' description when he returns from dining at the Beefsteak Club. Kitty is sitting up in bed, while he sits in a chair beside it, in full evening wear. After going on about the section of that night's performance he has watched from the wings ('Seemed to be going rather well, surprisingly'), he says, 'I'll leave you, you must be tired'. 'No, I'm not in the slightest', she says, and tries to persuade him to sit on the bed and talk to her. He demurs, saying that 'it's wrong of me to unburden myself on you', and goes. He seems emotionally frozen, channelling all his impulses into his work without actually enjoying the results ('Sometimes one wonders why one bothers'); again, this is in stark contrast to Sullivan's open enjoyment of their success, and to his licentiousness and infidelity to his married mistress Fanny (Eleanor David).

This early scene between Gilbert and Kitty is paralleled by another at the end, after the first night of *The Mikado*. This is the last we see of them, Kitty again soothing his ego after he admits: 'There's something inherently disappointing about success ... I don't quite know how to take praise'. 'It must be nice to receive it, nonetheless', she says, a little wistfully, before speculating that it would be 'wondrous if perfectly commonplace people gave each other a round of applause at the end of the day'. As she demonstrates, he briefly joins in before saying again: 'Well, you must be tired'. 'No, don't go', she says and, after hesitating, asks him if he has any ideas for his next piece. He invites her to suggest something, and she tells him her own scenario for a new musical, which includes a young and beautiful heroine who grows 'old and plain'; ladies chasing gentlemen who are 'far too busy' to talk to them; and hundreds of nannies with empty prams. He fails to respond to this expression of her insecurity and emotional needs; his self-absorption has been penetrated, but he has absolutely no idea how to react. Instead of responding to *her*, he sidetracks the conversation back onto his professional partnership: 'I shouldn't imagine Sullivan'd much care for that'.

It is no wonder that Kitty seems to despair of him; on at least one occasion her exasperation at his inability to take a compliment is evident. As he reads a draft of *The Mikado* to her, she comments ironically that it 'certainly is rich in human emotion and probability'. 'Hardly', he says, oblivious to the sarcasm. (Her reaction is in contrast to Sullivan's; rather unexpectedly, in the previous scene we have seen him laughing genuinely and appreciatively as Gilbert reads him the libretto.) Before the opening night, she is trying to keep him under control, in a scene conceived and choreographed by Leigh to accommodate a restless side-to-side tracking camera movement, reflecting Gilbert's compulsive pacing up and down. Their housekeeper says, 'You look beautiful, madam' and she is slightly taken aback before replying, 'Oh, thank you, Mrs Judd. Oh, it's most pleasant to be appreciated'. The moment is beautifully played by Lesley Manville, and our hearts go out to Kitty as we recognise that Gilbert's determined imperviousness to praise makes him unable to give it to anyone else. Even in the more artificial environment of the theatre, where Gilbert is more in control of people and events, he seems quite incapable, for example, of understanding how crushed Temple is when his solo, 'A More Humane Mikado', is cut after the dress rehearsal. 'My decision to cut the song in no way reflects upon your performance of it, which was fine in every respect', he says when pressed, but the cold formality of this reassurance takes no account of Temple's genuine disappointment, and it is only when the rest of the ladies and gentlemen of the chorus make a later appeal to Gilbert en masse that the song is reinstated. For the moment, Gilbert simply concludes that 'I have nothing more to say', and Temple, who was only minutes earlier chuckling somewhat theatrically at Gilbert's ironic witticisms, retires to his dressing room in distress. Sullivan's parting shot to the rest of the assembled company is characteristically much warmer: 'I am immensely proud of you all. I do not wish to tempt the fates, but I feel that we will have a great success. I have nothing further to add'.

Kitty, while selfless in her doomed attempts to bolster her husband's confidence, is not meekly submissive, however. An intriguing insight into their relationship is supplied by Leigh's use of a classic comic edit: on two occasions Gilbert says vehemently that he will under no circumstances do something – visit the dentist when he has an agonising toothache, and accompany Kitty to a Japanese exhibition in Knightsbridge – whereupon the film immediately cuts to him doing it. Clearly his obstinacy does not go unchallenged in matters unrelated to his work.

After that last glimpse of the two of them on *The Mikado*'s opening night – Kitty obviously distressed and Gilbert incapable of reaching out to her – we cut to the final scene between Sullivan and Fanny, which is equally shot through with melancholy. Sitting up in bed, Sullivan declares that he is 'proud of [him]self, triumphant, exhilarated, exhausted, revived, and fed up to the back teeth with these wretched kidneys'. Fanny tells him that she is pregnant again: 'An old demon has come back to haunt us at a most unwelcome time'. 'I shall make the arrangements', he says; but Fanny has made her own, which clearly involve a new method of termination: 'I couldn't go through that again ... Someone has been recommended to me. After all, it is 1885, Arthur'.

The mood and tone of *Topsy-Turvy*, then, are very consistent with Leigh's other work, even though his working methods might seem less fitted to the treatment of real lives and (largely) real events. Leigh, however, says this was not the case ('the actor still has to be the character in the flesh, in a three-dimensional way'[18]) and that in this instance it merely demanded research of a perhaps somewhat different kind to flesh out the characters and incidents. The research was as painstaking as one might expect. Gilbert and Sullivan's correspondence, both between themselves and to others, was readily available, as were Sullivan's extensive diaries. These reveal Sullivan to be, as in the film, a *bon viveur* much given to foreign travel and socialising with royalty and the nobility.

The hint of vanity in his artistic ambitions notwithstanding, it would seem that Sullivan was every bit as genial and companionable as in Corduner's endearing portrayal. Gilbert was likewise apparently every bit as irascible and insecure as the film shows him, although Leigh is at pains to demonstrate 'what a mad family he came from ... if he had any psychological problems himself, there was plainly a reason for it'.[19] His parents separated when Gilbert was nineteen, and what we see of them as individuals hardly encourages the view that they were any easier to deal with when apart than they would have been together. The cantankerous Gilbert senior alternately exasperates Gilbert with his eccentric behaviour and worries him with the fits he suffers (on the DVD commentary, Leigh justifiably highlights Charles Simon's performance as Doctor Gilbert as an extraordinary contribution to the film). Accused by his father of being 'in communication with' his mother, Gilbert replies stone-facedly that 'the very last person with whom I wish to have any communication at all is your estranged wife... the vicious woman who bore me into this ridiculous world'. The lady in question appears later in the film, played by Eve Pearce as a coldly domineering woman living with Gilbert's unmarried sisters, Maude (Theresa Watson) and Florence (Lavinia Bertram), and presiding imperiously over the household from her bed. There does not seem to have been much parental love in Gilbert's life, and the implication is that his emotional coldness is the result.

That said, Gilbert was also by all accounts a fundamentally kind and humane man – his death in 1911 was caused by his attempting to save a girl from drowning in the lake in his garden – and he inspired deep loyalty in the vast majority of those who knew him well. In that regard he certainly had something in common with Leigh himself, who nonetheless has also never disguised his sensitivity to criticism and consequently has gained a reputation with journalists for being prickly. As satirists, they might appear to have less affinity, since Gilbert's lampoons tended to be of the fallible humans who populate great social institutions rather than ordinary people in everyday situations. How interesting, though, that Clement Scott, a critic towards whom Gilbert bore a particularly long-standing grudge, should have written in *Theatre*, after the first performance of *The Pirates of Penzance* in 1880, that Gilbert's humour

> has been called topsy-turvy, deformed, exaggerated caricature, grotesque; it has been compared to the effect of a man looking at his face in a spoon, in a magnifying glass, or at the world through the wrong end of an opera glass; but none of these things hits the mark. It is a kind of comic daring and recklessness that makes fun of things ... In a comical way he shows us all that is mean, and cruel, and crafty, and equivocal even in the world's heroes; and he makes us laugh at them because we are convinced such faults are lingering even in the breasts of the best of us.[20]

Not at all a bad description of Leigh's own comic style, or of the criticisms that have sometimes been made of it!

While the raw material of Gilbert and Sullivan's lives was easily accessible to Broadbent and Corduner, other members of the cast had to look further afield. Kevin McKidd, for example, returned to his native Scotland, not far from where he grew up, to conduct his research into the life of Durward Lely, and found an unpublished biography in a local library; little was known about Richard Temple, on the other hand, and so Leigh and Spall consequently evolved him into a 'definitive Victorian actor character'.[21]

Temple aside, most of the other characters and incidents are recreated with meticulous accuracy. George Grossmith was addicted to morphine, and did indeed struggle on the first night of *The Mikado* – although he was by no means a spent force, being still a few years away from making his lasting contribution to British comic literature with *The Diary of a Nobody*, first published in *Punch* in 1888. Leonora Braham was indeed a widow with a young son and a weakness for alcohol; and Jessie Bond (Dorothy Atkinson), with whom Leonora is seen sharing a dressing room, did have problems with her legs, about which Leigh and Atkinson consulted a specialist who 'diagnosed that it was probably a varicose condition'.[22] Kitty did 'spy' for Gilbert, checking on audience numbers (not to mention any deviations in performance) for him. The oyster binge which lays low Grossmith and Barrington did happen. The call-boy at the Savoy was called Shrimp, and the theatre management did have a special code for communicating the box-office takings to Gilbert. The Japanese woman at the exhibition, whose only words of English were 'sixpence please' did exist, and Gilbert did bring her along to rehearsals to demonstrate Japanese deportment to the actresses.

Some details, one suspects, were simply too good to ignore: Gilbert did suffer from toothache at this time, and Leigh takes the opportunity to build this up into two wonderfully comical scenes – his anger with the women of his household as they nag him to visit a dentist, then his helplessness as the dentist passes undiplomatic comment on his work while he cannot speak. He also genuinely disliked the song he had written for the Mikado and did resolve to cut it. The chorus did get together and ask him to change his mind, an event which appealed to Leigh's 'sense of grass-roots politics'[23] as well as providing an excellent dramatic incident late in the narrative.

Gilbert always claimed that he conceived the idea for *The Mikado* when a Japanese sword fell from its place on his study wall. In the film, this occurs after he has visited the Japanese exhibition that he had initially insisted he would not attend 'for all the tea in China'. As a point of historical fact, he had already thought of the Japanese setting by the time the exhibition came to London (there was already a tremendous vogue for Japanese culture and fashion), but Leigh thought that it would be 'more fun'[24] to have him inspired by it. It is also, of course, more dramatically satisfying, and the exhibition thus leads smoothly into the lovely scene in which, late at night, the sword startles Gilbert by clattering to the floor. Jim Broadbent's reaction is hugely enjoyable, at first playing with the sword in swashbuckling style before wielding it in the more authentically Japanese manner he saw demonstrated at the exhibition. Then, as the inspiration for his next work dawns on him, there is a rapid track in with a slight tilt, and he looks into the camera and smiles, slowly and knowingly. Striking in itself, the shot is even more conspicuous as the only time in the whole of Leigh's work to date that a character has looked directly at the camera (and thus at the viewer).

For all this emphasis on the cultural specificity of its origins, Leigh points out that *The Mikado* is actually 'about as Japanese as fish and chips';[25] in keeping with the imperialism of the times, it is very much an appropriation and Anglicisation of Japanese traditions (the town of Titipu, populated by characters with names like Yum-Yum, Ko-Ko and Pish-Tush, might almost have come from a *Carry On* film). There is thus an irony in Gilbert's desire for authenticity, and indeed in separate scenes during the rehearsals he contradicts himself about the status of what they are doing. When Lely is reluctant to act without wearing his corset, Gilbert remonstrates with him: 'This is not grand opera in Milan. It is merely low burlesque in a small theatre on the banks of the River Thames'. Later, however, when D'Auban is arguing against the incorporation of an authentically Japanese style of movement, Gilbert is adamant that 'this is not low burlesque, this is an entirely original Japanese opera'.

These rehearsal scenes are among the wittiest and most entertaining in *Topsy-Turvy*. With very few exterior scenes in the film at all, the second half in particular takes place almost entirely in the theatre and its associated spaces – auditorium, back-stage areas, rehearsal rooms – and themes of class, hierarchy, leadership and teamwork are all explored through the backstage world. Apart from a very early shot of Sullivan arriving at the Savoy for the first performance of *Princess Ida*, we venture outside on just one occasion, as Gilbert, unable to remain in the theatre on the first night of *The Mikado*, walks around the nearby streets. Various sounds are heard coming out of the darkness: as itemised in the screenplay, 'bottles breaking, chains clinking, a dog barking, a man shouting and a baby crying'.[26] An old woman, whom the screenplay describes as 'filthy, dishevelled' and even 'mad',[27] suddenly appears and grabs his arm. Panicking, Gilbert shouts at her, 'Get your hands off me!' and 'You stinking bitch!' – the extremity of this latter insult emphasising how dangerous, how frighteningly out of control the world outside the theatre is to him. As he retreats, a group of men tear past him, pursued by a four-wheeled carriage, their flight seeming in this context frantic and threatening.

The predominance of interior spaces was initially a financial consideration, Leigh making the most of a still comparatively modest budget. This apparent limitation nevertheless becomes a stylistic virtue, lending the characters' lives an appropriately claustrophobic air, and also enabling Leigh to craft a piquant study of both the insularity *and* the solidarity of all those who work in the theatre. The very first shot in the film shows one of the theatre's more menial tasks, as first one man and then several throughout the auditorium are seen testing the tip-up seats by lifting and lowering each in turn – what Leigh describes as an initial 'whiff of the theatre as a working place'.[28] A later extract from the revival of *The Sorcerer* allows Leigh again to show the theatre as 'an industrial process',[29] emphasising the off-stage chorus, the orchestra and the stage hands creating sound effects, as much as the on-stage performers.

Following the melancholy final glimpses of Gilbert and Kitty and then Sullivan and Fanny, the film ends with 'a private moment'.[30] Leonora – who in an earlier scene has bemoaned her loneliness and the fact that whenever a suitor discovers she has a child 'he's off, quick smart' – is having a tipple alone in her dressing room, and quoting Yum-Yum's soliloquy from Act 2 of *The Mikado*: 'Yes, I am indeed beautiful! ... Can this be vanity? No! Nature is lovely, and rejoices in her loveliness'. From this bittersweet vignette, we cut to her alone on the Savoy stage, where an uplifting coda is provided as she sings Yum-Yum's song 'The Sun Whose Rays'. Shirley Henderson's lovely rendition amply bears out Caryl Brahms's assessment of the song as a 'charming lyric well matched by sensitive musical collaboration ... which held audiences spellbound a century ago, and still does';[31] it is majestically shot in a single take, the camera starting on a close-up of her and gradually craning upwards over the heads of the orchestra and audience, ending in a long-shot from the circle. The lyrics pick up on Fanny's parting comment to Sullivan, 'you light up the world', reminding us of Gilbert and Sullivan's legacy and allowing them the last word. Well, almost. As the picture fades to black, two captions appear before the closing credits:

> Gilbert and Sullivan wrote five more operas, including *The Yeomen of the Guard* and *The Gondoliers*.
>
> Sullivan only wrote one grand opera, *Ivanhoe*. Although moderately successful at the time, it is now mostly forgotten, and isn't as much fun as *The Mikado*.

That should banish any notion that the conflict depicted between Sullivan's grand ambitions and Gilbert's 'topsy-turvydom' represents any kind of inner struggle between Leigh's striving for documentary-style truth and his comic or satirical impulses, which co-exist harmoniously, indeed inseparably, throughout his work, including *Topsy-Turvy*. Leigh's most purely pleasurable film since *Life Is Sweet*, it is a scrupulous, vibrant celebration of the theatre, of theatre folk in general, and of these two men of the theatre and their associates in particular. Truly, all the world's a stage here, and Leigh observes it with all the wry affection that he has always brought to his observations of more contemporary lives and loves.

Notes

1 Quoted in Michael Coveney, *The World According to Mike Leigh* (London, Harper Collins, paperback edition, 1997), p. 49
2 Interview with the author, 5 April 2005
3 Richard Schickel, *Time Magazine*, 27 December 1999
4 Philip French, *The Observer*, 20 February 2000
5 Andy Medhurst, *Sight and Sound*, 10: 3 (March 2000), pp. 36–7
6 Director's commentary, *Topsy-Turvy* DVD (Pathe, 2000, P8968DVD)
7 Quoted in Ellis Davies, *Cardiff Post*, 17 February 2000
8 Quoted in Trevor Johnston, 'Taking the Mik?', *Time Out*, 9–16 February 2000, pp. 24–5
9 *Ibid.*
10 Interview at the National Film Theatre during the 43rd London Film Festival, 9 November 1999
11 Director's commentary, *Topsy-Turvy* DVD
12 See Brian Pendreigh, 'From Class A Drugs To a Little Light Opera', *The Guardian*, 4 November 1999
13 Matthew Sweet, 'The Very Model', *Independent on Sunday*, 30 January 2000
14 Andy Medhurst, *Sight and Sound*, p. 37
15 Director's commentary, *Topsy-Turvy* DVD
16 *Ibid.*
17 *Ibid.*
18 Interview, National Film Theatre, 9 November 1999
19 Director's commentary, *Topsy-Turvy* DVD
20 Quoted in Caryl Brahms, *Gilbert and Sullivan: Lost Chords and Discords* (London, Weidenfield and Nicholson, 1975), p. 96
21 Director's commentary, *Topsy-Turvy* DVD
22 *Ibid.*
23 *Ibid.*
24 *Ibid.*
25 *Ibid.*
26 Mike Leigh, *Topsy-Turvy* (London, Faber & Faber, 1999), p. 124
27 *Ibid.*
28 Director's commentary, *Topsy-Turvy* DVD
29 *Ibid.*
30 *Ibid.*
31 Caryl Brahms, *Gilbert and Sullivan: Lost Chords and Discords*, p. 150

'Life's too short': *All or Nothing* 10

After the unfamiliar period setting and comparatively large budget of *Topsy-Turvy*, Leigh returned to more recognisable territory for his next film, *All or Nothing*. Indeed, the opening shot almost looks like a parody of his style and mood – except that no parody could so succinctly convey the humanity and sense of mortality that pervade both this opening and the film as a whole.

We see a long, sustained shot of what the screenplay describes as an 'institutional corridor',[1] over which Andrew Dickson's melancholy music perfectly establishes the tone. A young woman is seen stoically mopping the floor; despite the wide-screen aspect ratio of the frame, the shot is centred so that the natural perspective of the corridor walls appears to hem her in. Interior features such as doorways will be used throughout the film to create a similar sense of claustrophobia (what Leigh calls a 'vertical frame within the horizontal frame'[2]); it is a device Leigh has used before, but never so often or so effectively as here. An older woman approaches her from behind, carefully making her way down the corridor, and shying away from the younger woman's outstretched hand as she offers to assist her. The scene is set; they are a cleaner and a resident in a care centre for the elderly.

We will meet this young woman again before long, and learn who she is; having been the first person we see on screen, she will also remain uppermost in our thoughts as the film ends. First, though, there is a range of other characters to whom we must be introduced, whose interrelated lives will be explored across the events of a long weekend, before the narrative is pared down to focus on a single family. Thus from the opening shot, over which the titles run, the film cuts immediately to a not obviously related scene, in which we recognise Timothy Spall, driving a saloon car. It rapidly becomes clear that he is a minicab driver, and throughout the film we see him carrying a variety of passengers in a series of vignettes, in rather the same way that Spall's character in

Secrets and Lies was periodically seen photographing a cross-section of different subjects.

This driver's name is Phil Bassett, and he lives with his partner Penny (Lesley Manville) and their two children, in a two-storey flat on a South London housing estate. (The film was actually shot in Greenwich on an estate that was scheduled for demolition and therefore empty, enabling Leigh to create 'a particular kind of look which was very controllable'.[3] The two-level design of the flats equally allows scenes to be choreographed with an unexpected spatial range inside as well as out.) Phil and Penny have never married – because 'he never asked me', Penny tells her friends. Phil is something of an armchair philosopher, genuinely able, in his lugubrious way, to rationalise things and articulate a perspective no doubt informed by his observations of and occasional conversations with the colourful mixture of people he meets in his cab. However, his ability to apply his philosophising to everyday life is shaky at best. Early on he muses to Ron (Paul Jesson), a neighbour and fellow driver who has just had an accident: 'You might have driven round the next corner and killed a little kid. It's whatsit, isn't it? Fickle finger of fate'. But his later attempt to apply this barroom philosophy to his family situation at a time of crisis is exposed as inadequate by both its irrelevance and his malapropisms. 'Whatsname – fate accompli. He might win the lottery tomorrow', he says of his son, who has just been hospitalised after a heart attack.

It is hard not to feel a good deal of sympathy for Penny, who manages to bring in a more dependable regular income than Phil from her job in Safeway, and simultaneously to attend to all matters in the home. She is mostly tight-lipped, sad-eyed and nervy, although she has not yet quite forgotten how to enjoy herself: 'It's a nice evening tonight', she hints in one scene. 'Yeah', says Phil. Penny persists: 'I ain't been for a walk in ages' and asks their daughter, Rachel, 'You fancy going for a walk later on?' 'No, not really', replies Rachel. Phil offers to 'take you out for a drink if you like' but Penny now declines. As Phil is later seen scrabbling about the flat for small change and borrowing money to pay the rental on his cab radio, we can assume that she would have been paying for the drink anyway – but even so it is quite clear that this is not the reason she turns down the offer of a trip to the pub; she simply does not want to be in his company. 'Why don't you get up earlier in the mornings?' she says when he asks to borrow money from her. 'Drive people to work, take 'em to the airport?' 'Yeah, know what you mean', he replies, rather uselessly. Trying to rebuild some kind of rapport, he asks for a clue to the crossword in her magazine (and one cannot help wondering whether Leigh, as a great film buff, was mischievously recalling the scene in *Brief Encounter* where a wife helps a husband with his crossword in an almost unimaginably different domestic setting). When she reads a clue out, he suggests two different answers and then refuses to commit himself when she says that the prize money is £1,000. He asks her for another clue, but Penny puts the crossword aside and says that she wants to go to sleep. She is rather brusque about it, and we perhaps begin to suspect here that she is harmfully shutting Phil out of her life; but all in all it is little wonder that Penny has retreated into herself, into a resigned world-weariness. Thoroughly brought down by her daily grind and by Phil's inability to take action or manifest any gumption, she has all but lost the ability to laugh, to love or to respond to anyone around her other than with the tired tetchiness that has become her default setting.

Although Phil himself seems more like a rather helpless child than a partner, he and Penny actually have two children: Rachel (Alison Garland), the woman seen mopping at the start of the film, and her younger brother Rory (James Corden), who suffers the heart attack. Both are, like Phil, overweight, and both still live at home with their parents. Rachel is withdrawn, taciturn and unsmiling, and does not appear to have any kind of social life. Although she does her job capably, she is quietly beleaguered at work, surrounded by the vulnerable elderly, a stressed female colleague (Michele Austin) who works at a permanent run, and a late-middle-aged male cleaner called Sid (Sam Kelly), who insidiously harasses Rachel. At first his comments seem at worst thoughtlessly ambiguous, such as his advice that she gets an early night prior to their weekend's work, but his later talk of sleeping 'stark naked' because of the heat and invitation to visit his flat and 'sit on the bed, watch a video' are more disturbing. Rachel clearly does not like this, though she denies it when he asks her 'Have I said something?' and prefers to remain silent.

Rory is unemployed, aimless and full of pent-up aggression. From what we see and hear, he sleeps late most mornings, then spends his days kicking a football against a wall on the estate and his evenings slumped across the sofa watching television with no discernible enjoyment, only briefly and resentfully joining the rest of the family at the table for meals. We first see him as Penny arrives home from her working day at the supermarket; another local youth, Craig (Ben Crompton), tries to kick Rory's football and Rory angrily turns on him, swearing at him and violently pushing him to the ground. When Penny remonstrates with him, he is equally aggressive towards her, and indeed she is on the receiving end of most of his abuse throughout. 'Fuck's sake, I'll get a job when I want', he tells her later that evening, 'it ain't got nothing to with you!' He then tells her to 'fuck off', even though she has only just pleaded with him, 'Rory, will you stop swearing at me, please', and she looks to Phil for support. None is forthcoming; Phil just turns away and hangs up his coat. In a later scene, Rory finishes his meal with the comment 'That was shit', and responds to Penny's protestations with another tirade: 'I only said I didn't like my dinner! I can't do nothing round here without you having a go at me! You're doing my fucking head in – why don't you fuck off?!'; again Phil fails to come to the defence of the shaken Penny, merely telling her to 'take no notice'.

Domestic life is no more harmonious among the other families we get to know on the estate, especially as regards relations across the generations: the younger characters tell their parents and each other to 'fuck off' with alarming regularity and venom. Ron's daughter Samantha (Sally Hawkins) despairs of both her parents, but especially of her mother Carol (Marion Bailey), who sits around the house all day in a dressing gown and an alcoholic haze. Ron, though earning a living, has a fairly negligent approach to life and is a somewhat accident-prone driver. Very early on in the film, we see him picking up a passenger from a terraced house. With the instincts of a great silent comedy director (and indeed he describes the moment as 'a bit of slapstick'[4]), Leigh emphasises a concrete post on the pavement by holding it in the centre of the frame so that Ron, in mid-three-point-turn, reverses into it with a glorious inevitability. 'I don't fucking believe it!' he bellows, for all the world as though the post has crept up behind him. He promptly radios in to the firm's boss, Neville (Gary McDonald), with a fictitious story about 'some bitch in a Volvo' who 'smacked me up the arse' and then drove off before insurance details could be exchanged. Faced with these two as parents, Samantha amuses herself by leading on the shy and dishevelled-looking Craig, who haplessly follows her around, silently watching her.

Another neighbour is Maureen (Ruth Sheen), who works with Penny in the supermarket. From their first appearance together, at adjacent check-outs, Maureen is shown to be as chirpy as Penny is careworn. She does not actually say 'You've gotta laugh'; following the logic of Leigh's films, this is because she *does* laugh, never losing her sense of humour and defiantly joking even in the face of indifference from those around her. When she asks her daughter Donna (Helen Coker) where she's going and gets the defensive reply 'Out!', Maureen's response is, 'Oh, I've been there ... gets a bit packed though, don't it?' When Maureen herself has a well-earned evening out with Penny and Carol (she makes extra money by taking in ironing as well as working at the supermarket), she joins in the pub karaoke and is relaxed and cheerful on stage as she sings 'Don't It Make My Brown Eyes Blue'. A fine singer, she thoroughly enjoys her moment in the spotlight – although when Carol takes a drunken tumble after trying to grope a man at the bar, Maureen immediately realises what has happened and rushes to help.

Her resilience is sorely tested by Donna's relationship with a repellent youth called Jason (Daniel Mays). As Garry Watson aptly says, 'From the moment we first see him, Jason gives the impression that he is physically bursting at the seams, having difficulty restraining himself from hitting something'[5] – and he convincingly threatens to 'fucking slice' poor old Craig. Jason obviously thinks he is doing Donna a favour by driving 'all the way round here – nearly two miles' or by taking her to the pub, but when we first see them together in the film it soon emerges that she has not seen him for the last two weeks. Her attempts to contact him by text message have not gone down well: 'I'm out with the boys, right, you're showing me up, you're making a right mug of me'. When Donna then drops the bombshell that she is pregnant, he is at first incredulous, then furious but practically in tears as well; his mixture of violent aggression and pitiful immaturity is encapsulated in the way Daniel Mays's wide-eyed, slightly babyish face is made up with a long scar close to the eye. He accuses her of deliberately not taking her contraceptive pill 'just to fucking keep me', then practically orders her to have an abortion ('I'll give you a little bit of money and, you know, I'll come along to the place and sort it with you'). When she refuses, he tells her that he has been thinking of ending their relationship anyway, taunts her with a story of casual sex with 'the best little bit of pussy ever' on a lads' trip to Newcastle, and finally threatens her: 'You lumber me with a kid, you won't know what's hit you! I'll make your life shit!' 'You already do!' yells Donna, and we believe her. Any viewers who have seen *Naked* or *Career Girls* and think that the most unpleasant characters in Leigh's films invariably have flashy cars, well-cut suits and upper-class accents would do well to look as closely at Jason as they can bear to.

Their argument, during which Jason only just seems to stop short of a serious physical assault on Donna, occurs on the same night as Maureen's night out at the pub, Leigh at one point cutting with bleak irony from Jason's vile parting shot of 'I'll bury you, you cunt! Fucking mug!' to a karaoke rendition of 'Stand By Your Man'. By the next morning Donna has been to his house, threatening to tell his mother of the pregnancy, and has received a black eye in retribution. Back home, she nevertheless defends Jason to an angry Maureen and, as they argue, we learn that Maureen had also been a single mother; she admits that she knew Donna's father for 'about five minutes'. Maureen guesses that her daughter is pregnant, and that this is why Jason hit her. As she goes to make them a cup of tea, Donna sends a text message, and Jason duly turns up at the flat shortly afterwards. Maureen stands up to his customary invective ('Just keep out of it, right, cause it's got fuck-all to do with you!') with a spirited mixture of indomitability and righteous anger. She even manages a feisty comeback when Jason tells her that Donna is 'the worst fucking shag I've had in my life', replying, 'Yeah? She said the same about you'. Ordering him to stay away from the flat and from Donna, she forces him outside, from where he hurls further abuse and kicks the door savagely. 'Bloody hell, Donna', she says, a little breathlessly, 'you don't half pick 'em!'

In the first half of the film, Leigh establishes and delineates all these characters with great skill and orchestrates their various appearances to maximum effect. Between Maureen's discovery of Donna's black eye and Jason's arrival at the flat, for example, is intercut the scene in which Rory describes his Sunday lunch as 'shit' and then launches into Penny. The effect is both slightly to mitigate Rory's abuse, since his aggression seems motivated by pent-up frustration rather than Jason's knee-jerk verbal and physical violence, and to point up the underlying affection in the relationship between Maureen and Donna. When Rory tells Penny to 'fuck off', he is lashing out in genuine, if unfocused, rage, and she is plainly upset by it. By contrast, Donna's 'fuck off' after Maureen has told her 'I thought you had more sense' is pained and vulnerable, and Maureen is able to recognise this and respond with an affectionate insult and an expression of concern: 'Oh, don't get the hump, you silly cow! Does your face hurt?'[6]

Roughly half way through the film, however, the narrative begins to move its attention away from the wider group of characters and to focus in on Phil and Penny, both with their family and, even more crucially, as a couple. The crisis point comes when Rory collapses on the estate after lashing out at some youths who kick his ball about and taunt him. Fortunately, it is Maureen's day off and, when she sees him clutching his chest, she runs to help. Carol is also around, but is of little use, since she does not realise what is going on (she ludicrously asks Rory, 'Do you want to cry?'). Maureen sends her home to phone for an ambulance, but Samantha discovers Carol shortly afterwards, staring at the phone, numb with fear and drink. Rapidly taking control, Samantha calls the emergency services and then rings the supermarket where Penny works.

While all this is going on, Phil is having a long conversation with his latest passenger – indeed the only passenger we see him with for any appreciable length of time – a smartly dressed French woman called Cécile (Kathryn Hunter). She is an antique dealer and is on her way back to her hotel, carrying a large Chinese vase, prior to attending a performance of *Don Giovanni*. Phil's habitual reluctance to commit himself is seen again when she asks if they will complete the journey in time: 'It's unpredictable, isn't it? You should be all right'. Travelling through the Blackwall Tunnel, he reminisces about walking through it with a friend when he was a boy, and then asks her about the Channel Tunnel. Cécile, who does not like tunnels, changes the subject and asks him about his family. Phil tells her that he is proud of Rachel and the work she does, and that Rory merely 'does a lot of nothing' except eating. 'He is fat, like you?' asks Cécile bluntly, and Phil chuckles as he replies, 'He's a big boy, yeah'. Unfortunately, as the film cuts to and fro between their conversation and events back on the estate, we are becoming aware that Rory's unhealthy diet and lifestyle have now had grave consequences.

Cécile tells Phil about her estrangement from her own son, and her divorce from her husband, then asks him outright, 'Do you love your wife?' With real affection, he says that he does, but oddly continues by saying, 'Love ... It's like a dripping tap ... Bucket's either half-full ... or it's half-empty. If you're not together, you're alone. You're born alone, you die alone. Nothing you can do about it'. Some thought seems to have come to the forefront of his mind, nagging away at him from this point onward. After dropping Cécile off, he turns off his radio and mobile – at precisely the time Penny is trying to contact him to tell him about Rory – and after some thought he drives out to the coast. In contrast to the claustrophobic environments deliberately emphasised elsewhere in the film, he pulls up amid a wide expanse of open land, the foreground full of wild yellow grass. (Although the location is not named in the narrative, these scenes were shot in Dungeness, on the coast of Kent, close to Derek Jarman's former home.) He walks along a lonely pebble beach and then stands looking out to sea, still deep in thought. It seems almost possible that he is about to walk out into the water – to cleanse himself of some emotion or other, or to keep going and commit suicide? – but eventually he walks away.

Meanwhile Penny has, of course, been trying to contact Phil. Ron has driven her to the hospital where Rory has been taken – although she completes the journey on foot after he has another accident on the way, colliding with a reversing car while overtaking an ice cream van. Rachel has also arrived at the hospital, just in time to hear a trendy, well-meaning young doctor (Robert Wilfort) tell them that Rory has a heart condition that will require continuous medication, regular check-ups and a significant change in diet. Penny is still struggling to take all this in when she finally gets hold of Phil and alerts him to what has been happening. Looking more haunted than ever, he drives on towards the hospital.

At this point in the film, we get our final glimpses of the other characters; for the last half an hour or so of the running time, all the focus will be on Rory, Rachel and, especially, Phil and Penny. Maureen and Donna are in their living room, united and mutually supportive. (Jason has already disappeared from the narrative, last seen about to have sex with Samantha in his car, shortly after being thrown out of Donna's life by Maureen.) Donna becomes anxious at the sound of a baby crying in an adjacent flat, and Maureen sits beside her, embracing and reassuring her. 'We'll be all right', she says, before being struck by a sudden thought: 'Here, what if it's a boy?'

We then cut to Carol and Ron, who are locked in a drunken embrace in their bedroom; Carol is as sozzled and incapable as ever, and Ron is moaning about his latest crash but putting off ringing the police, preferring instead to blame the world for his woes. Despairing of them both, Samantha walks out into the night, where she is confronted by Craig, who shows her that he has carved her initial into his chest. Shocked and tearful, she asks him why he has done such a thing, and he says that he loves her. Even more confused and agitated now, she tells him that she does not love him back and advises him to go to hospital, then strokes his hair and hugs him before running off in tears. Craig, smiling broadly at being hugged and at her concern over what he has done to himself, watches her go. We then see a brief shot of Samantha, back home in bed, sobbing. Leigh admits to a bit of 'cheating' in that these scenes, in particular the ones involving Carol, Ron, Samantha and Craig, look logically as though they take place much later at night than what follows; but in dramatic terms he was keen to bring the other characters' stories to a conclusion and then stay with Phil, Penny, Rachel and Rory until the end of the film.[7]

From the moment Phil arrives at the hospital, Penny is impatient and irritable with him. She interrupts him when he attempts to explain how he got lost on his way to the intensive care unit – 'Yeah, all right, Phil – you're here now, ain't you?' – and angrily asks him why he has had his radio and mobile turned off, telling him, 'It's pathetic!' Phil is thoroughly cowed by this, and sits sheepishly silent until Rory, emerging from his sleep, intervenes: 'Leave it out, Mum. Stop having a go at him'. Penny is shocked by this, and incredulous a few moments later when Phil asks Rory, 'Do you want to go on holiday? ... Disneyworld?' When they and Rachel finally have to leave the hospital, Phil puts his arm around Penny as they walk off down the corridor but, after a few moments, she shrugs him off and they drive home in silence.

When they get back to the flat, the three of them sit with drinks: Phil with a can of beer, Penny with a cup of tea, Rachel with hot chocolate.

Phil offers to run Penny up to the hospital first thing in the morning, and tells her his resolve to work longer hours so that he can fulfil his promise to take Rory on holiday. This is too much for Penny, and she turns on him, pouring scorn on the idea: 'Phil, it ain't about going on holiday. It's about getting by, week in, week out. It ain't a game'. Shrill and embittered, she berates him for suddenly getting 'a bee in your bonnet about getting up in the mornings and going to work', pointing out that she and Rachel have been managing to do this for some considerable time. She may have a point, but her throwaway 'You make me sick' and her suggestion that his family are to blame for Rory's heart condition ('All on your side, ain't it? Ain't none on mine') seem unduly harsh. She launches into another attack on him for making himself unavailable; he says that he turned off his radio and mobile because 'I'd had enough'. 'What can I switch off when I've had enough?' she asks. 'Had enough of getting up every morning, going to work, doing the shopping, coming home, cooking the tea, cleaning the house, doing the ironing, making sure everyone's got clean clothes on their back?' It is not an unreasonable question, but the sheer onslaught of her outburst, born of long-suppressed frustration, brings to the boil emotions that have been simmering away within Phil all afternoon. 'You don't love me no more, do you?' he says, and when she asks, 'What's that got to do with anything?' he replies with tears in his eyes that 'it's got to do with everything ... You ain't loved me for years. You don't like me, you don't respect me, you talk to me like I'm a piece of shit'. Penny, herself tearful now, denies this, but Phil's emotions are pouring out of him uncontrollably: 'I know I'm a disappointment to you – I know I get on your nerves. It's like ... like something's died ... if you don't want me, we ain't got nothing. We ain't a family. And that's it'.

He is sobbing now, and Penny goes to get him a tissue from her bag in the hall. To her surprise, Rachel, who had left the room during her earlier tirade, is sitting listening on the stairs. She runs to her room, and Penny follows her to see what is wrong. 'You do talk to him like that', Rachel tells her. 'Sometimes'. Stunned, but clearly disposed to believe Rachel's judgement (and perhaps remembering Rory's earlier admonishment from his hospital bed to 'stop having a go' at Phil), Penny kisses Rachel and goes back downstairs, deep in thought. She must face up to the fact that she has her share of blame in the breakdown of their relationship, contributing to its downward spiral. Phil's inertia may be exasperating, but by constantly shutting him up and putting him down, pushing him away and closing him out of her life, she has only made things worse. Moreover, he is a sensitive and fundamentally kind man, who may well feel every bit as defeated by life as she does, and she – and we – can see how crushed he is when he thinks that she no longer loves him.

The rest of the scene consists of a long two-shot, lasting around five minutes, in which Phil and Penny both admit that they feel lonely, hold hands and finally embrace tearfully. It is a superb scene, tenderly realised by all concerned: subtly directed by Leigh, with the camera moving gradually in to end on a tight close-up of the two characters, and exquisitely played by Spall and Manville. Indeed, it is all the more impressive given that, as Leigh points out, the two actors were surrounded by members of the crew busily moving boom mikes and the like, and facilitating the forward progress of the camera by removing items that had previously been in shot.[8] In a way, it is a pity that the publicity for the film in its various guises – lobby poster, screenplay, DVD – all focused exclusively on the instantly recognisable and much loved face of Timothy Spall, since no film that I can think of has depended more, especially in that final scene, on the rapport and chemistry between its two leading actors. (Ruth Sheen's superbly warm and endearing portrayal of Maureen nevertheless runs them a close third.)

Towards the end of the scene, revealingly, Penny says, 'You used to make me laugh', and Phil blows out his cheeks and allows her to push the air out, making a kind of raspberry noise. This trivial, silly action carries significant dramatic weight; only minutes ago, Penny was telling Phil that 'It's about getting by, week in, week out. It ain't a game'. Now she seems to remember that laughter and a spirit of play may be vital to 'getting by', and this moment of shared laughter is therefore a healing one. The only smile we have previously seen on Penny's face is a tiny, fleeting and slightly envious one during Maureen's karaoke performance in the pub; now we sense that she and Phil are rediscovering not only how to communicate but also how to laugh, and that the sharing of positive, joyful emotion will help to see them through their crisis and keep them together. 'Do you want to go to bed?' asks Phil. 'Yeah', she replies. 'Busy day tomorrow'. The suggestion of going to bed together does not necessarily carry a sexual connotation here – although there is certainly the suggestion that a restored sex life is one of the possibilities now open to them as they rediscover the pleasure of each other's company – but, given Phil's previous tendency to stay up late and sleep in, simply the fact of their going upstairs at the same time speaks volumes about the emotional renewal they have begun. (This is especially true in the context of Leigh's work, where healthy relationships are repeatedly denoted by scenes in which couples cuddle up in bed together.)

The scene concludes with the film's only fade to black, and the screen is blank for just a few seconds longer than we might expect – giving us some precious moments' breathing space after the catharsis of what we have just witnessed, and also subtly signifying that the coda to follow takes place a few days later, in contrast to the preceding narrative, which has unfolded over consecutive days. The notion of laughter as a manifestation of the human spirit that will bond and heal the family, and help them to survive, is reinforced as Phil, Penny and Rachel visit Rory in a spacious, sunny hospital ward. Penny is smiling now, albeit a little nervously, and is wearing lipstick; Phil, for the first time in the film, has shaved and washed his hair. When Rory tells them that he has eaten some fish in sauce, rather than in batter, Phil teases him: 'What, tie you down, did they?' He then makes Rory laugh with the story of an elderly Greek lady breaking wind in the back of his cab earlier that morning. Rory wheezes with laughter, rather to Penny's alarm, but she is still smiling. This is the first time we have seen the family laughing together and Rory, like Penny in the previous scene, is smiling for the first time in the entire film; like the humourless Frank in *Meantime*, we have previously seen him watching television in the flat, sitting frowning and unamused while gales of laughter come from the unseen programme's studio audience.

And yet, this being a Mike Leigh film, one would not expect the conclusion to be an artificial, feel-good assertion that things have magically changed and all will now be well. At the very end, after the last fully audible line of dialogue, the screenplay tells us that Penny 'has all sorts of thoughts and feelings and emotions. And she reflects on her lot'.[9] The moment is caught by Lesley Manville with beautiful sensitivity, and makes a subtle but significant impact, especially as we have been painfully aware that, as Leigh puts it, 'The big question mark that hangs over this scene is – Yes, but what about Rachel?'[10]

For Rachel is still withdrawn and troubled, remaining largely silent and smiling only momentarily. We learn that she is not sleeping, and has not been back to work. Almost the last lines in the film are Penny's 'You all right, Rach?' and her unconvincing reply, 'Yeah'. This is a near repetition of their first exchange; when Penny arrived home from work she asked Rachel, 'All right?' and on that occasion, too, Rachel's reply, 'Yeah, I'm all right', was mechanical and resigned, her expression betraying an inner sadness. Throughout the film, we never learn quite what is depressing her, although the stresses of her workplace, not least with Sid and his increasingly unsubtle innuendo, and of the fractious family who surround her at home, are clearly contributing factors. There is more than a hint that she is being neglected, that Penny's nagging of Rory is just one aspect of a long-standing tendency to pay him the most attention and to mother him; she rather ridiculously says of him, 'This is my little baby boy' and 'He's only little', as he lies in the intensive care unit. One could hardly call her blind to Rory's faults, but she is unaware that he smokes, for example, and it is left to Rachel to tell the doctor that 'he does, a bit'.

Although the narrative is dominated by the relationship between Phil and Penny, Rachel's role is scarcely less crucial, and the film does not forget her even in the extremely hectic section where Phil is driving to the coast, Rory being rushed to intensive care and Penny dashing out of work to get to him. In the middle of all this activity, there is a shot of Rachel walking by the Thames, with the Millennium Dome in the background. The shot goes unexplained – we never find out if this is the way that Rachel walks home, whether she is already heading for the hospital, or whether, like her father, she too has had a sudden urge to walk alone by water. Although Leigh's DVD commentary quite properly does not attempt to pin down its meaning, it is clearly a significant moment for him, and he makes a point of drawing attention to Alison Garland's 'sensitive, heartfelt' performance and Andrew Dickson's 'beautiful' music.[11]

Of course, the leaving of questions, of untied loose ends at the end of a film, is characteristic of Leigh's work. Human emotions and experiences are too complex to fit easily into neat and tidy narratives or orderly conventions of 'realist' drama. We are often reminded by Leigh's films that the story he is telling us is just one of many possible stories, all equally valid, and that his characters all have their own lives to be lived – and nowhere is this seen more clearly than in *All or Nothing*. It is right that our thoughts should be predominantly with Rachel at the end, but what of the other characters we have met? What will happen to Maureen and Donna? To Ron and Carol – or Samantha? To old Sid, with his loneliness and his bitter memories ('I was married once ... Four months. Bitch')? Or to poor, lovelorn, self-mutilated Craig? When Phil arrives home near the beginning of the film and enters the multi-storey block where he and Penny live, the camera tilts up the outside of the building. It is not just an efficient visual means of tracing Phil's journey and re-orientating us spatially; it also suggests that similar stories are happening in each of these homes. Lives are going on, and will continue to go on after the credits have rolled.

Leigh's collaborative methods naturally work to enrich this aspect of his films, the months of preparatory work with the actors creating precisely these sorts of rounded characters, all with credible histories ('back-stories', to use the industry jargon). He once reflected: 'Some [actors] I've met, when they're drunk in a pub, say things like, "Oh, it's all a load of method crap, Mike – just *do it*! What is the point of all that fucking information, if it's not in the film!" But of course it's in the film! ... It's not mentioned, *but it's there*!'[12] One might add that on the occasions when it *is* mentioned, as with Jason's lurid account of his sexual escapade in Newcastle, the details are that much more convincing, more right for the character. Much, however, remains unstated: Lesley Manville, for example, gave one interviewer a clear and detailed history of Penny, who had been an only child, lonely but not unhappy, played in a girls' football team and supported Arsenal; yet the only hint of this in the film is 'an Arsenal mug, fleetingly glimpsed in the kitchen'.[13] The creative process also enhances the supporting characters: the narrative *function* of the young doctor at the hospital is to explain to the family and to us the exact nature of Rory's heart condition, but as a *character*, rather like Lesley Manville's social worker in *Secrets and Lies*, he is recognisable as a professional doing his fallible best to deal on human terms with an institutional situation.

The care taken even with the conception and realisation of the supporting characters is another consequence of Leigh's humanism in action: 'The core of it is, for me, everybody is interesting'.[14] Sometimes the extensive groundwork leads to actors and scenes becoming casualties of the cutting room: in *Secrets and Lies*, for instance, the wedding sequence at the start was originally much longer, Maurice was seen working frantically throughout, and then later 'you finally see him asleep at the table in an Italian restaurant with Monica'.[15] And in *All or Nothing*, we were to have seen more of Carol drunkenly chatting up and groping two men at the bar during Maureen's karaoke performance, but this too was cut – which is why Mark Benton can just about be glimpsed as one of the men in question, his appearance in the film reduced from a cameo to a barely visible non-speaking role. Leigh always regrets this when it happens, but rightly sees it as an unfortunate part of the process of film-making – and perhaps, one could argue, particularly of his type of film-making, where even minor characters are developed with a concern for the all-important quality of truth. 'It doesn't happen very often, but that did happen', he says of the *Secrets and Lies* sequence, 'because it's all fascinating, basically. And I think it's important that whether a character is the main character or appears only for a split second, that you have to have the sense, as in real life, that each person, like you and me, is the centre of his or her universe and is completely not simply fulfilling a supernumerary role'.[16]

This truthful approach to characterisation goes hand in hand with Leigh's construction of dialogue. I have remarked earlier how his films eschew the pat, over-written conversation that bedevils so much 'realist' drama on film and television, and in *All or Nothing* there is a particularly joyous example, bringing the accurate representation of inarticulate everyday speech to something like its apotheosis. An extremely drunk passenger in the back of Phil's cab sits muttering, half to himself, half to Phil:

> Oh ... fuck it. I mean, what – it's er, all the stuff that ... I mean, it all – you know, like – it was supposed to ... and he was gonna bring round the ... just fucking, just kept thinking ... too much, you know. I mean, I don't know how it, you know – you seem like a nice bloke. And, erm ... oh, fucking wanker, you know? Fucking ... what can you ... ? Are we, um ... ? Round there, they used to, er ... someone ... see that door there? It used to open, inwards.

In fact, this is an extremely rare example in Leigh's work of a genuinely unscripted scene; knowing actor Allan Williams's ability to produce this kind of stream-of-consciousness (although Williams himself does not drink), Leigh was very happy to let him go for it and was delighted with the result.

All or Nothing received its premiere in competition at the 2002 Cannes Film Festival and, as noted in the introduction to this book, British reporters and critics alike were cheered by its enthusiastic reception. Writing in *The Guardian* on 20 May, Peter Bradshaw judged it the 'best film in competition so far',[17] while Nigel Reynolds reported for the *Daily Telegraph* that 'British flags were flying high in the south of France yesterday' and that *All or Nothing* had become 'a front-runner for the festival's Palme d'Or'.[18] In the event, the film failed to emulate the success of *Secrets and Lies*, and the top award went to Roman Polanski's semi-autobiographical *The Pianist*.

Subsequent reviews were, on the whole, cautiously favourable, while understandably finding the film a somewhat gruelling experience and, as Xan Brooks described it in *Sight and Sound*, 'surely the director's bleakest film since *Naked*'.[19] Anthony Quinn agreed in *The Independent*: recalling Woody Allen's division of life into 'the horrible and the miserable' in *Annie Hall* (1977), he summed up *All or Nothing* as 'the horrible, as experienced by the miserable'.[20] In the *Daily Telegraph*, Tim Robey, whose review I quoted in the introduction, found Leigh's new film 'almost heroically bleak even for him', but thought that 'by the end of *All or Nothing* Leigh has managed to pull us out of this total downer. It could hardly be described as a feel-good flick, but it's a feel-less-bad one: it gives its characters some measure of hope, and half mends what's most broken in their lives'.[21] Peter Bradshaw, in the *Guardian* review quoted above, took a similar tack, making the familiar criticisms that *All or Nothing*'s milieu was 'slightly caricatured' and the film as a whole 'vulnerable to charges of condescension and sentimentality', while still calling it 'a beautifully acted, meticulously controlled ensemble piece' and praising the 'outstanding confrontation scene' between Phil and Penny.[22] In those last two reviews, mostly favourable though a little ambivalent, both Robey and Bradshaw call attention to the redemptive nature of the ending, and therefore of the film, even while finding much of what leads up to that point a little hard to take. Even an appreciative Philip French remarked in *The Observer* that Leigh's previous film had been unusual in that it was an experience akin to actually meeting Gilbert and Sullivan: 'Few people would care to spend time with the characters in Leigh's other movies, and certainly not the three working-class London families in his excellent new picture, *All or Nothing*'.[23]

Since the success of *Secrets and Lies*, all of Leigh's films had opened in the UK in multiplex cinemas, as opposed to the independent subsidised sector (or 'the plush velvet enclaves of arthouses', as one *Guardian* reporter fatuously put it[24]). *All or Nothing* was guaranteed the same treatment when it became the first film to be picked up for UK distribution by UGC Films, who would consequently screen it in their chain of multiplexes. On stage at the National Film Theatre, Leigh told Derek Malcolm how pleased he was about this: 'The idea that a film like this, or any film I have ever made, should be dumped in what are regarded as arthouse cinemas isn't on'.[25] His enthusiasm for this exposure was tempered by disappointment 'that a younger audience won't be able to see it' because of its '18' certificate, awarded by the British Board of Film Classification due to the use of the most taboo of swear words. 'I realise that nobody under eighteen has ever heard the word "cunt"', he commented wryly.[26] (He also managed a sideswipe at multiplexes, 'where the film will only be shown as an accompaniment to the main activity of eating popcorn'.[27]) In the event, the film was not a big commercial success; as Leigh observes, it may have been shown in multiplexes, but most audiences were more interested in whatever Hollywood blockbuster was playing in the adjacent screen – 'people simply walked past it and went into the other picture'.[28]

Nevertheless, *All or Nothing* stands as yet another major work, showing Leigh continuing to develop his narrative and directorial skill and control. It is, as he says, a film 'about great feelings and great passions in ordinary lives';[29] a film in which happiness is to be found in the most unexpected moments, like the old lady trundling cheerfully out of the care centre and along the street on her motorised tricycle. It is also a film shot through with intimations of mortality, starting with the elderly man whom Phil takes to a cemetery in his cab. As the man walks through the cemetery to put flowers on one of the graves, Phil watches him, looking haunted. Later, hearing about his family, Cécile tells him,

'You're a very lucky man', to which his reply is, 'We're all going to die one day'. It is shortly after this that he tells her, 'You're born alone, you die alone'. As noted above, Rory is at that very moment suffering a heart attack, bringing the family face to face with the threat of mortality. For Rachel, by contrast, dealing with death on a daily basis in the care home can be rationalised as 'we've just got to clear out their rooms' – reflecting how her job and her life allow her precious little time to express her own feelings.

Above all, the film proved to be Leigh's most resonant assertion yet that human emotions and experiences are too intricate to be expressed through traditionally constructed dialogue and narratives; that real lives are too messy, too complicated to be squeezed into conventional dramatic parameters. The fact that it made this emphatic assertion precisely by means of a meticulously constructed narrative, involving characters who so clearly reflect the tragedies and triumphs of everyday life, testified to a writer and director at something like the height of his powers.

Notes

1 Mike Leigh, *All or Nothing* (London, Faber & Faber, 2002), p. 3
2 Director's commentary, *All or Nothing* DVD (UGC Films/Momentum Pictures, 2003, MP2450)
3 *Ibid.*
4 *Ibid.*
5 Garry Watson, *The Cinema of Mike Leigh: A Sense of the Real* (London, Wallflower Press, 2004), p. 171
6 Garry Watson discusses the use of language, and particularly violent language, in this film in greater detail in *The Cinema of Mike Leigh*, pp. 170–5
7 Director's commentary, *All or Nothing* DVD
8 *Ibid.*
9 Mike Leigh, *All or Nothing*, p. 152
10 Director's commentary, *All or Nothing* DVD
11 *Ibid.*
12 Quoted in John Hind, *The Comic Inquisition: Conversations with Great Comedians* (London, Virgin Books, 1991), p. 81
13 Mick Brown, 'Life Is Bittersweet', *Telegraph Magazine*, 12 October 2002, p. 40
14 Interview with the author, 5 April 2005
15 *Ibid.*
16 *Ibid.*
17 Peter Bradshaw, *The Guardian*, 20 May 2002
18 Nigel Reynolds, *Daily Telegraph*, 18 May 2002
19 Xan Brooks, *Sight and Sound*, 12: 11 (November 2002), p. 38
20 Anthony Quinn, *The Independent*, 18 October 2002
21 Tim Robey, *Daily Telegraph*, 18 October 2002
22 Peter Bradshaw, *The Guardian*, 20 May 2002
23 Philip French, *The Observer*, 20 October 2002

24 Angelique Chrisafis, 'Leigh Grateful as New Film Leaves Art House Ghetto', *The Guardian*, 16 August 2002
25 Interview at the National Film Theatre, 7 October 2002
26 *Ibid.*
27 *Ibid.*
28 Interview with the author, 5 April 2002
29 Director's commentary, *All or Nothing* DVD

'Out of the kindness of her heart': *Vera Drake*

11

Leigh's second cinematic venture into period drama was in a sense closer to home than *Topsy-Turvy*, being set within living memory for a substantial proportion of a 2004 audience; and dealing with a subject about which it is virtually impossible to remain neutral. In its way, it was clearly as personal a project as the earlier film, too: its dedication reads, 'In loving memory of my parents, a doctor and a midwife'.

The setting is London in 1950, when the Second World War still resonated in people's memories, and the continuing privations of the post-war period created a black market for commodities of all kinds. It is against this background that Vera Drake (Imelda Staunton) goes cheerfully on her way, cleaning for the upper classes, looking after her family, friends and neighbours – and helping young women to end unwanted pregnancies. The opening scenes show Vera cheery, chatty and with a permanent smile on her face as she bustles round the neighbourhood, helping people out. She visits a sick man in an adjacent tenement block, and makes him a cup of tea, something she is prone to do for anyone at the drop of a hat. On her way home she meets another neighbour, a young man named Reg (Eddie Marsan) and, on learning that he is planning to have 'a bit of bread and dripping' for his evening meal, she invites him round for supper the following night. She sings happily to herself as she arrives home, puts the kettle on and prepares the evening meal for her family.

The family – her husband Stan (Phil Davis) and their grown-up children Sid (Daniel Mays) and Ethel (Alex Kelly) – are cheerful and considerate as they return home from work and assemble around the dinner table. They ask each other how their day has been, chat, laugh and tease one another good-naturedly. Their life is clearly modest – they live in a small but well-kept tenement flat – but they are a happy and cohesive unit. The movement of the narrative will be the opposite of that in Leigh's last film. In *All or Nothing* a fractured, dysfunctional family was brought to crisis point and by the end the characters were *perhaps* (although we couldn't be sure) beginning to learn how to love and support each other. In *Vera Drake*, an already happy, mutually supportive family group will reach a different kind of crisis point, and the family unit we see at the beginning of the film will have been irrevocably changed and *perhaps* (although we can't be sure) left on the verge of disintegration.

The recreation of the 1950s goes way beyond just the period detail, although that is as meticulous as one would expect. The whole post-war setting is vital. Memories of the war and its shared experiences hang over all the characters; as Vera says, 'we all had it bad', and in discussing the hardships and the friends and colleagues they lost, the overwhelming feeling is one of gratitude for having survived it and for what they now have. But whereas Sid and his mates jokingly barter cigarettes and nylons in the pub, for Vera's friend Lily (Ruth Sheen), abortion is just one more commodity to be traded in this difficult environment, along with her black market sugar, sardines and boiled sweets.

It is Lily who puts Vera in touch with her clients, and from her first appearance in the film, complaining about the stairs as she arrives at Vera's flat, it is clear that she is a sour, hard-hearted woman – she could scarcely be more different from Sheen's last role for Leigh, as one of the few warm and cheerful souls in *All or Nothing* – and is certainly not motivated by compassion or fellow-feeling. 'Poor woman', says Vera as she learns that her next client already has seven children and cannot support any more. 'Serves her right', replies Lily. Later, we see her with another client (Rosie Cavaliero), and Lily is unsympathetic and abrasive, demanding immediate payment ('Well, I don't want paying next week, do I?') and snapping, 'Mind your own bleeding business' when the woman enquires how long Lily has been arranging abortions in this way. One thing becomes clear from this conversation: Vera does not realise that Lily is accepting money for arranging her services, and Lily carefully instructs her client to conceal the fact ('That's between me and you'). This woman's husband is away in Korea, and the baby she is expecting is the result of an affair; when Vera hears this she does not approve, but reasons, 'Still, got to help 'em out, haven't you?'

And that is Vera's rationale for doing what she does. While performing the terminations – an operation that involves filling the womb with soapy water and disinfectant via a rubber syringe – she is chatty, smiling, matter of fact and, above all, compassionate. She does not question the morality of what she does, but simply regards it as something that needs to be done. Abortion is available more or less on demand for the wealthy; as we will see, the procedure may be coldly commercial, controlled by men and calculatedly duplicitous, but it exists nonetheless. The less well off have no such recourse, and without Vera and others like her – even given all the health risks that such illicit practices entail – they would have nowhere to turn. Leigh 'thought it important to contrast these two cultures, given that anybody could accidentally fall pregnant, irrespective of class',[1] and the period setting is thus used to mobilise a tremendous anger, which underpins the narrative and the characters throughout the entire film.

A scene of Vera and Stan snuggling up in bed together establishes, in the Leigh tradition, their togetherness as a happy couple (perhaps all the more important to them, since we learn from a later bedtime conversation that Vera never knew who her father was and Stan's mother died when he was young), and also incidentally reinforces the companionship they are both tragically to lose. From this we cut to Susan Wells (Sally Hawkins), the daughter of one of the upper-class families that Vera cleans for, being seduced by David (Sam Troughton), a well-dressed, well-spoken young man who has taken her out for the evening. The scene is typical of Leigh, with David deliberately wrong-footing Susan by making jokes that she cannot be expected to understand: 'I do apologise ... I haven't got a gramophone', he says while trying to force her to dance, and laughs, a little manically; 'That's not funny', she replies uncomprehendingly, and he mocks this response before forcing her down onto the bed.

Susan becomes pregnant as a result of the rape, and seeks advice from an older friend (Fenella Woolgar). 'I have this ... friend, who ... she needs some help', she begins, and then starts to cry. Her confidante is not fooled for a moment – 'You've got yourself into trouble, haven't you?' – but she knows exactly what course of action to take, including advising Susan to 'make up a fearful fib about some potty aunt or other'. This refers to the legal loophole whereby 'a termination could be allowed if it could be demonstrated that the woman was in physical danger because of her psychological state'.[2] As Leigh points out, 'of course, a working-class girl wouldn't know that, and wouldn't have access to such an expensive and discreet system'.[3] For someone of Susan's background, the available procedures are smooth and well organised, although commercially driven and male-dominated: in another telling cut, the scene in which Susan first visits a private doctor (Nicky Henson) is immediately preceded by one in which a sick mother whose employers make no allowance for illness complains that 'They don't understand nothing, men. Bastards'. The doctor wastes little time before raising 'the delicate matter of money' and stipulating one hundred guineas 'in advance, in cash'; and the psychiatrist (Allan Corduner) whom she must subsequently visit is, while compassionate, thoroughly complicit in the pretence that her abortion is for the good of her mental stability; as advised, Susan invents a fictitious aunt as evidence of a family history of suicide.

From the obviously scared Susan in her well-appointed room at the clinic, with its open fire, we cut to an even more terrified Jamaican girl (Vinette Robinson), another of Vera's clients, in a sparsely furnished, rundown flat. It even appears that the bowl Vera has used as a container for her soapy water and disinfectant doubles as the chamber pot – our first reminder that the methods she uses, with the best will in the world, may frequently, subject to the vagaries of the various environments she operates in, be medically unsafe; something that Susan, no matter how scared she may be, need at least not worry about. Having gone through the usual procedures, Vera reassures the girl as best she can, and heads for the kitchen: 'What you need now is a nice hot cup of tea'. Again we are likely to smile at the cliché, since Vera's tea-making has already been established as something like a reflex action. A split second later, however, Leigh and Staunton turn the moment on a sixpence, as Vera glances back at the frightened girl with a heart-stabbing look of concern, compassion and pain. (She later recounts the girl's fear to Lily; 'What're they doing over here anyway?' grumbles Lily. 'They should stay where they are'.)

It is a stroke of bad luck and an unguarded moment that lead to Vera's arrest. She is performing an abortion on a girl named Pamela Barnes (Liz White); 'I know your face from somewhere', she says to Pamela's mother Jessie (Lesley Sharp), who is present, and Jessie recognises her as a pre-war colleague from the Sunlight Laundry, even remembering her name. It is this that will be Vera's downfall, making it possible for the police to trace her when this particular termination goes badly wrong.

Following this scene, shots of Vera contentedly stitching and drinking tea at home, and having a drink in the pub with Stan, are intercut with scenes of Pamela becoming gravely ill. When she is taken to hospital, her examination by a surgeon named Walsh (Anthony O'Donnell) confirms to us that what Vera is doing is not medically safe. 'Mrs Barnes, these people must be stopped', Walsh tells Jessie. He may well be right. But, even at this stage, we cannot honestly judge Vera as morally wrong. We have already seen that the procedures available to the wealthy and privileged are not open to the less well off; as Reg says later, after Vera's secret has been revealed, 'It's all right if you're rich, but if you can't feed 'em, you can't love 'em, can you?'

Reg and Ethel have by this time become engaged, much to the family's delight. Stan invites his younger brother Frank (Adrian Scarborough) and his wife Joyce (Heather Craney) round for Sunday tea to celebrate, and when they arrive they announce some good news of their own: Joyce is expecting a baby. 'This is a double celebration, ain't it?' exclaims Stan, unaware that the family's world is about to come crashing down around them.

The crucial sequence in which their Sunday tea is interrupted by the police arriving at the flat to arrest Vera is a good example of how Leigh's work evolves through improvisation in rehearsal. Imelda Staunton had no idea that actors playing policemen were going to turn up, the other members of her 'family' were not aware of her secret; and the 'police' themselves did not know that they would be interrupting a family celebration. Staunton has recalled her reaction when Phil Davis announced, 'It's the police': 'I got a pain in my chest, I thought I was going to have a heart attack ... we didn't film that until eight weeks later, but of course you had all that to draw on when you came to do it'.[4] She spoke to Leigh about how she had felt during the rehearsal, and 'he let that happen on screen';[5] her dominant memory was of not hearing what was going on around her due to the shock, and Leigh accurately reproduces the effect by cutting to a shot that holds Vera in the front of the frame, with other members of the family visible behind her. Her face immediately freezes, her smile vanishing and her eyes suddenly seeming not to see what is around her, alone with her thoughts and her fears.

From this moment in the film, Vera changes. Her contented smile never returns, and nor does her tendency to sing to herself; and in contrast to her previous bustling about, she becomes gradually more and more immobile. When she does move, she is stooped and shuffling, as though she were a much older woman. The day of her arrest is clearly one that she has always half-dreaded; the subsequent crumbling of her indefatigable chirpiness is truly tragic to behold, and Staunton makes her descent into tearful, anguished semi-articulacy painfully moving.

The chief investigating officer is Detective Inspector Webster (Peter Wight), who takes Vera away from the rest of her family, into her bedroom. 'I know why you're here', she says, and when pressed tells them that 'I help young girls out'. Webster puts it to her that she performs abortions. 'That's not what I do', she insists. 'That's what you call it – but they need help. Who else are they going to turn to?' She admits to 'helping' Pamela Barnes, and is horrified when Webster tells her that 'she nearly died'. It is at this point that he formally arrests her. They ask to see the equipment that she uses, and at this moment of truth, as Vera moves to retrieve her cloth bag from its hiding place in a cupboard above the wardrobe, we see her reflected in the bedroom dressing-table mirror. It is a cinematic convention that a mirror symbolises a secret identity or alter ego, and here, for a moment, we see four Veras – the real one and three reflections – hinting that there are at least that many ways of seeing and responding to her. She is the selfless neighbour and devoted family woman; the performer of a social service not available elsewhere to the girls she 'helps'; the misguided backstreet abortionist who conscientiously takes every precaution but does not seem to acknowledge that her procedures may still be fatally unsafe; the unworldly innocent who is being unwittingly exploited by a woman she regards as a friend. The story's social context is evoked in fastidious detail and with a piercing clarity, yet passing definitive moral judgement on Vera herself is virtually impossible.

Her acceptance of her arrest and imprisonment seems as much to do with her instinctive capitulation to the forces of social authority as with an awareness that what she has done is 'wrong' in anything other than the legal sense. She is, in her way, defiant (because she cannot accept that she was committing any moral crime), without actually seeming at all resilient or in any way fighting back. As Peter Bradshaw puts it, 'she is as hapless and hopeless as her victim-patients, with no way of defending or explaining herself. Her only response is mutely to absorb unimaginable quantities of shame'.[6]

Taken to the police station, Vera is treated compassionately but firmly. There is some exquisite acting involved here, even by the standards of a film in which every performance looks little short of faultless. WPC Best (Helen Coker), who is sympathetic but must follow procedures and take away Vera's stockings and even her wedding ring, is a character conceived and played with subtle excellence. Peter Wight likewise turns in a meticulous performance as Webster, perfectly blending compassion and world-weariness. Some fine touches are easy to miss: for example, later in the film, when Webster takes the oath before giving evidence in court, Wight manages to suggest a man who has said these words a hundred times before but still believes that they – and the truth – matter. At the station, he attempts to interrogate Vera, who is too distressed to respond, and his impatience shows. He asks her how long she has been performing terminations. 'I don't know, dear ... a long time', she says, unable to concentrate or to speak coherently. He asks her, 'How did you start ... did it happen to you when you were a girl?' – and she simply breaks down, sobbing uncontrollably. They continue to question her as gently as is possible, and she says that, as far as she knows, no other girls she has attended to have ever become ill or died, and that she always uses a rubber syringe, never metal objects in performing the abortions; 'I wouldn't do that', she insists. She is even more shocked at the suggestion that she receives payment for her services: 'I don't take money ... they need help'. Told that Lily does take payment from her clients, she cries out 'No!' partly in distress, partly in denial of such an unpalatable revelation.

Webster considerately brings through Stan, who has been waiting outside, so that Vera can tell him herself why she has been arrested and charged. (We never hear exactly what she says, as she is only capable of speaking to him in a whisper.) However, she must stay in a cell overnight, until bail can be requested for her release. As she is locked away, the heart-breaking sadness of the moment is reinforced when she is offered a cup of tea, and refuses. The inversion of what previously has been an amusing detail – her constant tea-making – speaks unexpected volumes about the disintegration of her life. As Ryan Gilbey says in his *Sight and Sound* review: 'The mention of a hot beverage has never sounded so cruel as when it is made by a WPC unaware that she has assumed Vera's defining function as bluntly as she has confiscated her wedding ring'.[7]

Back home, Stan breaks the news to the rest of the family that Vera has been detained overnight, although at this stage he does not tell anyone except Frank the reason. They are all worried and alarmed by the news – with the exception of Joyce, who has merely been irritated that the arrest has delayed her and Frank's departure; 'Thank God for that', she says, as Stan returns from the police station to find the rest of the family worried sick and her merely impatient to leave.

Throughout the film, Joyce is presented fairly unsympathetically. She is obviously very pleased to be living in a smart semi-detached house, and is glad they moved 'out here', a car ride away from the kind of tenement block where Vera and Stan live. She is anxious to kit the house out with whatever post-war luxury items come onto the market; when she first tells Frank that she is pregnant, she immediately follows it up by asking, 'Can I have my washing machine now, please?' She is also keen to move to somewhere larger, although Frank does not agree, since their present house is big enough, and in any case they have only been there a year. Her aspirations are slightly less superficial, however, than Beverly's in *Abigail's Party* or Valerie's in *High Hopes*, and up to a point we can sympathise with her over the friction caused by Frank's deep loyalty to Stan. When Frank insists on spending Christmas Day with Stan and Vera, she says a little tearfully, 'We ain't never going to have a Christmas by ourselves – just you and me', and we realise that her life has been dominated by Frank's attachment to his family. Yet we discover early on in the narrative that Stan's mother died when he was twelve, and that he went out to work whereas Frank, who is several years younger, went into an orphanage; we can understand why they are still extremely protective of each other. Stan and Vera looked after Frank when he was younger – 'paid for my apprenticeship ... all their savings' – and we sense a certain self-consciousness on the part of both brothers that Stan, the elder of the two, should now be working for Frank: he tells Reg that 'I work for him', then, in a moment of small pride, corrects this to '... with him'.

In any case, Joyce's attitude to Frank's family is generally patronising and selfish. Early in the film she says of Vera: 'She's a little busybody, bless her. She's going to get herself in trouble one of these days'. Of course, she is right about Vera in a way she cannot know at this stage – and as for being 'a little busybody', we might have noted Vera's urging Ethel to sit next to Reg when he comes round for his evening meal, and wondered if her invitation to him was entirely altruistic after all. However, we are never in any doubt that Vera's sympathy and concern for others, while shot through with a few human foibles, is preferable by far to Joyce's self-centred materialism. Again it is ironic, in view of her own self-centredness, that when Joyce does find out what Vera has been arrested for her judgement is a typically harsh one: 'stupid cow – how can she be so selfish?'

The other hostile reaction, when it is discovered that Vera has been performing illegal abortions, comes from Sid, who cannot cope with the revelations and insists that 'she's let us down'. As in *All or Nothing*, the characterisation is wonderfully reinforced by Daniel Mays's boyish face, and in particular his wide, expressive eyes. Sid is an outwardly confident young man, enjoying what opportunities he can in his post-war urban life, professionally and socially. We see him smoothly dispensing the patter of his trade – he works as an apprentice tailor – and taking the lead in chatting up girls with his friends at a dance hall. Yet beneath all this is the vulnerability of the boy who was thirteen when his father went off to war, telling Sid that he must now be 'the man of the house', and was forced to grow up – or rather to go through the motions of growing up – too soon.

Stan, equally well portrayed by Phil Davis as a stoic, decent and fair-minded man, is more compassionate. He does not agree with what Vera has been doing, and 'would've put a stop to it', but he knows that she did it 'out of the kindness of her heart'. Whereas Sid feels betrayed, Stan, while angry, makes the distinction that 'she never told us, but she never lied'. He insists that Sid must forgive Vera: 'God knows she's going to get punished enough for what she's done. We can't let her down'.

Vera is released on bail and the date of her trial is settled for January. She is therefore at home for Christmas, but the traditional family get-together at their flat is inevitably a subdued and tense affair – not least because of Joyce, who is only there at all under sufferance, perched on the edge of the sofa and scarcely making eye contact with anybody. Any sympathy we previously had for her evaporates as we see how she fails to recognise that Frank's loyalty and support have never been more necessary than now; and her not wanting to go was finally motivated more by knee-jerk moralism than any wish to spend Christmas alone with Frank. Amid the generally strained atmosphere, Reg, who has until now seemed little more than a shy, awkward loner, suddenly emerges as the film's most endearing character. We have previously been inclined to laugh at Reg, and at his slightly bumbling courtship of the equally shy Ethel. The claim that they 'become engaged without apparently exchanging a whole sentence with one another'[8] is a slight exaggeration, but it is certainly comical to see the pair of them walking in the park without holding hands, talking to, or even looking at, each other. That quaint old phrase 'walking out together' has never seemed more appropriate.

So when Reg, on that painful Christmas Day, says, 'This is the best Christmas I've had in a long time', our immediate instinct is to laugh at the incongruity, not to mention at the implication of what his other, lonely Christmases must have been like. But as he goes on, 'Thank you very much, Vera – smashing', we are caught off-guard. Our somewhat uncharitable impulse to find him funny is blown away by the simple decency and fellow-feeling of his attempt to show his appreciation as a guest *and* to offer some small solace to poor, doomed Vera. We recall that it was also Reg who was sensitive enough to realise and articulate the social imbalance that anchors the whole film with his reflection that 'It's all right if you're rich, but if you can't feed 'em, you can't love 'em, can you?' Eddie Marsan's finely judged performance did not go unrecognised: he deservedly won a Best Supporting Actor award in the British Independent Film Awards.

At Vera's trial, her barrister makes the plea that she accepted no money for her services and, having been so distressed by Pamela's near-fatal reaction, is extremely unlikely ever to re-offend. Nevertheless, the judge (Jim Broadbent) reminds her that she could well be facing the charge of murder 'but for the timely intervention of the medical profession', and concludes that 'the extreme seriousness of your crime is bound to be reflected in the sentence that I am about to pass, and that must serve as a deterrent to others'. Vera is sentenced to two and a half years in prison. Her family are naturally shattered, and we are reminded of the effect of her incarceration on the extended family when Stan visits Vera's elderly, sick mother (Sandra Voe) to tell her that Vera will not be able to come round and see her for a while.

Our last sight of Vera is in prison, talking to two other inmates (Angela Curran and Jane Wood), both abortionists who got longer sentences because their clients died. They try to reassure her, telling her, 'Cheer up, you'll only do half' and 'You'll be out before you know it' – but the realities of prison life are reinforced moments later when a prison guard tells Vera, 'Mind where you're going, Drake' as they pass on the stairs. As Ryan Gilbey noted in his review, the moment brings to a harsh conclusion the gradual stripping away of her previous identity that began in the police cell: 'Leigh gives the movie her name, but in the final line of dialogue, which hurts like a stubbed toe, a prison warden reduces her to "Drake"'.[9]

There is one final shot. Stan, Sid, Ethel and Reg sit around the dinner table over which Vera used to preside so cheerfully. In total contrast to the chatty familial banter that previously rang out, they sit silent and despairing. We remain on them for nearly half a minute, then there is a slow fade to black. The effect is devastating, both in itself and in the context of Leigh's work as a whole. We have become accustomed to his films ending on a bittersweet or quietly optimistic note. We are used to unanswered questions, but rarely such a stark one as 'What on earth are any of the characters going to do? How will they ever cope?' For most of Leigh's protagonists, a crisis that changes their lives irrevocably would look like an artificial dramatic conceit, a contrivance. In Vera's case the crisis is both profound and inevitable, and it is its inevitability that makes it so tragic.

Few viewers would deny that the overwhelming sense of tragedy derives to a considerable degree from Imelda Staunton's superlative performance as Vera. Leigh had never worked with Staunton before, but had met her and seen her work, and 'I just had an instinct, along with my long-time casting director Nina Gold, that this was the right actress for this part – and we were very, very right'.[10] Although a well-known face from films like *Peter's Friends* (Kenneth Branagh, 1992), *Sense and Sensibility* (Ang Lee, 1995) and *Shakespeare in Love* (John Madden, 1998), Staunton has the quality shared by all the best character actors, and especially those exposed to the merciless scrutiny of the film camera. She makes one forget all her previous appearances and seems to *inhabit* the role of Vera; as Phil Davis says of her, 'you don't see the wheels turning round'.[11] This is all the more impressive in a part which is required to be the physical and spiritual centre of a film, and a highly complex one at that. At times we admire Vera, at times we worry about her, at times we may disapprove of her, and Staunton never loses us, even, as noted above, appearing to change physically as the narrative enters its final phase following the arrest. She spends so much of the last hour of the film either fighting back or succumbing to anguished tears that it becomes hard to watch without one's face hurting in sympathy.

Staunton has said that she 'never in a million years' thought that she would work with Leigh: 'I've met him over the years and I've thought, oh, I don't think I'm his type ... I'm not in that league'.[12] When he approached her, she recalls that 'all I was told by Mike was, "I am setting a film in the 50s concerning abortion". He said, "You would be very heavily involved. Is this something you can handle?"'[13] She discussed the prospect with her husband, actor Jim Carter: 'Jim said, "Oh no, I am going to have some mad woman coming home each night." But he said, "You have to do it." I did not have any second thoughts either'.[14] Once the film had been completed, Staunton looked back on the experience of working with Leigh as 'the best job of my life. It's rather like falling out of an aeroplane with no parachute. But he's right there next to you ... he always has the big picture in his mind'.[15]

Many of the other actors were familiar faces in Leigh's films: Phil Davis, Peter Wight and Ruth Sheen could by now be regarded as part of his repertory company; the talented young actors Daniel Mays, Sally Hawkins and Helen Coker all returned from *All or Nothing*, as did Alex Kelly and Heather Craney, who had turned up among Timothy Spall's passengers in that film. So had Martin Savage, who previously excelled as George Grossmith in *Topsy-Turvy* and appears here as one of the arresting officers; another member of Leigh's Savoy troupe, Allan Corduner, also makes a brief but effective appearance as a psychiatrist. Among the cameos, Marion Bailey, Anthony O'Donnell, Paul Jesson, Tilly Vosburgh, Emma Amos, Elizabeth Berrington and Wendy Nottingham can all be spotted, and the stature and presence of Jim Broadbent reinforces the authority of the judge who sentences Vera. (As an indication of the dedicated research to which Leigh's actors willingly submit themselves, Broadbent spent three days visiting courtrooms and speaking with a judge, all for less than ten minutes of screen time). As Mrs Wells, Lesley Manville breezes in for a handful of lines, walks off with two of the biggest laughs in a film which is quite properly sparing with its humour, and deftly sketches in a portrait of monstrous upper-class heartlessness and indifference – to her own daughter as much as to domestic staff like Vera. When Susan returns from the nursing home, Mrs Wells is completely unaware of where her daughter has been – she can hardly be bothered even to reflect on her own weekend in Norfolk: 'Bearable. Terribly sunny. Extraordinary'. There were trusted colleagues behind the camera, too, including cinematographer Dick Pope, designers Eve Stewart and Christine Blundell, and composer Andrew Dickson.

As with *Topsy-Turvy*, the possibility of a large number of exterior scenes was ruled out by what Leigh calls 'a ridiculously tight budget'.[16] Fortunately he and his team, as they had for *All or Nothing*, found themselves a shooting environment that was both suitable and controllable: 'At first we had some flats lined up in Grays Inn Road but there was trouble with squatters so we moved to Stepney. A lot of the film was shot in a decommissioned hospital in Crouch End: we used it as a rehearsal space for six months, then for the hospital scenes, and then shot other scenes in the outbuildings'.[17] And as the budget would not stretch to the royalties for authentic songs of the 1940s on the soundtrack, Leigh had to ask Imelda Staunton to sing or hum instead – but to make sure that it was nothing recognisable.

Of the end result, Leigh has said: 'I hope I've made a film which is not crassly polemic or didactic and black and white; I made a film which invites people to take part in the debate'.[18] He does not see *Vera Drake* as being a radical departure from the treatment of ordinary lives that is his customary raw material – 'Most of my films have dealt with the whole issue of parents and children – having children, not having them, wanting them, not wanting them'[19] – but felt that, even more than usual, it was important for audiences to leave the film thinking about the issues raised rather than having been given an overt message: 'In this particular case the job was to confront the audience with a moral dilemma. People have to make their own decisions about how they see it. But having said that, it's also implicit in the film that backstreet abortionists cannot be a good thing'.[20]

By setting his story in 1950, Leigh highlights this moral choice at its starkest; as Robert Murphy has said, 'The peak for illegal abortions in Britain was probably between 1945, when the end of wartime conditions brought a reassertion of traditional social values, and 1960, when the moral climate began to change and contraception became more easily available'.[21] He also goes against the dramatic cliché of the backstreet abortionist who, in Imelda Staunton's words, is 'single, no children, pretty evil, in a basement, pretty grim'; as Staunton points out, 85 per cent of abortionists held in Holloway Prison in the 1940s and 1950s were themselves mothers and grandmothers.[22]

Leigh admits that 'I would have loved to have talked to my father about the sort of dilemmas the film broaches. Given that he had a one-man, working-class practice in Salford in the period that the film is set, he would undoubtedly have had to face the dilemma of unwanted pregnancies, the aftermath of abortions. I happen to doubt that he ever performed one'.[23] Abe Leigh did tell him that he had on occasions administered lethal injections of morphine to sick elderly patients who wished to end their lives. 'He put people out of their misery. Absolutely, but it was not a moral dilemma to him. He saw it as something that was positive, that had to be done, that was merciful. In that way, he was not unlike Vera'.[24]

Not surprisingly, the subject matter dictates a less overtly comic style than we have come to expect from Leigh. Yet the importance of a sense of humour remains central to the main characters. Their mutual teasing as they gather round the table for their evening meal tells us a great deal about their security in each other's company and their solidarity as a family unit. Edward Lawrenson found that in these moments 'the rhythms of family life are so well captured that we almost feel like intruders, and indeed DoP Dick Pope's camera hangs back, observing things from behind a door frame';[25] Leigh himself comments: 'If you're familiar with my films, you'll see I like the discipline of this kind of set-up, I love looking through doorways, that kind of thing'.[26] As that final shot of the characters silent around the same table emphasises, our sense of their loss is all the more tragic as a consequence of seeing their family routines so lovingly captured, just as with Vera and Stan's contentedness as they huddle together for warmth in bed.

Reg's integration into the family is also characterised by a certain amount of good-natured ribbing. During one of his visits, his growing acceptance by them is indicated by Ethel's offer to patch a hole in his trousers and Sid's teasing him: 'I'll get you a bit of cloth from the shop ... it'll cost you – half a crown'. Reg smiles happily, secure in the knowledge that the joking is part of the assimilation. That said, occasionally they do also laugh at him behind his back: in one scene Vera, Stan and Sid consider the possibility of his taking Ethel to a dance hall. 'Can't see Reg dancing', says Stan, and the three of them laugh at the very idea, as well as at Sid's suggestion that 'they might turn out to be a proper Fred and Ginger'.

Sometimes, however, the joke is on us rather than the characters. I have already noted a couple of instances of Leigh's ability to make us laugh one moment, then whip the rug out from under us: Reg's heartfelt words to Vera on Christmas Day, or Vera's advice to the Jamaican girl about needing a nice cup of tea. Vera's propensity for making tea at every opportunity is also well used the very first time we see Vera carrying out her abortion procedures. We have just witnessed a comical sex scene, in which Joyce, anxious to become pregnant, has to force a tired and reluctant Frank to climb on top of her. Leigh catches us unawares by immediately showing the darker side of sex and pregnancy, cutting to Vera's visit to a nervous and slightly tearful girl (Sinead Matthews). 'The first thing we've got to do is put the kettle on', she tells the girl, and we laugh or smile in anticipation of yet another cup of tea. Yet the smile is inclined to freeze on our faces with the realisation that the kettle is boiling this time for a very different reason; and the serious ramifications are brought home to us forcefully as Vera leaves, and the girl's husband or boyfriend, waiting ominously outside, tries unsuccessfully to get inside before the door is slammed. Leigh is able to manipulate our reactions back and forth between the richly comic and the deadly serious, although he admits he cannot always forecast what audiences will find funny: 'In the earlier part of the film people laugh uproariously at moments I don't think are particularly funny. But overall such a film must be open to different interpretations, short of anybody totally misreading it and thinking it's concerned with Egyptology or something similar'.[27] He also acknowledges that 'people laugh for a variety of reasons – with, or at, or out of embarrassment, or nervousness even. It's not always a function of mirth'.[28]

To widespread surprise throughout the film industry, *Vera Drake* was rejected by the organisers of the Cannes Film Festival, but promptly accepted instead by the Venice Festival, where it was screened in competition four months after Cannes, winning the Golden Lion as best film and the Volpi Cup for Imelda Staunton as best actress. Accepting his award, Leigh mischievously thanked 'most sincerely the Cannes Film Festival for rejecting this film'. As Peter Bradshaw remarked in his *Guardian* profile: 'That was Leigh all over. At the very summit of his success with his greatest masterpiece and a modern classic of British cinema, he was triumphant, gloomy, witty and curmudgeonly enough even to risk exasperating the Venetians with a joke reminding them they had been second choice'.[29]

Reviewing the film, Bradshaw found it 'as gripping and fascinating as the best thriller, as well as being a stunningly acted and heartwrenchingly moving drama' in which Staunton gave 'one of the most moving, haunting performances I have ever seen in the cinema'.[30] By contrast, in the *Daily Telegraph*, the less enthusiastic Sukhdev Sandhu raised what for some of us would have been a rather alarming prospect: 'Staunton is very good ... But I would have preferred Emily Watson to play her role, and possibly Lars Von Trier to direct the film, too'.[31] More positive comments came from two long-standing supporters of Leigh: Philip French thought the film 'outstanding' and 'provocative without presenting itself as a conventional problem play',[32] and Roger Ebert praised the 'pitch-perfect, seemingly effortless performances'.[33] In the *Village Voice*, J. Hoberman paid the film a tremendous compliment by saying that Vera's 'anguished solitude as she is judged by a world of powerful men in uniforms and wigs cannot help but invoke the passion of Carl Theodor Dreyer's Joan'.[34]

In *The Independent*, Anthony Quinn was impressed by the film's 'wonderfully tender portrait of proletarian togetherness' and thought that the performances of Staunton and Davis caught 'something quite elegiac about the virtues of charity and mercy'.[35] Recognising the centrality of these virtues, Quinn makes a point that others, including Sandhu, miss in their eagerness to find 'class caricatures' in the film: that wealthy characters like Mrs Wells or the young seducer David are indeed treated with scorn, but then so are Joyce's lower-middle-class aspirations and Lily's mercenary lack of compassion: 'In Leigh's vision, class allows no one to escape the freaks' roll-call'.[36] It is true that we see rather less of the upper-class characters than we do of Joyce or Lily, with the result that they are more like thumbnail sketches than fully fledged character portrayals. But what all these characters have in common is that for them money and material possessions take priority over care and concern for others, a fault which transcends class barriers, and for which the film will not forgive them. The upper-class character of whom we see most is, of course, Susan, who *is* portrayed sympathetically; she is, after all, a victim in the sense that her age and gender deny her – for the moment – the power that usually goes with wealth and privilege. One wonders whether her experiences at the private clinic will make her more compassionate to others in a similar plight, or whether she will simply end up like her mother. After Vera's arrest, some of her former employers provide written testament of her good character as an employee, while declining to appear as character witnesses; Mrs Wells, her solicitor reports sadly, 'has not even had the decency to respond to my second letter'.

Apart from minor complaints about caricatured upper-class characters *Vera Drake* opened to largely excellent reviews – indeed, it is hard not to conclude that the absence on the whole of stylised characterisation and broad comedy was one of the things that many critics most approved of; even the highly enthusiastic Peter Bradshaw noted that Leigh's 'trade-mark cartoony exaggerations of dialogue and characterisation are toned down almost to zero'.[37] The film was also widely seen in the UK, in both multiplexes and independent cinemas; Leigh puts this box-office success down to the nature of the subject matter, in the sense that 'My most successful film commercially was *Secrets and Lies*, and there's no doubt that was to do with the subject matter – adoption – which has an obvious hook. *All or Nothing* hasn't got a hook: it's about love and redemption, which are not as palpable as adoption or ... abortion'.[38] The awards at Venice were followed by many more: among others, British Independent Film Awards in six categories, London Critics Circle Film Awards in five, and further Best Actress awards for Imelda Staunton from the film critics associations in Chicago, Los Angeles, New York, San Diego, Toronto and Vancouver, as well as the American Film Critics Society, the *Evening Standard* and the European Film Awards. For Leigh, perhaps, the sweetest victory may have come courtesy of BAFTA, who at long last saw fit to name him as the year's best director. (*Vera Drake* was nominated for eleven BAFTAs in all, and won two others, one for Jacqueline Durran's costume design and the other – once again – for Staunton.)

So with great critical acclaim, good distribution and audience reaction, *and* awards at home and abroad, *Vera Drake* could fairly be described not only as a major work, dealing humanely and powerfully with a difficult and highly inflammatory issue, but also as, in Peter Bradshaw's words, a breakthrough with which Leigh 'shows every sign of entering a glorious late period of artistry and power'.[39] The recognition was deserved, almost certainly hoped for, though perhaps, after so many years, not really expected. Anyone who saw the television presentation of that year's BAFTAs will remember Leigh's genuine, open-mouthed astonishment when his name was announced. It was an endearing moment, as well as a heartening one. After all, a little incredulity could on such an occasion be allowed the man who had only recently insisted that he felt lucky purely because 'I get to make films without even showing a script. To be honest, the fact that I'm allowed to do what I do in the way that I do it never ceases to amaze me'.[40]

Notes

1 'Vera Drake', *The Movie Magazine: The Magazine of StudioCanal* (May 2004), p. 69
2 *Ibid.*
3 *Ibid.*
4 Cast and crew documentary, *Vera Drake* DVD (Momentum Pictures, MP399D, 2005)
5 *Ibid.*
6 Peter Bradshaw, *The Guardian*, 7 January 2005
7 Ryan Gilbey, *Sight and Sound*, 15: 1 (January 2005), p. 72
8 Anthony Quinn, *The Independent*, 7 January 2005
9 Ryan Gilbey, *Sight and Sound*, p. 72
10 Cast and crew documentary, *Vera Drake* DVD
11 *Ibid.*
12 Quoted in Emma Brockes, *The Guardian*, 8 October 2004
13 Quoted in Seamus Ryan, 'Fame at Last', *Saga Magazine* (January 2005), p. 112
14 *Ibid.*
15 Quoted in Peter Bradshaw, '*The Guardian* Profile: Mike Leigh', *The Guardian*, 7 January 2005
16 Quoted in Edward Lawrenson, 'Backstreet Revisited', *Sight and Sound*, 15: 1 (January 2005), p. 12

17 *Ibid.*
18 Cast and crew documentary, *Vera Drake* DVD
19 Quoted in 'Vera Drake', *The Movie Magazine: The Magazine of StudioCanal*, p. 67
20 Quoted in Edward Lawrenson, 'Backstreet Revisited', p. 15
21 Robert Murphy, 'Crime and Passion', *Sight and Sound*, 15: 1 (January 2005), p. 16
22 Cast and crew documentary, *Vera Drake* DVD
23 Quoted in Sean O'Hagan, 'I'm Allowed to Do What I Want – That Amazes Me', *The Observer*, 5 December 2004
24 *Ibid.*
25 Quoted in Edward Lawrenson, 'Backstreet Revisited', p. 12
26 *Ibid.*
27 *Ibid.*, p.15
28 Quoted in Sean O'Hagan, 'I'm Allowed to Do What I Want – That Amazes Me'
29 Peter Bradshaw, '*The Guardian* Profile: Mike Leigh'
30 Peter Bradshaw, *The Guardian*, 7 January 2005
31 Sukhdev Sandhu, *Daily Telegraph*, 7 January 2005
32 Philip French, *The Observer*, 9 January 2005
33 Roger Ebert, *Chicago Sun-Times*, 22 October 2004
34 J. Hoberman, *Village Voice*, 4 October 2004
35 Anthony Quinn, *The Independent*, 7 January 2005
36 *Ibid.*
37 Peter Bradshaw, '*The Guardian* Profile: Mike Leigh'
38 Quoted in Edward Lawrenson, 'Backstreet Revisited', p. 15
39 Peter Bradshaw, *The Guardian*, 7 January 2005
40 Quoted in Sean O'Hagan, 'I'm Allowed to Do What I Want – That Amazes Me'

Conclusion
'The journey continues'

This book leaves Leigh on something like the crest of a wave. The success of *Vera Drake* was almost immediately followed up by a triumphant return to the theatre, a medium in which he had not worked since 1993's *It's a Great Big Shame!* Still, even after an absence of twelve years, it is hard to imagine him refusing an invitation from the Royal National Theatre – although it had taken him a few years to find the time, Nicholas Hytner having asked him every year since taking over as the National's artistic director in 2001. Hytner gave him carte blanche to follow his usual working methods through a six-month rehearsal period, with the unusual result that until a matter of days before it opened, the piece could only be advertised as a 'New Play by Mike Leigh', since he was still evolving it with his chosen cast. Not that this lack of information seemed to worry anyone, since *Two Thousand Years*, as it was eventually titled, was sold out for its entire run – some 16,000 advance tickets – over two weeks before the opening night. In the event, previews were delayed by a couple of days while Leigh and his actors continued to get the play – which dealt with some highly topical issues – the way they wanted it, but if anyone expected a critical mauling as a result, they would have been disappointed, since the reaction was overwhelmingly positive. Suddenly, it seemed, Leigh's unique method of organically developing new work was not only accepted as a given, but regarded as both appealing and highly effective.

This recent flurry of acclaim makes it easier to summarise his achievements to date than to predict what he will get up to in the future. We can say with certainty that he will continue to aspire to the all-important quality of truth; as he told *The South Bank Show* at the time of *All or Nothing*'s release: 'All any of us who make things want to do is to try and get better ... the journey continues'. (He did qualify this, reasonably enough, by adding that 'I think retrospectively there's nothing particularly wrong with any of the previous pieces of work'.)[1] He will, of course, continue to work in his own unique way, developing characters and narratives through the processes of improvisation in preparation and rehearsal that have left actors exhausted and exhilarated for over thirty years. Through these methods, he has led his various collaborators in creating a body of work that is both utterly distinctive and impressive by any standards.

Leigh's many fans cherish his matchless ability to perceive life's funny side at one and the same time as its tragedies. To treat his protagonists as human beings, and therefore as both flawed *and* admirable. To deal with big themes through recognisable characters rather than self-conscious spokespersons. To acknowledge that life is too messy, too complex to fit comfortably within conventional parameters of narrative art. He has created films that can stand comparison with some of the great cinematic works he most admires – such as Ozu's *Tokyo Story* (1953) or Olmi's *The Tree of Wooden Clogs* (1978) – in avoiding dramatic contrivance and instead appearing simply to drop in on ordinary people and then move on, leaving them continuing to live their lives.

While pursuing his own career uncompromisingly, he has helped the progress of a number of others. Liz Smith, who came to prominence in *Bleak Moments* and *Hard Labour* and is now a much loved veteran in the tradition of Irene Handl or Thora Hird, says: 'I owe everything to Mike. I could still be behind a counter in Dickens and Jones on a zimmer frame had he not plucked me from that slavery'.[2] More recently, director Greg Hall, who was twenty-three at the time, had cause to be grateful when Leigh's championing of his low-budget film *The Plague* (2004) led to its inclusion in the London Film Festival and a subsequent limited run in independent cinemas.

A British institution? Perish the thought. A talent to be prized; most certainly. And, best of all, still a fully paid-up member of the awkward squad who, just when we think we've got him sussed, remains capable of totally surprising us with whatever project he chooses to work on next.

Notes

1 *The South Bank Show*, first broadcast ITV1, 13 October 2002

2 Quoted in 'The Amazing Miss Smith, Revelling in the Despair of Beckett', *Daily Telegraph*, 6 March 2004

Filmography

All the features and shorts listed here were directed by Mike Leigh and, unless otherwise indicated, written by him. He is credited with the 'scenario' as well as direction on *Bleak Moments*; his on-screen credit reads 'devised and directed' on the films made for television, and 'written and directed' on *The Short and Curlies* and all subsequent features.

Bleak Moments, 1971, 111 mins, col.

Production company: Autumn Productions/Memorial Enterprises/BFI Production Board
Producer: Leslie Blair
Photography: Bahram Manoochehri
Editing: Leslie Blair
Art direction: Richard Rambaut
Sound recordist: Bob Withey
Cast: Anne Raitt (Sylvia), Eric Allan (Peter), Sarah Stephenson (Hilda), Joolia Cappleman (Pat), Mike Bradwell (Norman), Liz Smith (Pat's Mother), Malcolm Smith, Donald Sumpter (Norman's Friends), Christopher Martin (Sylvia's Boss), Linda Beckett, Sandra Bolton, Stephen Churchett (Remedial Trainees), Una Brandon-Jones (Supervisor), Ronald Eng (Waiter), Reginald Stewart (Man in Restaurant), Susan Glanville (Enthusiastic Teacher), Joanna Dickens (Stout Teacher), Christopher Leaver (Wine Merchant) and Peter Chandler, Brian Chenley, Ina Clough, Pat Ferrand, Sandra Jewell, Lin Layram, Ruth Lesirge, David Marigold, Marion Turner, Ken Wheatcroft and P. A. Rowley

Hard Labour, 1973, 75 mins, col.

Production company: BBC TV
Producer: Tony Garnett
Photography: Tony Pierce-Roberts

Editing: Christopher Rowlands
Designer: Paul Munting
Costumes: Sally Nieper
Sound: Dick Manton
Cast: Liz Smith (Mrs Thornley), Clifford Kershaw (Jim Thornley), Polly Hemingway (Ann), Bernard Hill (Edward), Alison Steadman (Veronica), Vanessa Harris (Mrs Stone), Cyril Varley (Mr Stone), Linda Beckett (Julie), Ben Kingsley (Naseem), Alan Erasmus (Barry), Rowena Parr (June), June Whitaker (Mrs Rigby), Paula Tilbrook (Mrs Thornley's Friend), Keith Washington (Mr Shaw), Louis Raynes (Tallyman), Alan Gerrard (Greengrocer), Diana Flacks (Mrs Rubens), Patrick Durkin (Frank), Ian East (Dick), Dennis Barry (Old Man), Sonny Farrar (Publican), Surya Kumari (Sikh Lady), Irene Gawne (Sister), Hal Jeayes (Priest)

The Five-Minute Films, 1975 (broadcast 1982), 5 x 5 mins, col.

Production company: BBC TV
Producer: Tony Garnett
Photography: Brian Tufano
Editing: Chris Lovett
Sound recordist: Andrew Boulton

The Birth of the 2001 F.A. Cup Final Goalie
Cast: Richard Ireson (Father), Celia Quicke (Mother)

Old Chums
Cast: Tim Stern (Brian), Robert Putt (Terry)

Probation
Cast: Herbert Norville (Arbley), Billy Colvill (Sid), Anthony Carrick (Mr Davies), Theresa Watson (Secretary), Lally Percy (Victoria)

A Light Snack
Cast: Margaret Heery (Mrs White), Richard Griffiths (Window Cleaner), Alan Gaunt (Talker), David Casey (Listener)

Afternoon
Cast: Rachel Davies (Hostess), Pauline Moran (Teacher), Julie North (Newly Wed)

The Permissive Society, 1975, 30 mins, col.

Production company: BBC TV
Producer: Tara Prem
Designer: Margaret Peacock
Cast: Bob Mason (Les), Veronica Roberts (Carol), Rachel Davies (Yvonne)

Knock for Knock, 1976, 30 mins, col.

Production company: BBC TV
Producer: Tara Prem
Designer: Myles Lang
Cast: Sam Kelly (Mr Bowes), Anthony O'Donnell (Mr Purvis), Meryl Hampton (Marilyn)

Nuts in May, 1976, 80 mins, col.

Production company: BBC TV
Producer: David Rose
Photography: Michael Williams
Editing: Oliver White
Designer: David Crozier
Costumes: Gini Hardy
Sound recordist: John Gilbert
Cast: Roger Sloman (Keith), Alison Steadman (Candice-Marie), Anthony O'Donnell (Ray), Sheila Kelley (Honky), Stephen Bill (Finger), Richenda Carey (Miss Beale), Eric Allan (Quarryman), Matthew Guinness (Farmer), Sally Watts (Farm-girl), Richard Ireson (Policeman)

The Kiss of Death, 1977, 80 mins, col.

Production company: BBC TV
Producer: David Rose
Photography: Michael Williams, John Kenway
Editing: Oliver White
Designer: David Crozier
Music: Carl Davis
Costumes: Al Barnett
Sound recordist: John Gilbert
Cast: David Threlfall (Trevor), John Wheatley (Ronnie), Kay Adshead (Linda), Angela Curran (Sandra), Clifford Kershaw (Mr Garside), Pamela Austin (Trevor's Mum), Philip Ryland (Froggy), Frank McDermott (Mr Bodger), Christine Moore (Mrs Bodger), Karen Petrie (Policewoman), Brian Pollitt (Doctor), Eileen Denison (Mrs Ball), Marlene Sidaway (Christine), Elizabeth Hauck (Shoeshop Customer), Elizabeth Ann Ogden (Bridesmaid)

***Abigail's Party*, 1977, 104 mins, col.**

Production company: BBC TV
Producer: Margaret Matheson
Editing: Ron Bowman
Designer: Kenneth Sharp
Sound recordist: Derek Miller-Timmins
Cast: Alison Steadman (Beverly), Tim Stern (Laurence), Janine Duvitski (Angela), John Salthouse (Tony), Harriet Reynolds (Susan)

***Who's Who*, 1979, 80 mins, col.**

Production company: BBC TV
Producer: Margaret Matheson
Photography: John Else
Editing: Chris Lovett
Designer: Austen Spriggs
Costumes: Robin Stubbs
Sound recordist: John Pritchard
Cast: Richard Kane (Alan), Joolia Cappleman (April), Philip Davis (Kevin), Adam Norton (Giles), Simon Chandler (Nigel), Graham Seed (Anthony), Catherine Hall (Samantha), Felicity Dean (Caroline), Jeffrey Wickham (Francis), Souad Faress (Samya), David Neville (Lord Crouchurst), Richenda Carey (Lady Crouchurst), Lavinia Bertram (Nanny), Francesca Martin (Selina), Geraldine James (Miss Hunt), Sam Kelly (Mr Shakespeare), Angela Curran, Roger Hammond (Couple in Window)

***Grown-Ups*, 1980, 90 mins, col.**

Production company: BBC TV
Producer: Louis Marks
Photography: Remi Adefarasin
Editing: Robin Sales
Designer: Bryan Ellis
Costumes: Christian Dyall
Sound recordist: John Pritchard
Cast: Philip Davis (Dick), Lesley Manville (Mandy), Brenda Blethyn (Gloria), Janine Duvitski (Sharon), Lindsay Duncan (Christine), Sam Kelly (Ralph)

***Home Sweet Home*, 1982, 90 mins, col.**

Production company: BBC TV
Producer: Louis Marks
Photography: Remi Adefarasin

Editing: Robin Sales
Designer: Bryan Ellis
Music: Carl Davis
Costumes: Michael Burdle
Sound recordist: John Pritchard
Cast: Eric Richard (Stan), Lorraine Brunning (Tina), Kay Stonham (Hazel), Timothy Spall (Gordon), Su Elliott (June), Tim Barker (Harold), Frances Barber (Melody), Lloyd Peters (Dave), Sheila Kelley (Janice), Heidi Laratta (Kelly), Paul Jesson (Man in Dressing Gown)

Meantime, 1983, 90 mins, col.

Production company: Central Television/Mostpoint Ltd
Producer: Graham Benson
Photography: Roger Pratt
Editing: Lesley Walker
Designer: Diana Charnley
Music: Andrew Dickson
Costumes: Lindy Hemming
Sound recordist: Malcolm Hirst
Cast: Marion Bailey (Barbara), Phil Daniels (Mark), Tim Roth (Colin), Pam Ferris (Mavis), Jeff Robert (Frank), Alfred Molina (John), Gary Oldman (Coxy), Tilly Vosburgh (Hayley), Paul Daley (Rusty), Leila Bertrand (Hayley's Friend), Hepburn Graham (Boyfriend), Peter Wight (Estate Manager), Eileen Davies (Unemployment Benefit Clerk), Herbert Norville (Man in Pub), Brian Hoskin (Barman)

Four Days in July, 1985, 96 mins, col.

Production company: BBC TV
Producer: Kenith Trodd
Photography: Remi Adefarasin
Editing: Robin Sales
Designer: Jim Clay
Music: Rachel Portman
Costumes: Maggie Donnelly
Sound recordist: John Pritchard
Cast: Bríd Brennan (Collette), Des McAleer (Eugene), Paula Hamilton (Lorraine), Charles Lawson (Billy), Brian Hogg (Big Billy), Adrian Gordon (Little Billy), Shane Connaughton (Brendan), Eileen Pollock (Carmel), Stephen Rea (Dixie), David Coyle (Mickey), John Keegan (Mr McCoy), John Hewitt (Mr Roper), Ann Hasson (Sister Midwife), Geraldine Lidster, Stephen Lidster, Lisa Mullan, Kerry O'Neill (Children), Emma Hamilton, Mark Lawless (Babies)

***The Short and Curlies*, 1987, 18 mins, col.**

Production company: Film Four/Portman
Producers: Victor Glynn, Simon Channing-Williams
Photography: Roger Pratt
Editing: Jon Gregory
Designer: Diana Charnley
Music: Rachel Portman
Costumes: Lindy Hemming
Sound recordist: Malcolm Hirst
Cast: Alison Steadman (Betty), Sylvestra Le Touzel (Joy), David Thewlis (Clive), Wendy Nottingham (Charlene)

***High Hopes*, 1988, 110 mins, col.**

Production company: Portman/Film Four International/British Screen
Producers: Simon Channing-Williams, Victor Glynn
Photography: Roger Pratt
Editing: Jon Gregory
Production designer: Diana Charnley
Music: Andrew Dickson
Costumes: Lindy Hemming
Sound recordist: Billy McCarthy
Cast: Philip Davis (Cyril), Ruth Sheen (Shirley), Edna Doré (Mrs Bender), Philip Jackson (Martin), Heather Tobias (Valerie), Lesley Manville (Laetitia), David Bamber (Rupert), Jason Watkins (Wayne), Judith Scott (Suzi), Cheryl Prime (Martin's Girlfriend), Diane-Louise Jordan (Chemist Shop Assistant), Linda Beckett (Receptionist)

***Life Is Sweet*, 1990, 102 mins, col.**

Production company: Thin Man/Film Four International/British Screen
Producer: Simon Channing-Williams
Photography: Dick Pope
Editing: Jon Gregory
Production designer: Alison Chitty
Music: Rachel Portman
Costumes: Lindy Hemming
Sound recordist: Malcolm Hirst
Cast: Alison Steadman (Wendy), Jim Broadbent (Andy), Claire Skinner (Natalie), Jane Horrocks (Nicola), Timothy Spall (Aubrey), Stephen Rea (Patsy), David Thewlis (Nicola's Lover), Moya Brady (Paula), David Neilson (Steve), Harriet Thorpe (Customer), Paul Trussel (Chef), Jack Thorpe Baker (Nigel)

A Sense of History, 1992, 28 mins, col.

Production company: Thin Man/Film Four International
Producer: Simon Channing-Williams
Screenplay: Jim Broadbent
Photography: Dick Pope
Designer: Alison Chitty
Music: Carl Davis
Sound recordist: Tim Fraser
Cast: Jim Broadbent (23rd Earl of Leete), Stephen Bill (Giddy), Belinda and Edward Bradley (Children)

Naked, 1993, 126 mins, col.

Production company: Thin Man/Film Four International/British Screen
Producer: Simon Channing-Williams
Photography: Dick Pope
Editing: Jon Gregory
Production designer: Alison Chitty
Music: Andrew Dickson
Costumes: Lindy Hemming
Sound recordist: Ken Weston
Cast: David Thewlis (Johnny), Lesley Sharp (Louise), Katrin Cartlidge (Sophie), Greg Cruttwell (Jeremy), Claire Skinner (Sandra), Peter Wight (Brian), Ewen Bremner (Archie), Susan Vidler (Maggie), Deborah Maclaren (Woman in Window), Gina McKee (Café Girl), Carolina Giammetta (Masseuse), Elizabeth Berrington (Giselle), Darren Tunstall (Poster Man), Robert Putt (Chauffeur), Lynda Rooke (Victim), Angela Curran (Car Owner), Peter Whitman (Mr Halpern), Jo Abercrombie (Woman in Street), Elaine Britten (Girl in Porsche), David Foxxe (Tea Bar Owner), Mike Avenall, Toby Jones (Men at Tea Bar), Sandra Voe (Bag Lady)

Secrets and Lies, 1996, 140 mins, col.

Production company: Thin Man/CiBY 2000/Channel Four Films
Producer: Simon Channing-Williams
Photography: Dick Pope
Editing: Jon Gregory
Production designer: Alison Chitty
Art direction: Eve Stewart
Music: Andrew Dickson
Costumes: Maria Price
Make-up: Christine Blundell

Sound recordist: George Richards

Cast: Brenda Blethyn (Cynthia), Timothy Spall (Maurice), Phyllis Logan (Monica), Claire Rushbrook (Roxanne), Marianne Jean-Baptiste (Hortense), Elizabeth Berrington (Jane), Lee Ross (Paul), Michele Austin (Dionne), Lesley Manville (Jenny), Ron Cook (Stuart), Emma Amos (Woman with Scar), Brian Bovell, Trevor Laird (Hortense's Brothers), Claire Perkins (Hortense's Sister-in-Law), Elias Perkins McCook (Hortense's Nephew), June Mitchell (Senior Optometrist), Janice Acquah (Junior Optician), Keeley Flanders (Little Girl in Optician's), Hannah Davis (First Bride), Terence Harvey (First Bride's Father), Kate O'Malley (Second Bride), Joe Tucker (Groom), Richard Syms (Vicar), Grant Masters (Best Man), Annie Hayes (Mother in Family Group), Peter Wight (Father in Family Group), Jean Ainslie (Grandmother), Daniel Smith (Teenage Son), Gary McDonald (Boxer), Lucy Sheen (Nurse), Frances Ruffelle (Young Mother), Felix Manley (Baby), Alison Steadman (Dog Owner), Liz Smith (Cat Owner), Nitin Chandra Ganatra (Potential Husband), Metin Marlow (Conjuror), Amanda Crossley, Su Elliott, Di Sherlock (Raunchy Women), Alex Squires, Lauren Squires, Sade Squires (Triplets), Sheila Kelley (Triplets' Mother), Dominic Curran (Little Boy), Angela Curran (Little Boy's Mother), Linda Beckett (Pin-up Housewife), Stephen Churchett, Philip Davis, David Neilson, Peter Stockbridge, Peter Waddington (Men in Suits), Rachel Lewis (Graduate), Wendy Nottingham (Glum Wife), Paul Trussell (Grinning Husband), Anthony O'Donnell, Denise Orita (Uneasy Couple), Margery Withers (Elderly Lady), Theresa Watson (Daughter), Ruth Sheen, Gordon Winter (Laughing Couple), Jonathan Coyne, Mia Soteriou (Engaged Couple)

Career Girls, 1997, 87 mins, col.

Production company: Thin Man/Matrix Film & Television Partnership/ Channel 4

Producer: Simon Channing-Williams

Photography: Dick Pope

Editing: Robin Sales

Production and costume designer: Eve Stewart

Music: Marianne Jean-Baptiste, Tony Remy

Make-up: Christine Blundell

Sound recordist: George Richards

Cast: Katrin Cartlidge (Hannah), Lynda Steadman (Annie), Kate Byers (Claire), Mark Benton (Ricky), Andy Serkis (Mr Evans), Joe Tucker (Adrian), Margo Stanley (Ricky's Nan), Michael Healy (Lecturer)

Topsy-Turvy, 1999, 160 mins, col.

Production company: Thin Man/Greenlight Fund/Newmarket Capital Group
Producer: Simon Channing-Williams
Photography: Dick Pope
Editing: Robin Sales
Production designer: Eve Stewart
Music: Carl Davis, from the works of Arthur Sullivan
Costumes: Lindy Hemming
Make-up: Christine Blundell
Sound recordist: Tim Fraser
Cast: Jim Broadbent (William Schwenck Gilbert), Allan Corduner (Arthur Sullivan), Timothy Spall (Richard Temple), Lesley Manville (Lucy Gilbert), Ron Cook (Richard D'Oyly Carte), Wendy Nottingham (Helen Lenoir), Kevin McKidd (Durward Lely), Shirley Henderson (Leonora Braham), Dorothy Atkinson (Jessie Bond), Martin Savage (George Grossmith), Eleanor David (Fanny Ronalds), Sam Kelly (Richard Barker), Andy Serkis (John D'Auban), Charles Simon (Gilbert's Father), Vincent Franklin (Rutland Barrington), Cathy Sara (Sibyl Grey), Nicholas Woodeson (Mr Seymour), Jonathan Aris (Wilhelm), Stefan Bednarczyk (Frank Cellier), Mark Benton (Mr Price), Eve Pearce (Gilbert's Mother), Lavinia Bertram (Florence Gilbert), Theresa Watson (Maude Gilbert), Kenneth Hadley (Pidgeon), Dexter Fletcher (Louis), Kate Doherty (Mrs Judd), Michael Simkins (Frederick Bovill), Louise Gold (Rosina Brandram), Sukie Smith (Clothilde), Mia Soteriou (Mrs Russell), Togo Igawa (First Kabuki Actor), Naoko Mori (Miss 'Sixpence Please'), Akemi Otani (Dancer), Kanako Morishita (Shamisen Player), Eiji Kusuhara (Second Kabuki Actor), Alison Steadman (Madame Leon), Roger Heathcott (Stage Door Keeper), Geoffrey Hutchings (Armourer), Francis Lee (Butt), William Neeman (Cook), Adam Searle (Shrimp), Keeley Gainey (Maidservant), Gary Yershon (Pianist in Brothel), Katrin Cartlidge (Madame), Julia Rayner (Mademoiselle Fromage), Jenny Pickering (Second Prostitute), Philippe Constantin (Paris Waiter), David Neville (Dentist), Matthew Mills (Walter Simmonds), Nick Bartlett, Gary Dunnington (Stage Hands), Amanda Crossley (Emily), Kimi Shaw (Spinner), Toksan Takahashi (Calligrapher), Neil Humphries (Boy Actor), Angela Curran (Miss Moeron), Millie Gregory (Alice), Shaun Glanville (Mr Harris), Julian Bleach (Mr Plank), Neil Salvage (Mr Hurley), Matt Bardock (Mr Tripp), Bríd Brennan (Mad Woman), Heather Craney (Miss Russell), Julie Japp (Miss Meadows), John Warnaby (Mr Sanders), Kacey Ainsworth (Miss Fitzherbert), Ashley

Artus (Mr Marchmont), Richard Attlee (Mr Gordon), Paul Barnhill (Mr Flagstone), Nicholas Boulton (Mr Conyngham), Lorraine Brunning (Miss Jardine), Simon Butteriss (Mr Lewis), Wayne Cater (Mr Rhys), Rosie Cavaliero (Miss Moore), Michelle Chadwick (Miss Warren), Debbie Chazen (Miss Kingsley), Richard Coyle (Mr Hammond), Monica Dolan (Miss Barnes), Sophie Duval (Miss Brown), Anna Francolini (Miss Biddles), Teresa Gallagher (Miss Coleford), Sarah Howe (Miss Woods), Ashley Jensen (Miss Tringham), Gemma Page (Miss Langton-James), Paul Rider (Mr Bentley), Mary Roscoe (Miss Carlyle), Steven Speirs (Mr Kent), Nicola Wainwright (Miss Betts), Angie Wallis (Miss Wilkinson), Kevin Walton (Mr Evans)

All or Nothing, 2002, 128 mins, col.

Production company: Thin Man/Les Films Alain Sarde/Studio Canal
Producer: Simon Channing-Williams
Photography: Dick Pope
Editing: Lesley Walker
Production designer: Eve Stewart
Music: Andrew Dickson
Costumes: Jacqueline Durran
Make-up: Christine Blundell
Sound recordist: Malcolm Hirst
Cast: Timothy Spall (Phil), Lesley Manville (Penny), Alison Garland (Rachel), James Corden (Rory), Ruth Sheen (Maureen), Marion Bailey (Carol), Paul Jesson (Ron), Sam Kelly (Sid), Kathryn Hunter (Cécile), Sally Hawkins (Samantha), Helen Coker (Donna), Daniel Mays (Jason), Ben Crompton (Craig), Robert Wilfort (Doctor), Gary McDonald (Neville), Diveen Henry (Dinah), Jean Ainslie (Old Lady), Badi Uzaman, Parvez Qadir (Passengers), Russell Mabey (Nutter), Thomas Brown-Lowe, Oliver Golding, Henri McCarthy, Ben Wattley (Small Boys), Leo Bill (Young Man), Peter Stockbridge (Man with Flowers), Brian Bovell (Garage Owner), Timothy Bateson (Harold), Michele Austin (Care Worker), Alex Kelly (Neurotic Woman), Allan Williams (Drunk), Peter Yardley (MC), Dawn Davis (Singer), Emma Lowndes, Maxine Peake (Party Girls), Matt Bardock, Mark Benton (Men at Bar), Dorothy Atkinson, Heather Craney, Martin Savage (Silent Passengers), Joe Tucker (Fare Dodger), Edna Doré (Martha), Georgia Fitch (Ange), Tracey O'Flaherty (Michell), Di Botcher (Supervisor), Valerie Hunkins (Nurse), Daniel Ryan (Crash Driver)

Vera Drake, 2004, 125 mins, col.

Production company: Thin Man/Les Films Alain Sarde/Inside Track/ UK Film Council
Producers: Simon Channing-Williams, Alain Sarde
Photography: Dick Pope
Editing: Jim Clark
Production designer: Eve Stewart
Music: Andrew Dickson
Costumes: Jacqueline Durran
Make-up: Christine Blundell
Sound recordist: Tim Fraser
Cast: Imelda Staunton (Vera), Phil Davis (Stan), Peter Wight (Detective Inspector Webster), Alex Kelly (Ethel), Daniel Mays (Sid), Adrian Scarborough (Frank), Heather Craney (Joyce), Eddie Marsan (Reg), Ruth Sheen (Lily), Sally Hawkins (Susan), Fenella Woolgar (Susan's Confidante), Lesley Sharp (Jessie Barnes), Anthony O'Donnell (Mr Walsh), Helen Coker (WPC Best), Martin Savage (Detective Sergeant Vickers), Allan Corduner (Psychiatrist), Nicky Henson (Private Doctor), Lesley Manville (Mrs Wells), Wendy Nottingham (Ivy), Paul Jesson (Magistrate), Sandra Voe (Vera's Mother), Leo Bill (Ronny), Gerard Monaco (Kenny), Chris O'Dowd (Sid's Customer), Sam Troughton (David), Elizabeth Berrington (Cynical Lady), Sinead Matthews (Very Young Woman), Rosie Cavaliero (Married Woman), Vinette Robinson (Jamaican Girl), Tilly Vosburgh (Mother of Seven), Liz White (Pamela Barnes), Jim Broadbent (Judge), Richard Graham (George), Anna Keaveney (Nellie), Simon Chandler (Mr Wells), Marion Bailey (Mrs Fowler), Sid Mitchell (Very Young Man), Alan Williams (Sick Husband), Heather Cameron, Billie Cook, Billy Seymour (Children), Nina Fry, Lauren Holden (Dance Hall Girls), Emma Amos (Cynical Lady), Joanna Griffiths (Peggy), Angie Wallis (Nurse Willoughby), Judith Scott (Sister Beech), Lucy Pleasence (Sister Coombes), Tracey O'Flaherty (Nurse), Tom Ellis (Police Constable), Robert Putt (Station Sergeant), Craig Conway (Station Constable), Jake Wood (Ruffian), Vincent Franklin (Mr Lewis), Michael Gunn (Gaoler), Paul Raffield (Magistrate's Clerk), Philip Childs (Clerk), Jeffrey Wickham (Prosecution Barrister), Nicholas Jones (Defence Barrister), Stephan Dunbar (Usher), Angela Curran, Jane Wood (Prisoners), Eileen Davies (Prison Officer)

Select bibliography

Published screenplays and playscripts by Mike Leigh

Abigail's Party/Goose-Pimples, London, Penguin Books, 1983
Naked and Other Screenplays, London, Faber & Faber, 1995 (contains screenplays for *High Hopes*, *Life Is Sweet* and *Naked*)
Smelling a Rat, London, Nick Hern Books, 1996
Career Girls, London, Faber & Faber, 1997
Secrets and Lies, London, Faber & Faber, 1997
Ecstasy, London, Nick Hern Books, 1999
Topsy-Turvy, London, Faber & Faber, 1999
All or Nothing, London, Faber & Faber, 2002

On Mike Leigh

Carney, Ray and Quart, Leonard, *The Films of Mike Leigh: Embracing the World*, Cambridge, Cambridge University Press, 2000
Coveney, Michael, *The World According to Mike Leigh*, London, Harper Collins, 1996 (paperback edition 1997)
Dacre, Richard, 'Devised and Directed: The Television Work of Mike Leigh', *Primetime*, 1: 2 (Autumn 1981), pp. 23–5
Fuller, Graham, 'Mike Leigh's Original Features', in *Naked and Other Screenplays*, London, Faber & Faber, 1995, pp. vii–xlii
Lawrenson, Edward, 'Backstreet Revisited', *Sight and Sound*, 15: 1 (January 2005), pp. 12–15
Medhurst, Andy, 'Mike Leigh: Beyond Embarrassment', *Sight and Sound*, 3: 11 (November 1993), pp. 6–10
Movshovitz, Howie (ed.), *Mike Leigh Interviews*, Jackson, University Press of Mississippi, 2000
Watson, Garry, *The Cinema of Mike Leigh: A Sense of the Real*, London, Wallflower Press, 2004

On British cinema

Adair, Gilbert and Roddick, Nick, *A Night at the Pictures: Ten Decades of British Film*, London, Columbus Books, 1985

Auty, Martyn and Roddick, Nick (eds), *British Cinema Now*, London, BFI Publishing, 1985

Babington, Bruce, *Launder and Gilliat*, Manchester, Manchester University Press, 2002

Barr, Charles (ed.), *All Our Yesterdays: 90 Years of British Cinema*, London, BFI Publishing, 1986

Burton, Alan, O'Sullivan, Tim and Wells, Paul (eds), *The Family Way: The Boulting Brothers and British Film Culture*, Trowbridge, Flicks Books, 2000

Catterall, Ali and Wells, Simon, *Your Face Here: British Cult Movies Since the Sixties*, London, Fourth Estate, 2001

Durgnat, Raymond, *A Mirror for England: British Movies from Austerity to Affluence*, London, Faber & Faber, 1970

Hill, John, *British Cinema in the 1980s*, Oxford, Oxford University Press, 1999

Lay, Samantha, *British Social Realism: From Documentary to Brit Grit*, London, Wallflower Press, 2002

McFarlane, Brian, *An Autobiography of British Cinema*, London, Methuen, 1997

——, *The Encyclopaedia of British Film*, London, BFI Publishing, 2003

Murphy, Robert (ed.), *The British Cinema Book*, London, BFI Publishing, 1997

——, (ed.), *British Cinema of the 90s*, London, BFI Publishing, 2000

Perry, George, *The Great British Picture Show*, London, Pavilion Books, 1974 and 1985

Richards, Jeffrey and Aldgate, Anthony, *Best of British: Cinema and Society 1930–1970*, Oxford, Blackwell, 1983

On comedy, humour and satire

Banks, Morwenna and Swift, Amanda, *The Joke's On Us: Women in Comedy from Music Hall to the Present Day*, London, Pandora Press, 1987

Bergson, Henri, *Le Rire*, 1900, translated by Cloudesley Brereton and Fred Rothwell, London, MacMillan & Co., 1913

Carpenter, Humphrey, *That Was Satire That Was: The Satire Boom of the 1960s*, London, Victor Gollancz, 2000

Freud, Sigmund, *Jokes and Their Relation to the Unconscious*, 1905, translated by James Strachey, London, Penguin Books, 1976

Galton, Ray and Simpson, Alan, *The Best of Hancock*, London, Robson Books, 1986

Glendinning, Victoria, *Jonathan Swift*, London, Hutchinson, 1998

Hind, John, *The Comic Inquisition: Conversations with Great Comedians*, London, Virgin Books, 1991

Louvish, Simon, *Stan and Ollie: The Roots of Comedy*, London, Faber & Faber, 2001

Midwinter, Eric, *Make 'Em Laugh*, London, Allen & Unwin, 1979

Skynner, Robin and Cleese, John, *Life and How to Survive It*, London, Methuen, 1993

Index

Note: page numbers in *italics* refer to illustrations.